Attack of the 50 Ft. Women

Attack of the 50 Ft. Women

How Gender Equality Can Save the World!

Catherine Mayer

ONE PLACE. MANY STORIES

HQ
An imprint of HarperCollinsPublishers Ltd.
1 London Bridge Street
London SE1 9GF

1
First published in Great Britain by
HQ, an imprint of HarperCollinsPublishers Ltd. 2017

A catalogue record for this book is
available from the British Library

ISBN: HB 978-0-00-819115-3
TPB 978-0-00-821980-2

Printed and bound by in Great Britain by
CPI Group (UK) Ltd, Croydon, CR0 4YY.

To sisters, mine especially.

And in memory of Sara Burns, Sarah Smith and Michael Elliott.

If we were socially ambisexual, if men and women were completely and genuinely equal in their social roles, equal legally and economically, equal in freedom, in responsibility, and in 'self esteem', then society would be a very different thing. What our problems might be, God knows. I only know we would have them. But it seems likely that our central problem would not be the one it is now: the problem of exploitation – exploitation of the woman, of the weak, of the earth.

URSULA LE GUIN

'Is Gender Necessary?', The Language of the Night: Essays on Fantasy and Science Fiction, 1976.

Contents

Introduction: The Shoulders of Giants

A COLOSSAL ZOMBIE Scarlett Johansson commandeered London's red buses a few years ago. She sprawled across the upper deck of a fleet of vehicles, face slack with simulated desire, mouth gaping wide enough to swallow a small terrier, breasts threatening to smother passengers seated in the lower tier.

Dolce & Gabbana's advertising campaign intended to evoke Marilyn Monroe's heyday, and it succeeded. The apparition recalled Nancy, the title character of a 1958 film, *Attack of the 50 Ft. Woman*. Nancy's encounter with a space alien transforms her into a giant ('Incredibly Huge, with Incredible Desires for Love and Vengeance'). The patriarchal authorities – doctors, police, spouse – chain her, but she breaks free and, naked but for an arrangement of bed sheets, embarks on a murderous rampage. Behold the dreadful power of woman unleashed ('The Most Grotesque Monstrosity of All')!

Zombie Johansson captured the inadvertent humour of the B-movie, but she was properly scary too. In her human incarnation she is the only woman to break through Hollywood's diamond ceiling to claim a place among the ten top-grossing actors of all time. She chooses intelligent roles and has more than once pushed back against the chauvinism of Hollywood and its media ecosystems. Her dead-eyed alter ego belonged to the monstrous regiment of billboard women in perpetual march across the world. Nancy gained agency as she grew. Today's 50-footers, hypersexualised and supine, promote a retrograde ideology alongside brands and products.

We're so marinated in this imagery that we seldom stand back to parse its meaning and impact. It is all-pervasive, not just on hoardings and print and broadcast but metastasised into myriad digital forms. The underlying messaging is little different to the drumbeat that helped return women to pliant domesticity after World War II. From earliest childhood, girls are taught to value themselves for their abilities: desirability, marriageability, tractability.

There are, of course, other role models, women of stature and astonishing achievement, but still they break through against the odds. Globally women own less and earn less than men, often in the worst and worst regulated jobs, undertake the lionesses' share of caregiving and unpaid domestic labour, and are subject to discrimination, harassment and sexual violence.

Every woman navigates a world fashioned by and for men. Female drivers are more vulnerable to serious injury from accidents in many models of car because until recently crash test dummies were built only to male dimensions. Some pharmaceuticals fail us because they are tested on male animals to avoid having to account for hormonal cycles. We shiver at our workplaces because thermostats are set to temperatures that suit male metabolisms.

We're left in the cold in other ways too. The Organisation for European Economic Co-operation (OEEC) logs the gap between women's earnings and men's at 17.48 per cent in the UK, 17.91 per cent in the US and 18 per cent in Australia. Women have long been blamed for this gap. We don't ask for raises often enough or we don't ask right. Studies identify the real culprits: job segregation and discrimination.[1]

Jobs traditionally performed by men attract higher wages than those held by women. Female employees of Birmingham City Council working as care home attendants, cooks and cleaners discovered they were paid less than the mostly male refuse collectors and street cleaners on the council payroll. Although women are the main breadwinners in many households, and dual-earner households are also common, the paradigm of the husband as the head of the household and chief provider remains firmly lodged in the public imagination. One reason some employers pay men better may be that they think the men have greater need of the money. In the US, men in nursing are vastly outnumbered by their female colleagues, by nine to one, yet earn $5,100 more on average per year than female nurses.[2] These disparities are echoed across the world.

Every woman lives with the constant tinnitus hum of low-level sexism. Most of us have been leered at or leched over and told we should be flattered by the attention. For one in five women in Europe, that flattering attention takes the form of sexual assault. Almost a fifth of US women will be raped in their lifetimes, with close to half reporting other forms of sexual violence. One in three women worldwide will be subjected to violent sexual attack.[3] The response to this epidemic is muted and muddled.

In the US, prosecutors ask a judge to send a college athlete to prison for six years for sexually assaulting an unconscious woman; the judge decides on six months, concerned a longer period of incarceration will have a 'severe impact' on the perpetrator. He is freed halfway through his sentence. In India, a woman is gang-raped to death; one of her rapists says: 'A decent girl won't roam around at nine o'clock at night. A girl is far more responsible for rape than a boy.' In Pakistan, 14 men rape a woman on the orders of their village council, as punishment for her brother's supposed liaison with a local woman. The majority of the 276 schoolgirls kidnapped by terrorists in northern Nigeria are still missing; those who escape bearing tales of mass rape and slavery find themselves social outcasts. Egyptian lawmakers finally approve a draft bill that would dole out five- to seven-year jail terms for people carrying out female genital mutilation (FGM), an operation to remove part or all of the clitoris. The procedure – often called circumcision by those trying to minimise its brutality – has been inflicted on more than 90 per cent of the country's women and girls. 'We are a population whose men suffer from sexual weakness, which is evident because Egypt is among the biggest consumers of sexual stimulants,' an MP protests. 'If we stopped circumcising we will need strong men, and we don't have those.'[4] Up to 1,000 women are sexually assaulted on the streets of the German cathedral city of Cologne on New Year's Eve 2015; the attacks trigger condemnation not of women's oppression but of migration, reinforcing the false narrative that sexual violence is imported, rather than native to white European society.

In South Africa, a Paralympian shoots his girlfriend, a would-be lawyer and successful model; newspapers across the world use an image from a bikini photoshoot to illustrate coverage, which focuses on his achievements and barely mentions her. A court in China finds Zhang Yazhou guilty of strangling 24-year-old Li Hongxia, whom he had abused for years, but gives Zhang a lesser sentence than is standard for murder cases because Li was his wife.

And on 8 November 2016, US voters choose their President. The front-runners are a female candidate and a man who has been recorded boasting of assaulting women. 'You know I'm automatically attracted to beautiful … I just start kissing them. It's like a magnet. Just kiss. I don't even wait. And when you're a star they let you do it. You can do anything … Grab them by the pussy. You can do anything,' he says.[5] After the recording emerges, ten women come forward to accuse him of assault. He insists that they are lying. After all, two of them were too ugly to grope.

Many other aspects of his candidacy should also repel any voter who values equality. The candidate appears to believe only in himself, but panders to Christian social conservatives by promising to roll back women's reproductive rights. He lets it be known that he will back a law to permit discrimination against gays and lesbians by anyone who claims religious grounds for their stance. He stirs up racism and gains the support of the Ku Klux Klan by pledging to ban Muslims from the country and force Mexico to build a wall to keep its own citizens from crossing the border into the US. He refuses to condemn his supporters for racist violence.[6]

He is the worst would-be President we have seen in our lifetimes or read about in history books – dangerous, incoherent and vain. He cosies up to Russian autocrat Vladimir Putin, publicly invites the Russian secret service to hack US government emails to damage his opponent and announces he will unpick years of international negotiations to limit climate change – which he calls a 'hoax'.

He wins the election.

A majority of men votes for him, by 53 per cent to 41 per cent.

A majority of white people votes for him, by 58 per cent to 37 per cent.

Eighty-one per cent of white evangelicals and born-again Christians vote for him.

Women vote against him, by 54 per cent to 42 per cent. Yet a majority of white women supports him: 53 per cent.[7]

A dual US and UK national, I cast a ballot in my home state of Wisconsin. I am not one of the white women who helped Donald Trump into the White House, but like all white American women, I am implicated. Through researching this book, I also understand the mechanisms that encourage turkeys to vote for Christmas.

This book aims to set out those insights and to make something else abundantly clear. The skewed status quo serves almost nobody – certainly not most men.

The world is full of decent men who strive to be allies to women. It's a safe bet that most men who are engaged enough in these issues to read these pages fall into this category, though you may not always be sure how best to support us. Many of you want change, for women and girls and for yourselves, but you don't always understand that 'women's issues' are your issues. You observe your own sex suffering within patriarchal cultures and structures but don't always join the dots. Because of these structures, boys struggle at school; suicide rates are highest among young males, who are also more likely to murder and more likely to be murdered; and men drink more heavily and more frequently end up in prison. Fathers yearn to be with their children, but the enduring pay gap means they cannot afford to stay home, while social norms sometimes deter them from pushing for change. Businesses, institutions and economies underperform.

The twenty-first century wasn't supposed to be like this.

Late boomers like me grew up believing history was going our way. We assumed progress to be linear, counting ourselves lucky to be born to an era that had all but vanquished the great scourges of humanity. Racism and homophobia proved susceptible to education and so would wither. Wars were still prosecuted, but at a distance. Hunger, too, seemed confined to far-away lands, and technology must surely deliver fixes, just as it would soon banish cancer, ageing, death and clothes moths. As for women's rights, the heavy lifting had been done by the women, and their male allies, who came before us. A liberal consensus held sway and growing up in comfort, largely surrounded by the white middle classes, I had no idea of the limits or vulnerabilities of our progress.

After a peripatetic early childhood, I attended a girls' school in Northern England that proudly counted among its alumnae all three daughters of the magnificent, if flawed, Emmeline Pankhurst. We learned that the Suffragettes' achievements marked the beginning of the end of the gender wars. In 1918, as Europe made its fragile peace, the Representation of the People Act granted some British women the right to vote. A decade later that right was extended to all adult females. New Zealand had led the way in 1893. The US followed suit in 1920. When I was seven and still living in the US, the doughty women of Ford Dagenham fought and won the battle for equal pay. Women's libbers and the Pill were finishing the job. As teenagers my contemporaries and I saw shimmering on the near horizon a fully gender-equal society in which every inhabitant could stand as tall as the next person.

I named this place 'Equalia', and like a querulous child on a family outing, I've spent much of my life asking 'When will we get there?'

There's always someone prepared to claim we've already arrived. Such people rarely describe themselves as feminists because they misunderstand the term as a doctrine of suppression. 'There is a mistaken conception that feminism is somehow dour,' says Sandi Toksvig, broadcaster, writer, comedian, and, in the pungent prose of a *Daily Mail* columnist, 'a vertically challenged and openly lesbian mother'. '"Aren't you all about burning your bras?" one man asked me. "Yeah, that's right," I said, "and thank goodness the manufacturers thought to make all women's underwear out of combustible material. Why I practically set fire to myself if I break into too fast a jog."'[8]

The media maintains lists of pundits who can be relied on to declare that Western women already have enough equality. After all, the largest and second-largest economies in Europe are run by women, and most Western countries have legislated for equal pay, even if the legislation hasn't achieved the desired result. The laws and their application cannot be faulty; women must be choosing their lower status. Sex discrimination and sexual harassment are outlawed, so women must deserve this treatment. We never had it so good. We should stop whingeing and worry about Saudi Arabia. (It is axiomatic among these useful idiots that you cannot advocate for the rights of women in your own country *and* in Saudi Arabia.) Feminism can go home and put its feet up.

Broadcasters are particularly fond of pitting women against women. The anti-feminist female is as persistent a breed as the clothes moth. Typically white and middle class, she either doesn't believe in gender equality or else she doesn't believe in gender inequality – because she's too cocooned and myopic to see it. She routinely seeks to strengthen her case by co-opting a tenet of feminism: that the personal is political. She feels no kinship with younger and less privileged women still fighting the old battles while simultaneously picking their way through new and dangerous territories. She declares that she has never experienced sexism or discriminatory behaviour she couldn't handle. She is thriving.

Let us celebrate the advances that enable her complacency even as we sometimes doubt her sincerity. Her protests are too vigorous, her unease in her own skin too obvious. Her mind has hardened with habit into narrow pathways and she cannot conceive how her own discomfort might relate to a wider pattern. The men around her give succour to her views.

'The war has been won,' one such tells me. 'It's just a mopping up operation now. You can't even kick your dog now much less your wife.' Yet, make no mistake, we haven't reached Equalia. The Most Grotesque Monstrosity of All? We're still a long, long way from Equalia.

We live, wherever we live, under a patriarchy, a system that excludes women. Not a single country anywhere on the planet has attained parity. The Nordic quartet of Iceland, Norway, Finland and Sweden tops the rankings of the best places to be female. Even in these countries, though, girls start life as second-class citizens and will be demoted further down the unnatural order with every year beyond their socially determined prime, or if poor or non-white or disabled or daring to combine any of these factors.

There is increasing awareness that gender is not binary but a spectrum, yet this awareness has neither diminished gender conflict nor created acceptance for people transitioning along the spectrum or sitting at junctions that challenge bureaucratic or social labels. Groups that are themselves disadvantaged unconsciously incorporate patriarchal pecking orders. Gay men have a habit of crowding out the other letters in the LGBTQ movement. Civil rights activists have form too. In 1964, Stokely Carmichael, a leader of the Student Nonviolent Coordinating Committee, batted away a question about women volunteers. 'The position for women in SNCC is prone,' he said.[9] It was, he later explained, a joke, but one that closely matched the experience of women in progressive movements. Black Lives Matter, founded by three women , Patrice Cullors, Alicia Garza and Opal Tometi, to illuminate the high − and under-reported − toll of racially motivated killings of black Americans by whites, focuses increasingly on the killings of black males by law enforcement officers. This is hugely important but killings of black women get less attention, prompting a separate movement to take up the cause, #SayHerName.

The elites that might be expected to forge solutions are themselves part of the problem. There is a startling lack of any kind of diversity in politics, and the gender imbalance is stark. There are more male MPs in the Westminster parliament than there have ever been female MPs elected. America blew its chance to elect Hillary Clinton as its forty-fifth President amid barbs about blow jobs. 'Hillary sucks, but not like Monica' read T-shirts and badges flaunted by Trump supporters. Clinton not only suffered the consequences of her husband's dalliance with White House intern Monica Lewinsky. She, like Lewinsky, continues to be vilified for it. Still, women had cause to celebrate the elections according to the US media outlets that trumpeted 'the highest number of women of colour on record' to win seats in the Senate. That record-breaking grand total equals just four: Catherine Cortez Masto, Tammy Duckworth, Kamala Harris and Mazie Hirono. The number of female representatives in both houses remained static at 104, a mere 19.4 per cent.

Business is just as bad. Among CEOs of the biggest companies in the UK and the US there are more men called John than women of any name. Financial institutions in both countries are overwhelmingly white, male and middle class. Other key institutions – the judiciary, the police, the media – share the same weaknesses.

Here's something else they share: most of them claim, institutionally and individually, to support gender equality. The liberal consensus is still alive but it is under concerted attack from different expressions of political and religious extremism. The forces ranged against it aim not only to destroy it, but to dismantle its legacy of rights and protections. Progress is not, after all, linear, and it is far too easily reversed.

We would not have so much to lose if not for the achievements of feminism. Its Western incarnation loosely divides into four eras, or waves. The first, in the late nineteenth and early twentieth centuries, coalesced around the battle for votes for women. The second kindled in the 1960s, and asserted reproductive rights as a tool of liberation that would enable women to define their own being and sexuality and participate alongside men outside the home. It often rejected the possibility of equality within existing systems and structures. A third iteration in the 1990s grappled with the movement's own failings to address systemic inequalities in its own ranks, while another strand attempted to seize ownership of male ideals of womanhood and recast them as female empowerment. The 1993 remake of *Attack of the 50 Ft. Woman*, starring Daryl Hannah, becomes a parable of emotional as well as physical growth, and gets a happy ending.

We're now well into a fourth era, more of a torrent than a wave thanks to the proliferation of digital media, and too fast-flowing to analyse easily. It doesn't help clarity that so many people lay claim to be part of that flow. Business leaders insist that finding and retaining female talent is essential to success. Economists hail increasing gender balance in the labour force as the key to growth. One recent report estimates a boost to global GDP of £8.3 trillion by 2025 simply by making faster progress towards narrowing the gender gap.[10] Two large-scale pieces of research by Credit Suisse suggest that companies with significant numbers of women in decision-making roles are more profitable.[11] Multiple studies also suggest that giving women a greater say – and a greater stake – in the planet is essential to building a healthier planet. Trump may doubt the reality of climate change, but among the rural poor, women are at its sharp end, because females are most often tasked with sourcing water, food and energy for their families and communities. In 25 sub-Saharan countries, 71 per cent of the water collectors are women and girls who every day spend an estimated 16 million hours fetching water, compared to six million hours spent by men. The worse the drought, the longer the journeys and the greater the vulnerability of those women and girls. In India, 75 per cent of rural women work in agriculture but own only nine per cent of arable land. Bina Agarwal, Professor of

Development Economics and Environment at the University of Manchester, posits that increased female participation in business decision-making improves environmental outcomes.[12]

Agarwal rejects the romantic idea that this is because women are in some way closer to nature than men, but much of the current orthodoxy identifies women as a corrective to testosterone-driven cultures. The Credit Suisse studies find companies steered by women take fewer risks. 'Where women account for the majority in the top management, the businesses show superior sales growth, high cash-flow returns on investments and lower leverage,' says the 2016 report.

Politicians of many stripes laud women and profess to fight for us. Congresswoman Ann Wagner went so far during the US election campaign as to call on her own party's nominee to stand aside because of his misogyny. 'I have committed my short time in Congress to fighting for the most vulnerable in our society,' Wagner said in an October 2016 statement. 'As a strong and vocal advocate for victims of sex trafficking and assault, I must be true to those survivors and myself and condemn the predatory and reprehensible comments of Donald Trump.' Less than a week before polling day, she urged voters to back Trump.

Wagner was unlucky. Political commitment to gender equality is often little more than skin deep, but a great many politicians get away without their commitment being publicly tested. This is not to paint all politicians as hypocrites. Many of them believe in women. It's just that when push comes to shove, they believe in other things more – and they also make the mistake I once did, of assuming that gender equality is already well on its way, without any extra help from them.

If there is a sliver of a silver lining to Trump's victory, it is that it dented this myth. It did not destroy it. Clinton's defeat seemed to contrast a regressive US with feminising cultures elsewhere. Former Attorney General Patricia Scotland had recently taken office as the Commonwealth's first female Secretary-General. Estonia had its first female president. Rome and Tokyo for the first time had elected female mayors. After a campaign dominated by male voices tore up the UK's membership of the European Union, British eyes had turned to women to save the day. Some looked with envy at Germany and its unflappable Chancellor Angela Merkel. More than a few English voters discovered a new reason to beg Scotland not to secede; they wanted the country's clever First Minister Nicola Sturgeon to be Prime Minister of England too. Britain's two biggest parties, the governing Conservatives and Labour, turned hopeful eyes to senior women in their ranks. There was, after all, precedent. In 1979, the British economy seemed locked into a downward spiral of a weakening currency and blooming inflation, amid industrial unrest that saw even gravediggers down tools. Then a general election returned Margaret Thatcher to Downing Street, the first female Prime Minister not only of the UK but of any major industrial democracy. Within a few years, her economic policies had laid waste whole communities and sectors but galvanized other quarters and, more than that, revived a sense of potential that had long been missing.

She set a template for the female leader who sweeps in to sort out the mess created by men. Cometh the hour, cometh the woman. The press dubbed Merkel Germany's Margaret Thatcher. Inevitably Sturgeon has become Scotland's Margaret Thatcher, Angela Eagle briefly flew as Labour's Margaret Thatcher and Theresa May is Margaret Thatcher in kitten heels or, when that comparison wears thin, Britain's Merkel. 'Women are such rare creatures that they can only be understood through the prism of one another, like unicorns or sporting triumphs by the England football team,' observed the journalist Hadley Freeman.[13]

The female half of the population may be better able to tell each other apart but that doesn't mean we're immune to sweeping assumptions about how women use power. 'If Lehman Brothers had been Lehman Sisters, today's economic crisis clearly would look quite different,' IMF chief Christine Lagarde told an interviewer in 2008.

Whenever economies falter or politics stutters, the refrain starts again. Men plunder the environment; women manage it. Men start wars; women make peace. We need more women in high and influential positions. We need more women to tower. Bring on the new breed of 50-foot women!

With so many people making this argument, not just rebels and advocates of social justice, but great swathes of the political classes, pillars of the establishment, corporate bigwigs and analysts focusing so hard on the bottom line that they walk into lampposts, surely we must be able to make substantial progress? With the dangers of failure laid bare in countries that are shredding hard-won rights, surely we have no choice but to redouble our efforts? Where are the traps and barricades obstructing the road to Equalia? Does anyone even know the way? And will it take 50-foot women to get us there?

In 2015, I kicked off a process that would provide fascinating and unexpected answers to those questions.

I accidentally started a political party.

Westminster's first-past-the-post voting system reliably delivered single-party victories until a Conservative–Liberal Democrat government emerged from the 2010 elections. Five years later, as fresh elections hove into view, the coalition partners sought to win voters' favour by vilifying not only the Labour opposition but each other.

For that reason alone, the political debate I attended at London's Southbank Centre on 2 March 2015 felt excitingly unorthodox. As part of the Women of the World (WOW) Festival, the Conservatives' Margot James, the Lib Dems' Jo Swinson and Labour's Stella Creasy described overlapping experiences and ambitions. They debated companionably, listening intently, nodding appreciatively and applauding each other's points.

This should have been thrilling. Instead it was dispiriting. In 66 days we faced a choice not between these vibrant women but their parties.

The Lehman Brothers' collapse in 2008 had ushered in an age of deficit-cutting measures that often hit the poorest hardest, and that meant a disproportionate impact on women. In the UK, as in most other countries, the male-dominated mainstream that steered towards the crisis also took the wheel to direct the recovery.

There were significant dividing lines, of course. Tories, Lib Dems and Labour disagreed over the degree, speed and targets of proposed cuts, but not one of them made serious efforts to apply a gender lens to the discussion. They needed only to look over to tiny Iceland to see the difference that could make. Prime Minister Jóhanna Sigurðardóttir did attract international attention – she wasn't just Iceland's first female Prime Minister, she was the world's first openly lesbian premier. Less noted, and at least as noteworthy, her coalition took a consciously gender-aware approach to the economic crisis. The country's three largest banks had failed, its currency collapsed, the stock market plummeted and interest on loans soared. As businesses bankrupted, jobs vanished. Cuts in state spending were inevitable, but in planning them, Jóhanna's coalition tried to diminish the pain by spreading it thinner.[14] Where other nations cut state sector jobs and prioritised capital investment, effectively supporting male employment at the expense of sectors employing and serving women, Iceland took a different tack. It asked a simple question: why build a hospital, but cut nursing staff?

'The typical reaction of a state to a crisis is to cut services because they're seen as expenses,' says Halla Gunnarsdóttir, who served as a special adviser in the Icelandic coalition. 'The state puts money into construction because it's seen as investment. So basically it cuts jobs for women, and also takes away services and replaces them with women's unpaid labour: care for the elderly, care for the disabled, caring for children and those who are ill. Then it creates jobs for men so that they can continue working.'[15] This is often done through public–private partnerships in which the state takes the risk but the private sector benefits. Women's unemployment goes up as the state focuses on preserving jobs for men.

Such perspectives — and women themselves — were never more conspicuous by their absence from British political discourse than during the election campaigns of the post-Lehman years. During the 2010 elections, the media invented a new top-shelf category, Leaders' Wives, framing the electoral choice as one between sultry Samantha (Cameron), magnificent Miriam (Gonzáles Durántez) and sexy Sarah (Brown). Five years later, three near-identikit white male 40-something party leaders semaphored their commitment to change by giving speeches in shirt sleeves.

The 2015 elections threatened to be an entirely women-free zone and the broader landscape looked bleak. Of 650 electoral constituencies, 356 had never elected female MPs. Labour did better on getting women into Parliament, but the Tories remained the only major party to have chosen a female leader, and that had been 40 years earlier.

Labour women did try to elbow their way into the front line of the campaign. Harriet Harman, the party's deputy leader, long saddled with the nickname 'Harperson' by sections of the press hostile to her feminist politics, commissioned research that revealed that 9.1 million women had chosen not to exercise their votes at the previous election. 'Politics is every bit as important and relevant to the lives of women as it is to men. Labour has set itself the challenge to make this case to the missing millions of women voters,' she said.

In truth, Labour had done no such thing. Harman couldn't get her male colleagues to treat gender as a core issue, and ended up scrambling together a separate campaign. Her party had a proud heritage on women's equality: it appointed the first ever female cabinet minister (Margaret Bondfield in 1929), pioneered equal pay legislation, made strides on early years provision for children, and in introducing all-women shortlists in 1997 engineered the biggest single increase in female representation in the Commons. Of the intake of 418 Labour MPs elected in Tony Blair's first landslide victory, 101 were women. The total number of female MPs in the previous parliament across all parties had been just 60.

Yet these achievements sit alongside more problematic strains, a culture descended from a struggle for the rights of the working man that often viewed female workers not as part of that struggle but as competition, and an ideological underpinning that in seeing gender inequality as fixable only by fixing all power imbalances too often sends women to the back of the queue to wait their turn. In every vote for the leadership involving women, the female candidates have come last. Angela Eagle's bid to oust Jeremy Corbyn ran into the sand after the MP Owen Smith put himself forward, in a brain-twisting piece of logic, as an alternative unity candidate. 'If Labour had an all-women leadership race, a man would still win,' tweeted the journalist Stephen Daisley after Eagle's withdrawal.

Harman had climbed higher in Labour than any other woman, elected the party's Deputy Leader when Gordon Brown succeeded Tony Blair in Downing Street. Her predecessor as Deputy Leader, John Prescott, had also served as Deputy Prime Minister. She never got that status and further slights followed. 'Imagine the consternation in my office when we discovered that my involvement in the London G20 summit was inclusion at the No. 10 dinner for the G20 leaders' wives,' Harman said later.[16] Heading into the 2015 election, now deputy to Ed Miliband, Harman found herself sidelined by male advisers, consultants and politicians. Her riposte trundled into view in February of that year, apparently blushing with shame that such a stunt should be necessary.

'That pink bus! Oh my god, the pink bus!' Sitting in a café in the Southbank Centre, I listened to a table of women holding their own debate ahead of WOW's. They, like me, found the political choices on offer to voters about as exciting as a limp egg-and-cress sandwich. They, too, cringed to see Harman's pink bus touring constituencies with its cargo of female MPs. For all its noble intent – and its effectiveness; the negative publicity generated what spin doctors call 'cut through', drawing voters who might otherwise not have engaged – it was tough to get past that pinkness.

The women at the Southbank Centre were weighing exactly the response Harman's pink bus was supposed to head off. They were considering not voting at all. 'There's nobody to vote for,' said one of them.

A tube train rumbled beneath us, or perhaps it was Emmeline Pankhurst spinning through the soil of Brompton Cemetery. Then again, Pankhurst overestimated the transformative power of suffrage. 'It is perfectly evident to any logical mind that when you have got the vote, by the proper use of the vote in sufficient numbers, by combination, you can get out of any legislature whatever you want, or, if you cannot get it, you can send them about their business and choose other people who will be more attentive to your demands,' she declared in 1913. Yet here we were, 86 years after full enfranchisement, still waiting to be fully enfranchised.

This proved to be the inescapable subtext of the whole evening. For all that James and Swinson and Creasy had won admission to the House of Commons, they had not thrived as their talent suggested they should. Swinson was a junior minister, Creasy held the equivalent position on the opposition benches. James served as a Parliamentary Private Secretary, two rungs below a junior minister.

If Westminster didn't value them enough to put them at its top tables, the media helped to reinforce that view. I understood the reasons for this. After 30 years as a journalist, latterly a decade at *TIME* magazine, I was well aware that media companies – like political parties – were still far from closing the gender gap. Male cultures inevitably produce distorted and inadequate coverage of women. For female journalists, sexual harassment by colleagues or interviewees is an occupational hazard as routine and inescapable as a stiff neck from too much time at the computer. Pay and promotional structures value male staff over their female colleagues and, in admitting too few women to decision-making, maintain a male sensibility about which stories should be covered and how. This can be insidious – women receive less coverage than men and what they do often appears labelled 'lifestyle' – or it may express itself in hostility and mockery.

Swinson gave an example of the latter during the WOW discussion: her observation during a parliamentary debate that boys might want to play with dolls mutated in the *Sun*'s reporting into a proposal to mandate boys to play with Barbies.[17] New media also meant new challenges. Creasy had become the target of virulent Twitter trolls spewing rape and death threats, simply by virtue of being female.

The trio set out the problems of women in politics compellingly. They had some answers. Yet it was equally evident that they had little power to make change and little prospect of more power. So when Jude Kelly, the artistic director of the Southbank Centre and moderator of the event, invited the audience to volunteer proposals to speed gender equality, I found myself clutching the microphone.

I explained that when Jude conceived of WOW in 2009, she had recruited me to the founding committee. I talked about the sense of female community and commonality the festival always generates, and congratulated the MPs on demonstrating their spirit despite party political differences.

I continued: 'I, like many other people, come to this election knowing that whatever the outcome, it will be disappointing. It would be so much more exciting – we would be spoiled for choice – if the three of you were the leaders of the parties.'

The audience whooped in agreement.

'The questions you've all been asking this evening are about not only how we make progress but how we hold onto progress. So what I would like to do is invite anybody who wants to come to the bar afterwards or interact with me on Twitter to consider whether one way of doing this might be to actually found a women's equality party, one that works with women in the mainstream parties that are doing the good things, and indeed with men in those mainstream parties who are doing the things that need to be done, but works rather in the way of some fringe parties that we've seen coming up to push [gender equality] so that it finally really is front and centre of the agendas of mainstream parties. At which point we'd happily dissolve our party, go away and leave the mainstream parties to what they should be doing.'

'So that is my question. I will be at the bar afterwards.'

'Are you buying, Catherine?' asked Creasy.

I could have reduced that whole rambling, unplanned intervention to two observations: old politics was failing and its failure was creating room for change; mainstream parties had lost their core identities and were therefore primed to copy anything that looked like it might be a vote winner. If you build it, they will come.

The growth of the Green Party had provided mulch for green shoots in other parties. When the United Kingdom Independence Party started winning serious support, the other parties gave up challenging its anti-immigration rhetoric and started contorting themselves into UKIP-shaped positions. It wouldn't be until the results of the EU Referendum the following year that we would begin to see the full consequences of the copycat syndrome, but it was already clear that UKIP didn't need to be in government to transform Britain. The threat to women posed by a surging UKIP and the success of similar parties in other countries was also becoming evident. UKIP, Tea Party Republicans and France's Front National, to name just a few, all stood for the backlash against a whole range of values, including gender equality. 'The European Parliament, in their foolishness, have voted for increased maternity pay,' UKIP leader Nigel Farage had tweeted in 2010. 'I'm off for a drink.' Why couldn't a women's equality party steal from their political playbook to assert the opposite view? Why couldn't a women's equality party trigger copycat impulses in the established parties and finally push the interests of the oppressed majority to the top of the political agenda?

People enthused about the idea the moment the words came out of my mouth. They also assumed, to my alarm, that I was proposing to do something to make it a reality. Some followed me to the bar and yet more joined the discussion in the perpetual pub of social media. I returned home to an empty house and an empty fridge and before going to sleep left a message on Facebook to amuse friends who knew of my musician husband's dedication to eating well. 'Andy's only been on tour for 24 hours and I've already had a sandwich for dinner. And started a women's equality party.' I added: 'Want to join? Non-partisan and open to men and women.'

'I'm in!' replied the writer Stella Duffy almost instantaneously. 'Me too,' declared Sophie Walker, a Reuters journalist who could not anticipate just how deeply in she would soon find herself. By the next morning, the thread had lengthened considerably and all the responses were similar.

I called Sandi. She too was on the WOW founding committee and two weeks earlier we had talked at a committee dinner about how to channel the energy the festival always generated into transformative politics. We hadn't discussed specific mechanisms, so I thought she might be interested to hear about my spontaneous proposal at the Women and Politics event. Her response wasn't quite as anticipated.

'But that's my idea,' she said. Each year she concocted a show called Mirth Control as a finale for WOW and for 2015 was planning to bring onto the stage cabinet ministers from an imaginary women's equality party. She'd been on the point of ringing me with a proposition. 'Darling,' she said. 'Do you want to be foreign secretary?'

The idea of someone with no Cabinet experience and a habit of making off-colour jokes becoming the UK's premier advocate abroad made me laugh, but that was before Theresa May appointed Boris Johnson to the role. Both Sandi and I aspired to see more female secretaries of state.

Days after WOW's glorious finale, we sat down together and lightly took decisions over a few beers that would disrupt our lives and many others. We decided to give it a go, try to start a party. We swiftly concluded we weren't the right people to lead it. Both of us are outsiders, born and bred. Our parents shuttled us back and forth across the Atlantic and plunged us into a series of new schools and social groups. Sandi is the funniest woman in the world but her wit is a shield that conceals an enduring shyness. She would never have willingly put into the public domain details about her private life – she came out in an interview with the *Sunday Times* in 1994 – had she not faced twin pressures. Tabloids threatened to reveal her 'secret', and she felt compelled to campaign for lesbian and gay rights and equal marriage. Her revelation earned death threats that sent her into hiding with her young children. The last thing she wanted was more disruption. 'Can we go home yet?' she asks me, often and plaintively. It's a joke but there's always truth to Sandi's humour.

We also feared we were too metropolitan, too media, to rally the inclusive movement we envisaged. For the party to be effective, it had to be as big and diverse a force as possible. That meant getting away from the assumption that the left had sole ownership of the fight for gender equality. It meant a commitment to a collaborative politics dedicated to identifying and expand-ing common ground, and that in turn demanded a serious effort to build in diversity from the start. That diversity had to include a wide range of political affiliations and leanings.

Sandi also realised she'd have to give up her job as host of the BBC's satirical current affairs show, *The News Quiz*. Only once during the process of negotiating her exit did she privately admit to a wobble. '*News Quiz* wasn't just a radio show for me, it was a kind of family,' she says now. 'I'd been involved with the show for nearly a quarter of a century. I was passionate about our accuracy and our fearlessness in tackling anyone and anything without fear or favour.' She knew she couldn't maintain that principle as the passionate proponent of the Women's Equality Party. 'At the last recording we all wore black tie and there was a great party atmosphere but leaving was one of the hardest things I have ever had to do.' It was a move her fans didn't easily forgive. After the announcement, the ranks of my regular trolls swelled with angry Radio Four listeners venting their displeasure.

Even before Sandi's public involvement, our meetings, advertised only on Facebook and by word of mouth, drew hundreds. From the first such gathering, on 28 March 2015, came confirmation of the party's name. Some participants argued for 'Equality Party', but that risked diffusing the message while potentially reinventing the Labour Party. Others favoured Gender Equality Party as an easier sell to male and gender non-binary voters, but that had the ring of a student society in a comedic campus novel. Sandi has little patience for the discussion, which has continued to flare. 'When I'm asked why it's called the Women's Equality Party, I always say "We just thought we'd be clear. We're busy women and we didn't really want our agenda to be a secret."' 'Women's Equality Party' is direct, unambiguous and produces the acronym WE, pleasingly inclusive if apt to spark toilet humour. Politics, as we would learn at first hand, involves compromise.

Speakers at that first meeting included Sophie Walker, later elected WE's first leader by the steering committee that also emerged from that meeting. At the second meeting on 18 April we signed off on six core objectives jotted down on a napkin during a meal with friends: equal representation, equal pay, an education system that creates opportunities for all children, shared responsibilities in parenting and caregiving, equal treatment by and in the media, and an end to violence against women and girls. In June, our first fundraiser at Conway Hall in London sold out within hours of ticket sales going live. In July 2015, WE registered as an official party. October saw the launch of our first substantial policy document, compiled in close consultation with experts, campaigning organisations and grassroots support that already amounted to tens of thousands of members and activists. WE raised over half a million pounds by the year end. In May 2016 we secured more than 350,000 votes at our first elections for London Mayor, the London Assembly, the Welsh Assembly and the Scottish Parliament.

A month later, I encountered Boris Johnson's father, Stanley, a former Member of the European Parliament, at the birthday gathering of another politician. 'Catherine,' he shouted across the room. 'I heard some terrible news about you!' The room fell silent, heads swivelled. 'I heard you'd become a feminist!' Later that evening I talked to a Labour peer who berated me for splitting his party. This was a feat Labour was managing without external help. What the peer meant was that we'd taken Labour votes. At the same event, prominent members of Labour and the Conservatives confessed they'd voted for us. Westminster was no longer patronising and dismissing us, but it wasn't yet sure what to make of us either.

WE's second year has seen the transition from scrappy start-up, with an ad hoc and necessarily fluid structure, to fully-fledged party with more than 70 branches and many more in the works, driven by its members. Our first party conference in Manchester, attended by 1,600 delegates, adopted a raft of new policies including a seventh core objective, equal health, and ratified an internal party democracy devised to give branch activists a guaranteed presence on decision-making bodies and ensure real diversity on those bodies. Throughout the year we ran campaigns that had significant impact such as #WECount – mapping sexual harassment, assault and verbal abuse directed against women – and #NoSizeFitsAll, highlighting the link between the fashion industry and negative body image. We began detailed work with other parties too. The Liberal Democrats asked for help in drafting legislation to combat revenge porn – the disclosure of intimate images without consent. Several parties and politicians opened conversations with us about much closer cooperation, including the possibility of alliances and joint candidacies.

This book isn't intended as a history of the party. These are still early days for us – and could be the end of days too. The challenges to the survival of our upstart initiative remain acute in a political system designed, like zombie Johansson's breasts, to smother movement in the lower tiers. These challenges are also shifting and shape-changing with unprecedented speed since the UK began disentangling itself from the European Union and tangling instead with the demons the process is unleashing. The Referendum was conceived to reconcile internal strains within the Conservative Party, but did no such thing. Labour's fault lines were deeper still; things fell apart, the centrists could not hold on. As its factions grappled with each other, fugitives from the fighting found a haven in the Women's Equality Party but some of them dreamed of repositioning us. 'What I'd like is for the Women's Equality Party to remake itself as the Equality Party,' wrote the novelist Jeanette Winterson in the *Guardian*. 'It's a relevant name, a powerful name, and naming matters. I'd like to drop Labour and New Labour as words that don't mean anything anymore. If you still needed proof of that after the last election, Brexit just gave it to you.'[18]

We did consider changing the name but most of us opposed the idea of dropping 'women' from our brand – that would mean becoming like all other parties and relegating women's interests. A fresh danger emerging, as Britain finally got another female Prime Minister, was that people would see her and think 'job done', even though the mechanisms and back rooms of all the mainstream parties remained in the same old hands. And Brexit posed a danger to women as the process of decoupling raised questions over rights and protections anchored in Europe and guaranteed by Europe. Our vision was more relevant than ever. Whenever we shared it, we won new support, new members. Our first problem was, and remains, how to get the message out on meagre resources. The second problem is how to raise the money to keep going.

So a monograph on the Women's Equality Party would be premature. I will, however, share insights from the process of starting the party. Journalists often suffer from the delusion of being intimately acquainted with the world. Work had taken me to six continents, war zones and pleasure domes, theatres and operating theatres, palaces and prisons, to interviews with dictators and democrats. It's quite a lot like being married to a rock musician. You enjoy Access All Areas: ringside seats for big events, freedom to roam backstage and go behind the ropes. These experiences foster understanding, but they don't make you part of the band. As a journalist, I imagined I understood politics. As a journalist-politician-whatever, I now understand how imperfect that understanding was.

But my primary aim in writing *Attack of the 50 Ft. Women* is not just to mine lessons from the recent past and present, but to think about Equalia. What can today's world tell us about the way to this promised land and what we might find when we get there?

'Circumstantial accounts of the future are idealistic and, worse, static,' observed Germaine Greer in *The Female Eunuch*, the text that woke me and many others to feminism. As is often the case with Greerisms, their author is both right and wrong.

No such account makes sufficient allowance for the impact of quakes, natural or of human origin, or the intended consequences that flow even from planned events. Technology is shaking up our lives in ways no seer foresaw (though science fiction writers came close to predicting whole chunks of it). How, for example, can we talk about gender in the future workplace if the workplace – if work itself – might disappear?

The answer cannot be to avoid such discussions, but to recognise the limits of our knowledge and imaginations and to try to expand both. Politics is all about shaping the future, yet political movements succumb too easily to the Happily Ever After syndrome. Gender equality advocates are no exception, focusing on the big, fat, equal wedding of genders, the moment equality is reached, and not what lies beyond. Confetti drifts and then the picture fades.

Knocking on doors for the Women's Equality Party ahead of the London elections proved revealing on that issue and, on occasion, literally. A resident of a Southwark tower block responded cautiously to my knock: 'Who is it?' 'I'm here about the elections.' 'Electricity?' In evident alarm, perhaps fearing I had come to cut his energy supply, he threw open the door, naked.

Campaigning also uncovered a generational split in male attitudes. Men in their fifties, finding WE canvassers on the doorstep, often responded 'I'll fetch the wife'. Younger men engaged directly. We didn't need to explain this was a party for them, pushing a platform that would also benefit them.

That was encouraging; so too was the enthusiasm we encountered. People told us they had literally danced when they heard about WE. But they also asked difficult questions that we were already grappling with, both personally and as a party. Would gender equality encourage other kinds of equality? Did we want an improved version of our current society – gender equality within existing structures – or something more radical? How much change might be achieved through nudging? In what circumstances might prohibition or coercive legislation be necessary?

You can see why people would shy away from Equalia if they imagine it to be a brave new world that, like Aldous Huxley's addled dystopia, requires a sublimation of the individual to a supposed greater good. You can see why they might lack enthusiasm for building Equalia if they sense that it will simply enshrine old injustices within a new pecking order. Would the new race of 50-foot women create a fairer system or form a new elite?

If only we could poke around Equalian homes and businesses, check what's on the telly and in the news, find out how people are having sex and if anyone is selling it, taste the air to verify that it's cleaner, and confirm that the shadows of conflict have receded. If only we could find out who does the dishes or the low-paid work in Equalia and whether such work is more highly valued. Will a society that allows everyone to take up as much space as they like produce giants, or might the absence of adversity diminish creativity, or obviate the need for ingenuity? We don't even know what gender would mean in a society freed from gender programming. So how do we begin to answer questions so fundamental, not just to the Women's Equality Party, but to everyone affected by the global imbalance between the sexes? And that's all of us.

The ambition of this book is just that – not to answer these fundamental questions but to begin to answer them. There are clear limits to how definitive any such inquiry can be, not only because of the paucity of hard information, but because of the confines of my own experience. I am a product of my own background and socialisation, of a particular confluence of genes and influences, of luck – or privilege – and half a century of racketing about the planet and poking into other people's business. For this book I travelled as far as time and resources permitted, interviewed as widely as possible, read and kept reading, thought and kept thinking. I needed to learn in order to find out how much I didn't know. The Equalia I describe, and the pathways I discovered, are located in the cultures that produced me. It may well be that the routes and outcomes look different in other hemispheres.

My quest took me to Iceland, the nation that comes closest to Equalia, and to countries and continents that have made less progress on gender equality, to ascertain the factors and people promoting or retarding change. Angela Merkel, like Sandi, is a tiny woman who takes up a lot of space. Germany, under her Chancellorship, has become a better place for women – yes, even for the women of Cologne. Is she the kind of giantess we need, a *15-Meter Frau*? Does she lead differently because she is a woman? Now it's May every month in Downing Street. Is this a sea change or just proof of the so-called glass cliff, the phenomenon first identified by researchers at the University of Exeter that sees leadership opportunities open up to women at times of crisis when the odds against successful leadership peak. And what should we make of Hillary Clinton's fate and the rise of Trumpism and related strains of populism in Europe? These signal fresh challenges for women and minorities and to any consensus on gender equality. In France this movement is led by a woman, Marine Le Pen, who aims to secure the country's presidency, a position conferring executive powers unrivalled in the democratic world. Yet the first day of Trump's presidency also triggered the biggest women-led marches in history, with 3.5m protesters on US streets and millions more in 20 other countries determined to resist the rising world order.

We will survey the predictable changes heralded by science and technology, and by global shifts in power and population. China's growth is endangered by the legacy of a one-child policy within a Confucian culture that values boys more than girls and, in acting out these preferences, has ended up with a surplus of discontented single men. India has 43 million more men than women. Rwanda's population tilts in the other direction because genocide killed off scores of men. It now ranks higher than Iceland, indeed highest in the world, on female representation in politics. So, is it a paragon of gender equality?

We'll examine the media, its power and potential. We'll go to Hollywood and Facebook. We'll visit citadels of privilege and ghettos of oppression. We'll talk to experts, leaders, people in public life and in their most private pursuits. The personal *is* political and for that reason let us start this journey in that most personal of spaces, at home.

Please join me at my kitchen table.

Chapter One: Gate-crashing the club

DOWNTRODDEN PEOPLES CLAIM superior qualities to compensate for inferior status. Women cling to a belief in essential, female difference. We are emotionally intelligent. We are nurturing. We work together rather than against each other. We can multitask. Want something done? Ask a busy woman.

The early months of the Women's Equality Party appeared to reinforce this thesis. Each successive gathering of our newly formed steering committee brought a banquet to the table, of energy, ideas, sweet concord and food – so much food.

Sandi came with herrings: pickled herrings, herrings in a sweet mustard and dill sauce, herrings in soured cream, and pumpernickel already cut to carry satisfactory consignments of herring from plate to mouth without need of forks. Others baked cakes from scratch. I supplied alcohol.

Each meeting also brought long lists of tasks completed without reminders, despite multiple commitments tugging at sleeves. One of the most time-consuming jobs involved answering the unstanchable flow of emails that news of WE had triggered. Volunteers often worked through the night, their exhaustion mitigated by the enthusiasm of the correspondence.

'Thank you for giving me something to believe in again.'
'At last, something to get excited about in politics!'
'For the first time in my 14 years of not bothering to vote I am inspired.'

'I am 16 years old and passionate about feminism. I would love to be a bigger part of the worldwide fight for women's equality!'

'I am so excited about this party – I've waited my whole adult life for it.'

'YES PLEASE, this is just what we have needed for such a long time. I'm on board, we have much work to do, please delegate.'

To delegate, you need a structure. We created an organisation from scratch and then scrambled to update it as needs and priorities changed, sprouting subcommittees to formulate policy and deal with press, social media, outreach, fundraising, finance and the demands that bureaucracy ladles onto the political process.

Britain is generous with its portions of red tape, far more so than many other nations. In July 2015, I met up with Sunniva Schultze-Florey, who had also co-founded a new political party four months earlier. Inspired by Sweden's Feminist Initiative, she and a small group of friends started a Norwegian offshoot, Feminist Initiative Bergen-Hordaland, and they were already preparing for their first elections, for local government, in September. They didn't need to do much more to make the party official than to announce its existence; they didn't have to raise money for deposits to run, just collect a certain number of signatures. Norway's proportional voting system meant the entry level for new parties didn't seem too daunting – only a few thousand votes to win a council seat.

As our Norwegian counterpart plunged into campaigning, we jumped through hoops just to secure the right to campaign, an exercise as questionable as a dolphin show at a water park – and as anachronistic. Politics in the UK doesn't just look and sound like a club. It is a club, with rules designed to exclude the wrong type of person as defined by the type of person who already belongs to the club. A new party cannot open for membership or put up candidates for election until registered with the Electoral Commission. That involves writing a constitution and rules of association and appointing officers. You must also establish a company and then find a bank willing to accept your business, because a party is also an enterprise. Quite a few bankers sucked pens and stared skywards when confronted by a start-up enterprise without a business plan or guarantee of income.

You can see why they might worry. The club rules ensure it's hugely expensive to do politics. There are deposits to be paid for each candidate – £10,000 to stand for Mayor of London! A further £10,000 to appear in the official brochure that goes out to voters! Turn again, Whittington: the road to London's City Hall is truly paved with gold.

Campaign costs are eye-watering, especially in first-past-the-post elections such as Westminster's, where the overall number of votes across the UK matters less than the concentration of votes in individual constituencies. In the May 2015 general election, UKIP picked up one in eight votes, almost 3.9 million in total, but won only a single seat. The Scottish National Party gained 1.5 million votes and 56 seats. To successfully challenge old parties, newcomers must finance not only profile-raising marketing and PR campaigns but also street-by-street, door-by-door drives, reliant on volunteers and paid expertise, and underpinned by pricey technologies.

There's another way in which money talks. One reason politics is dominated by affluent men in suits is that candidacy is expensive and risky. It's far easier for people with private incomes or salaried jobs that grant leave of absence to run, and that's assuming they aren't caring for children or elderly relatives. The Women's Equality Party wanted to support women to become candidates, not only by paying their deposit money but also by providing bursaries to help with childcare and other costs.

So we were eager to open for membership as soon as possible to establish the revenue stream necessary to do this – any of this. We needed funding just to collect funds. The Electoral Commission allows political parties to accept donations over £500 only from permissible donors: UK-based companies and individuals registered on a UK electoral roll. The regulations are intended to stop foreigners and tax exiles from buying influence in British politics – no representation without taxation, as it were – but do nothing of the kind. Any global corporation with a UK subsidiary is entitled to donate, no matter how breathtaking its tax-minimising schemes. Any person rich enough to stash wealth offshore is probably also rich enough to find channels to donate.

Yet WE risked penalties if, say, a British national living in the UK but not registered to vote gave a series of small donations that in total breached the £500 threshold. The only way to guard against such accidents is to check would-be donors against the electoral register, which inevitably isn't a conveniently centralised electronic list, but a series of lists held by local authorities. Sian McGee, a new law graduate and youngest member of the original steering committee, became WE's first paid employee, hired to perform these checks. She immediately spotted a potentially dodgy transaction. The party had launched a time-limited founding membership scheme, ranging from £2 a month to £1,000 and upwards for lifetime membership. Sandi enrolled online for the latter option but Sian could find no Toksvigs on the electoral roll. She could not know that Sandi's information is withheld since a stalker broke into her house. Sian diligently rang Sandi to query her eligibility to help found the party she had founded.

The final hurdle to gaining official party status involved seeking the Electoral Commission's approval for our logo and slogan for use on ballot papers. Two wonderfully talented designers, Sara Burns and Jeanette Clement, volunteered to produce a logo for us. They had never met before joining the steering committee, but instantly devised a way of working together, and celebrated that collaborative spirit, and the party's aims, with a design that turned the E of WE into an equal sign. They chose a palette not in use by any other party – green, white and violet, the colours of the Suffragette movement. The committee then voted on a range of slogans and landed back on the one I had written for the public meeting back in March: 'Because equality is better for everyone.'

This book aims to test that proposition. It might appear that the only point of debate relates to men and whether by ceding their dominance they would really gain more than they lose. The rest seems self-evident.

Inequality is yawning and its impact is disfiguring. The gap between rich and poor countries, and between rich and poor, is widening. One per cent of the global population owns more wealth than everyone else on the planet combined. Not even the one per cent look happy about this state of affairs as they transfer from one hermetically sealed bubble to the next, ringed with security lest real life accost them. In rich countries, the poor struggle daily to survive. As many as a fifth of Britons live below the poverty line, as do more than 15 per cent of Americans. Social mobility is stalling. Social unrest is deepening. Conflicts spill across borders and reach out violently into distant city centres. Many of the people displaced by those conflicts, some 65.3 million on current estimates, seek shelter in countries already lacking resources; 86 per cent of the world's refugees are lodged in the developing world. Migrants reaching Europe should expect a mixed reception. Any dreams of universal live-and-let-live tolerance are dissipating as populist hate-mongers and extremist movements find, in their supposed polarities, common cause against liberalism.

Surely if we successfully dismantle the patriarchy, the biggest structural injustice of all, other structural injustices must also begin to crumble. Surely a more gender-equal world will be a more equal world in other ways too.

Yet from the start of WE, easy assumptions frayed. Our first steering committee meeting took place at my central London flat, in my kitchen. We sat around an extendable table owned by my family since 1933, when my widowed great-grandmother started dealing antiques from her front room in a Chicago suburb during the city's Century of Progress International Exposition (a World's Fair with the motto 'Science Finds, Industry Applies, Man Adapts'). The table tells a story not just of female entrepreneurship, but of comfort. My middle-class family, émigrés to the US, not refugees, lived in homes large enough for such a table.

There were ten of us at the first steering committee meeting. Not every woman (and neither of the men who joined us) had been born to the same level of advantage, and none of us had problem-free lives. Between us we wrestled with disability, physical and mental health issues, had experienced racism, homophobia, ageism and abuse. Still, we all enjoyed the luxury of political activism. Entry to the steering committee rested on two qualifications: an enthusiasm for the idea of the party and a commitment to getting it started. Many women are too busy with low-paid work or unpaid caregiving to spend time trying to fix the problems of women in low-paid work or unpaid caregiving. Our participation in the committee defined us as an elite, and we knew that to build a representative party we needed to be a representative party at the core. It would take us longer to appreciate the scale and complexity of that task.

As the committee recruited additional members, and culinary contributions became more elaborate, we had to look for other venues. The size of my table wasn't the issue. Mandy Colleran, an actor and activist, used a motorised wheelchair that could not navigate the narrow doorway to my flat. Other members volunteered to host, but every alternative venue revealed structural impediments that able-bodied residents hadn't appreciated. A lift in one apartment block proved too small. Another disabled committee member offered her flat but its front steps defeated Mandy's chair. There are degrees of disability as there are degrees of inequality. Many impediments are visible only to those whose path they block.

Mandy is a coruscating speaker, painfully and often hilariously direct in her opinions. She spoke up at our first public meeting and again at the second, held at Conway Hall, since 1929 the home of the Ethical Society and a fulcrum of liberal activism. Its CEO, Jim Walsh, had quickly decided to support the nascent Women's Equality Party by making the auditorium available to us for events at low rates with deferred payment. Unfortunately, Conway Hall's precarious income and listed building status meant that, although it is fully accessible for audience members in wheelchairs, there is no ramp to the stage. We decided against using the stage for that event and anyone who wanted to speak did so from the floor. Sometimes equality is about finding a level that works for everyone. A lot of the time, it's more complicated than that.

At first we plundered our own address books to grow the party but our London base risked a London bias. It has been exciting to watch the idea spread to other parts of England and to Scotland, Wales and Northern Ireland, and in each context to define different sets of priorities within our unified commitment to change. Committee members' combined circles encompassed a wide range of professions and experiences, even if they were a little heavy on entertainment, media and politics. My friends and contacts came in all shapes, sizes and flavours. If asked, I might well have described them as diverse.

That's because it's easy to misunderstand diversity. One friend, a senior figure in the media, explains it well. He is hugely talented, but knows that the fact he ticks some 'diversity boxes' made the companies that employed him look good without actually challenging their culture. He speaks and acts like a member of the establishment club despite a mixed-race heritage and comprehensive-school background. He learned to minimise differences, to put people, including people like me, at ease. 'Frankly, as one black friend who has risen a long way in politics put it to me, we don't frighten the horses,' he says. The point he is making is that for organisations to benefit from diversity, be they corporations or political parties, they must accept and value the discomfort of difference. It's pleasant when your colleagues agree. It's often more productive when they challenge.

Diversity isn't always visible, and, as my friend pointed out, visible diversity is by no means enough, but it does matter. Groucho Marx famously sent a telegram to a Hollywood club: 'Please accept my resignation. I don't care to belong to any club that will have me as a member.' Most people aren't by instinct Marxists. They care to belong only to clubs that appear to accept them.

Women aren't just excluded from politics by a lack of time and money. Many are put off by the way it looks and sounds because they cannot see or hear themselves in its monotone braying. In launching a political party that took as one of its core objectives the equal representation of women – that itched to throw open the doors of public institutions and of private enterprises not just to more women but to a wider range of women – we needed to ensure we didn't replicate the deficiencies of the existing system. This couldn't be just a party for friends and friends of friends, for like-minded people who felt comfortable together. We had to incorporate visible and invisible diversity, to attract the widest possible engagement, and to engage as an organisation with all of those perspectives.

One form of diversity you can't see is that of political allegiance. By having people of divergent political persuasions around the table and opening our membership to members of all other democratic parties, we intended to identify the tracts of common ground between those parties on gender equality, and either work with them or, by winning votes away from them, spark them into copying our policies.

It wouldn't be enough to be a broad church – and we were anyway unlikely to become one – if we failed adequately to address the issues that divide the women's movement within itself and from other movements. 'When feminism does not explicitly oppose racism, and when anti-racism does not incorporate opposition to patriarchy, race and gender politics often end up being antagonistic to each other and both interests lose,' wrote American academic and civil rights activist Kimberlé Williams Crenshaw in 1992.[1] She had coined a term, 'intersectionality', to describe the ways in which disadvantages such as race, gender, class, religion and age intersect and intensify, and she also proposed frameworks to enable collaborative and mutually beneficial advocacy among disadvantaged groups. Her observation was both true and prophetic, in good ways and bad. America's 2016 elections highlighted deep splits among female voters, and the sharpest related to race. Ninety-four per cent of black women voted for Hillary Clinton; 53 per cent of white women voted for Donald Trump.[6] Black women needed no coaching to understand the dangers a Trump presidency represented to them. Large numbers of white women succumbed to a cocktail of ingrained misconceptions and prejudices.

They – we – are taught throughout our lives that white men have a grip on power and wealth and that the easiest way to share in those benefits is to align with them. We are inculcated with the lie that equality is like a cake: if you take a piece, there is less for me. We also absorb the propaganda that calls into question the abilities of our own sex to lead, just as we will all have picked up racist attitudes.

No wonder feminism divides along these lines – and how urgent it is that white women learn, fast, to recognise where our true interest lies, in building a world that works better for all women and, indeed, for all genders. Kimberlé Crenshaw created an essential framework for thinking about how we should do this. The most effective organisations combatting misogyny and racism take an intersectional approach, but women of colour are apt to recoil from the embrace of white feminists who presume to speak for them rather than giving them the floor.

Long before white women helped put Trump in the White House, anger at clumsy patronage, and at the allied phenomenon of wealthy women presuming to understand the priorities of the poor, had become so intense in corners of feminism that the phrase 'white, middle-class feminist' emerged as a potent insult. In 1983, the novelist Alice Walker coined the term 'womanist' as an alternative to white feminism. 'How can you claim the label of those who would oppress you to see their goals realised, even when commonality exists in some areas?' asked the blogger Renee Martin three decades later, in an essay explaining why she, as a black woman, rejects the term 'feminism'.[2] Commonalities are not enough to stop movements that can only succeed through cohesion and volume from splintering.

Sandi and I – undeniably white, irretrievably middle class and irrevocably feminist – of course drew fire. The criticism helped us to focus on the issues underpinning it. Just as men lack a visceral understanding of the female condition, so women leading reasonably comfortable lives may not automatically grasp what it is to suffer multiple oppressions. How could we as activists in our own flurry of activity avoid taking up space that others, less privileged struggle to claim? Were we entitled to found a party or was this action proof of entitlement, in the negative sense of the word?

The answer — or at least one answer — is that it depends what the party does and achieves. Another is that the appropriate response to critics of white, middle-class feminism cannot be for every white, middle-class feminist to down tools. That would be to fall into a similar trap as the white, middle-class anti-feminists who deny the evident and urgent need for greater gender equality at home because there are more acute examples of misogyny elsewhere. Nimco Ali, co-founder of Daughters of Eve, a non-profit organisation focused on raising awareness and education regarding FGM, was one of the first members of the steering committee and attacked in some quarters for joining the Women's Equality Party. She points out that the black, Asian and minority-ethnic population of the UK stands at less than 12 per cent. This means, she says, that 'there are going to be women at the forefront who are white, but it's how they use their privilege and platform to have that conversation.'[3] To acknowledge that some women need less help than others is not to deny that all women need help. The question is how to be helpful.

I got to put that question to Kimberlé Williams Crenshaw herself in May 2016. She had come to the UK as a guest lecturer at the London School of Economics, on furlough from an extraordinary range of jobs and commitments: her law professorships at UCLA and Columbia, and the recently formed Congressional Caucus on Black Women and Girls, as well as from her executive directorship of the organisation she co-founded, the African American Policy Forum (AAPF), and from #SayHerName, the campaign she and the AAPF had started the previous year with other organisations to draw attention to the black women killed by police and overlooked by the Black Lives Matter movement. She'd arrived in London just two days before but managed to lead me to one of the few good, tourist-free bars in Covent Garden.

She laughed at my question, then sighed. 'Well, you have your work cut out for you,' she said. 'I think there has to be a lot of work on all sides and that's the work of coalition and that's hard.' She gave generous, practical advice about how to do the work, and much encouragement, but also slipped in a warning. 'I'm suspicious of privileged women who just go: "Yes, you're absolutely right." And have nothing to say beyond that. You have to engage deeply. I want people to ask and question if they don't feel it, so that you can have the fight, you can try to resolve it. So, it's kind of about having to find some agreement among those of us who feel Othered and are Othered: What is it that we want to see? What is it that we want to find agreement on? What is it that shapes our agenda?'[4]

It took an effort of will not to respond 'you're absolutely right', for the sake of the gag and because she absolutely was. It would never have been possible to build an effective organisation from my kitchen table. We had to go out and reach out, involve an ever wider demographic and, crucially, find ways to create an internal democracy that gave full weight to each of those voices without slowing momentum or losing sight of the reasons for starting the party in the first place.

We've made progress but nowhere near enough. Pushing for diversity isn't the same as achieving it – an obvious point but one that bears repeating because of the frequency with which organisations quote their diversity policies as supposed evidence of diversity. The process can be long and is littered with obstacles that I have come to understand much better

Right at the beginning, perhaps two days after proposing the party, I called a friend and fellow journalist, Hannah Azieb Pool, and attempted to persuade her that she should lead it. My thinking was simple – to the point of naivety. I asked myself 'would I vote for her?' and the answer was a resounding yes. Would she appeal to voters of all genders, classes and ethnicities? I thought so. Eritrean-born, adopted by a white family in Manchester, she was in a position to speak to the universalities of female experience and to the specifics of intersectionality – the ways in which that experience is changed or impacted by other factors.

Hannah thanked me, and said she'd ponder. A few days later she declined, with expressions of regret. She had too much going on, too many commitments. Straining to hear her as I stood in a noisy airport, phone clasped to ear, I tuned out the background hum of things unsaid. It was only recently that I summoned up the courage to ask her if she had spared me a more brutal response. She explained that the reasons she gave were genuine but that the deciding factor had been risk – and the risks would always be greater for black women. The animus she'd attract from trolls and anti-feminists would comingle with racism, while some strands of black activism would inevitably label her a sell-out.

WE represented a leap in the dark and, while she trusted Sandi and me, she couldn't be sure how the party would evolve around us. After working at the *Guardian*, she knew that organisations sometimes mistake good intentions for good practice. I also hadn't factored in the economic hit she'd take in spending time party-building. If we asked her now, she might be more inclined to say yes, she added kindly.

There were other barriers to overcome. Some people who came on board kept their support quiet because they were members of parties less enlightened about collaborative politics. Even so, every day brought a fresh crop of outrageous talents to my kitchen table. This, we realised, is what politics might be if it weren't such a narrow club. The candidates WE fielded at the elections in May 2016, all new to politics, were extraordinarily gifted and extraordinarily different to each other. The steering committee crackled with ideas and energy.

Even in this crowd, Sophie Walker was an obvious standout. I had invited her to speak on equal parenting at our first ever public meeting. She held the attention of the room in a way that only natural communicators can do. In April 2015 the steering committee elected Sophie leader. The vote was unanimous and unanimously enthusiastic. In August, on the day she came to work at the party full time, leaving a job at Reuters to do so, she and Sandi and I lined up for a joint portrait in the King's Cross offices of the *Guardian*.

We might have been re-enacting the '*Class Sketch*'. First performed in 1966 on David Frost's satirical TV show, *The Frost Report*, the skit featured tall, gaunt John Cleese peering down his nose at the shorter, stockier comedian Ronnie Barker. 'I look down on him, because I am upper class,' Cleese says. Barker returns his gaze: 'I look up to him, because he is upper class. But …' He swivels to stare at five-foot-nothing Ronnie Corbett. 'I look down on him because he is lower class. I am middle class.' 'I know my place,' deadpans Corbett.

Sophie, at well over six foot and skinny, is Cleese to my Barker and Sandi's Corbett. Stand us next to each other, and the effect is pretty funny. Some of our critics laughed at us, rather than with us. They depicted the Women's Equality Party as a joke and the joke was that we were all middle class. 'Sandi Toksvig's Women's Equality Party is a middle-class ladies' campaign group doomed to fail,' read one headline.

That neatly summarised the message of the *Guardian* feature that accompanied the photos, written by a journalist called Paula Cocozza.

We arrived for the interview and photo shoot after a full morning of meetings in my kitchen. We'd strategised our approach to a fundraiser that evening and discussed Stella Duffy's proposals for extending our reach beyond our initial catchment. The first person to sign up to the party on Facebook, and an original member of the steering committee, Stella was our branch-builder and queen of email-answering, directing the enthusiasms of would-be supporters into practical steps, and often pulling all-nighters as she attempted to combine her commitment to WE with her work as an author and the founder of the community arts and science project, Fun Palaces.

A chunk of the morning before the *Guardian* interview had also been devoted to making progress on policy, a consultative process harnessing the input of our rapidly expanding branches, grassroots organisations, campaigners and experts. We ran through a to-do list that included pinning down the date and detail of our autumn policy launch, and figuring out the logistics for a series of membership and fundraising drives, including a potential partnership with the producers and distributor of the movie *Suffragette*. We discussed merchandising possibilities too. We needed money, we needed staff and we needed offices.

The flow of emails, far from slowing, had multiplied and diversified. In addition to offers of help and declarations of enthusiasm, we now received endless press bids, queries from organisations working in overlapping fields, and approaches from politicians from other parties wanting to scope us out. Many of these communications betrayed false assumptions about the size and resourcing of WE. Correspondents complained if they didn't get a response within 24 hours. One group asked *us* for a donation.

We were certainly more organised than we had been. Our subcommittees still relied heavily on volunteers, but this situation was clearly unsustainable – for the party and the exhausted volunteers. In addition to Sian, we now had a fierce and forensic Treasurer, Samantha da Soller, and a secret weapon, Polly Mackenzie, a Liberal Democrat who had until the recent elections served as Deputy Director of Policy at 10 Downing Street for the coalition government and had come to us as a consultant. Marketing and public relations support came from Andrea Hartley and her company Skating Panda. She had apologised to me after the March public meeting: she loved the idea of the party but didn't have time to help. A few days later she emailed to say she didn't have time to help but would do so anyway.

In Sophie we had that most precious of assets – a leader, a natural and inspirational leader. When she spoke, people listened and wanted to listen. She could run meetings, an underrated skill essential to an evolving organisation. She had already cut her campaign teeth pushing for better treatment for her daughter Grace, whose Asperger's Syndrome went undiagnosed for years, in part because the condition is assumed not to affect girls.

Sophie had become a potent advocate and activist, and ran marathons to raise money for autism charities. In her blog, *Grace Under Pressure*, later published as a book, she documented struggles with public services and schools, and her daughter and herself. Running had also helped to rescue her from depression. Divorced from Grace's father, and for a considerable time a working single mother, she remarried, acquiring two stepsons and a second daughter. She spoke at the first WE meeting about her experiences of juggling work and family in a system and society that sees childcare as a matter for mothers alone.

Her parents attended university, the first members of working-class families to do so. After state school in Glasgow, Sophie also went to university, Reading. She found a way into Reuters via a short-term contract and remembers her conversation with her future boss when the company decided to move her onto permanent staff. 'I'm always interested in people who get in by the back door,' he told her.

Cocozza didn't see in Sophie a woman who got in by the back door. If the author's impressions aligned with her expectations, we carried some of the blame – literally. Three 'white, middle-aged, middle-class' women, we arrived with bags of white, middle-aged, middle-class food.

Sandi, handing out Pret A Manger sandwiches, appeared to Cocozza's eyes 'mum', whereas I defined myself as 'the most obvious politician of the three'. This is not a compliment, nor is it ever the business of the *Guardian* to dole out compliments.

That didn't stop us from wincing as we read the piece because it reinforced precisely the narrative we'd been hoping to change. 'Listening to Toksvig, Mayer and Walker, clues arise that suggest they may not be able to hear how their assumptions can shade into complacency,' Cocozza had written. 'Their language is encoded with a privilege they appear not to notice … It all suggests difference of the wrong kind: that the life experiences of Mayer, Toksvig and Walker may be alienatingly divergent from the people they want to reach.'[5]

On the day of publication, membership applications skyrocketed. The only thing worse than being talked about is not being talked about.

While Cocozza and others, ourselves included, worried whether we were too privileged to pursue politics effectively, another school of thought predicted the Women's Equality Party would dissolve into a puddle of sugar. An article in *Spiked* greeted our founding with a call for an end to feminism under the headline 'The Women's Equality Party: for ladies too nice for politics'. 'Women's Equality Party needs a strong dose of Nigel Farage', advised the *Telegraph*. 'The Women's Equality party has a problem – no one hates it', a second *Guardian* piece declared.

If any of us resented these accusations – how dare they call us nice! – we bit back the responses that might have punctured our ladylike image. Several of us had tweeted our criticisms of Cocozza's piece and then regretted doing so. For one thing, we were determined to treat journalists with courtesy, and not only because some of us were journalists. We were setting out to do politics differently and to develop a style and sensibility distinct from the male-dominated old guard. That difference showed itself in small touches. Sandi accepted the title of 'MC', a role hitherto absent from party politics. Would she be master or mistress of ceremonies, I asked her? 'It depends on the day,' she replied.

More ambitious was our desire to resist the combative culture that simultaneously unites and divides Westminster hacks and media managers. Like most members of the parliamentary lobby, I'd learned to expect abusive calls and texts from special advisers as part of my job. Parties often employ human attack dogs who attempt to secure the coverage they want by shouting or threatening to remove access. After reading Cocozza's piece, I couldn't help laughing at a memory that bubbled to the surface. In 2008, I'd gone to the pub after putting to bed my first long *TIME* cover story on David Cameron. The feature explained that the Conservative leader looked set to become Prime Minister, but his rise in the polls and a recent by-election win by a posh Tory candidate did not mean that his gilded past had lost the power to haunt him. I'd tracked down a contemporary of Cameron's in Oxford University's Bullingdon Club who described a night on the tiles with the wealthy student and his similarly privileged fellow members as 'Brideshead Regurgitated'. 'Champagne memories and social deprivation could make for an uneasy juxtaposition, especially in such tough times. Can someone marinated in plenty viscerally understand what it feels like to be poor or excluded?' I wrote. '[Cameron] brushes the question aside with visible irritation. "I don't have this deterministic view of life that you can only care about something if you directly experience it," he says. "You can't walk a mile in everybody's shoes."'[6]

Before leaving my office, I'd emailed a copy of the cover image, but not the text, to Cameron's then director of communications, former *News of the World* editor, Andy Coulson. In UK editions, the cover would run with the gnomic headline 'Behind the Smile'. Outside Britain we'd chosen a more direct line, assuming people might not recognise our cover star: 'David Cameron: A Class Act'. Coulson didn't like the pun at all. He called me to deliver a long ticking off. I recall standing outside the Fox and Anchor as his voice issued tinnily from my mobile phone: 'Class no longer matters to voters!'

At the Women's Equality Party, we resolved to handle media politely but also firmly. One of our core objectives is equal treatment by and in the media, a huge and urgent issue for women and for democracy that I'll explore in depth later in this book.

A small but significant part of that objective relates to the ways in which political coverage skews against women. The gladiatorial contests that broadcasters prefer over reflective, conversational interviews benefit neither politics in general nor women in particular. Why should politicians be judged on their ability to withstand a barrage of questions, or the same question repeated as the interviewer attempts to extract an answer that he – aggressive interviewers are most often men – likes better? Do we prefer leaders who speak quickly or think deeply? This style of journalism reflects male priorities, male socialisation, and even women skilled at debating are always at a disadvantage. Studies show that audiences react quite differently to men and women taking the floor. Men gain respect, women attract animosity.[7]

Hillary Clinton speaks more softly than either Bernie Sanders or Donald Trump, yet she was accused throughout her presidential campaign of shouting. As Secretary of State, Clinton's popularity ratings were high. They dropped as soon as she confirmed her run for the White House.[8]

This response wasn't confined to male voters. Women are products of the same sets of social messaging, programmed in varying degrees to defer, to support, and that's only the start of the problem. The harder we try to slough off patriarchal programming and determine for ourselves what it means to be female, to be a woman, the more our synapses begin to fry. Where does biological sex end and constructed gender begin? What are intrinsically female qualities?

We know that it is an insult to be called 'nice' in the political context, yet in that same context, as feminists, many of us would go to the barricades to assert our niceness. We assume it is the superpower the new breed of 50-foot women could bring to bear. We imagine Equalia would be a nice place because a gender-balanced society would enable men to relax and discover their own niceness in a gentler, feminised culture.

The ease with which the steering committee achieved consensus at its earliest meetings seemed to bear out this notion. Then came an argument. We tussled over the future shape of the organisation, and afterwards everyone around the table looked stricken. In raising our voices to defend beliefs, we had inadvertently challenged one of the unspoken shared beliefs that brought us together. True, the disagreement led to better decisions, but maybe the sexes weren't so different after all.

Did we, as women, really bring something unique to the table? The next chapter looks at what happens if those tables are not kitchen tables but Cabinet tables.

Chapter Two: Votes for women

IN 2008, A YOUNG Labour Party activist from London travelled to Raleigh, North Carolina, to help Barack Obama win the White House. Hannah Peaker believed in descriptive representation – that it isn't enough to elect lawmakers to advocate for us; at least some of our representatives must also share characteristics and perspectives with us if legislation is to be properly attuned to our needs. The Democratic primaries posed a quandary in this respect. Did the United States more urgently require a black President or a female one? Both firsts seemed long overdue, and the debate had quickly descended into rancour.

'Gender is probably the most restricting force in American life,' wrote Gloria Steinem in a piece arguing for Hillary Clinton.[1] This sentiment from one of the most prominent leaders of second-wave feminism kicked off a self-mutilating game of Who's More Oppressed Than Whom. After it rumbled on for nearly a month, Kimberlé Crenshaw co-authored a riposte with the author of *The Vagina Monologues*, Eve Ensler, pointing out the false polarity. 'We believe that feminism can be expressed by a broader range of choices than this 'either/or' proposition entails ... For many of us, feminism is not separate from the struggle against violence, war, racism and economic injustice.'[2]

Hannah did not believe that misogyny trounced racism or that getting any woman elected would inevitably help women. Her view was that descriptive representation creates better democracies by more closely reflecting the complexity of the voting populations. However, she had already witnessed in British left-wing politics the magical queuing system that keeps gender from ever reaching the head of the line. She had also seen women held to higher standards than men – and judged more harshly than men – because of their rarity. She wasn't enthused by Hillary Clinton, but she didn't think Clinton deserved the venom spat in her direction. In choosing to help Obama, Hannah hoped to support a politician who seemed as if he might, in Crenshaw and Ensler's terms, 'work to abolish the old paradigm of power'. Patriarchy lies at the core of that paradigm.

By the time Hannah headed to the States, Obama had defeated Clinton and teamed up with Joe Biden. They were rising in the polls against the Republican Party's John McCain and his surprise choice as a running mate, Sarah Palin. Obama's ground campaign looked impressive. Hannah arrived in North Carolina with just a change of clothes and an address on a piece of paper. Within 24 hours, she had digs in a house loaned to Obama's local team by supporters, a bellyful of barbecued meat from a fundraising cookout, boxes of Obama t-shirts, hats, stickers and leaflets, and an itinerary. She would be working in Raleigh campaign headquarters but her new colleagues wanted her to meet the voters first.

'They sent me out canvassing because they thought this whole thing was hilarious: this British girl knocking on people's doors,' says Hannah. 'People just couldn't understand what on earth I was doing there. Why had I come to campaign for their President? There's very little travel outside of the state much less the US.' Door-knocking in North Carolina held dangers she had never encountered on the other side of the Atlantic. After a brace of gun-toting Republicans bared their teeth and set their dogs on her, she approached the task with circumspection.

When yet another red-faced man answered the door with a shotgun in the crook of his arm and dogs circling his legs, Hannah instinctively began backing away. Still she delivered her opening line. 'Hey, sorry to disturb you. Are you going to be voting for Obama?'

'He's like "What?"'

'Are you going to be voting in this election, sir?"' Hannah mimics herself, the question starting softly and tapering to a near-whisper. 'He's like "You with Obama?" I'm like "Yeah".' She mimes cowering. 'I was wearing an Obama jumper and baseball cap.'

She had started to calculate the time it would take to sprint from his porch to the gate when he spoke again. 'So me and my boys, we've voted Republican our whole lives. But Sarah Palin is on the ticket. I said to them "Would you want your wife to be President?" And they said "Hell no." So we're going to be voting for Obama.'

'OK,' Hannah replied, simultaneously relieved and horrified. 'Have a badge. Welcome on board.'

This attitude wasn't isolated. The racism that flamed so fiercely through-out Obama's two terms of office sometimes tried to mask itself during his initial run at the presidency, even in North Carolina, a state that between 1873 and 1957 operated 23 so-called Jim Crow laws enforcing racial segrega-tion. On the doorsteps, people avoided talking directly about race, although they regurgitated racist conspiracy theories that Obama might be a secret Muslim or lack a US birth certificate. They made no effort to cloak their hostility towards women in politics. 'The gender stuff you could be explicit about. You could just be anti-women,' Hannah says.

She stayed in Raleigh until the election and watched the count in a funeral parlour hired as campaign headquarters by the Democrats 'because it was the cheapest thing on the block. The night of the election I passed out on the floor of the embalming room with a bottle of scotch. It was the absolute best feeling in the world.' Back in the UK, she wanted to recapture that feeling and, more than that, find a way to open up politics to women. She successfully applied for a Kennedy scholarship, and spent a year at

Harvard researching the topic she had pitched: the feasibility of a women's equality party.

Five years later, back living in London and working for the Cabinet Office after stints helping the Labour Party to get more female candidates elected, she went with friends to the Women of the World Festival at the Southbank Centre, but all the events that interested her were sold out. 'So we drank lots of wine and had this massive discussion. "WOW is great but this has to move into the political space. How do we do that and should we act on that?" It didn't go anywhere and a couple of weeks later someone said to me "This party's been set up".' Hannah laughs at the memory. 'I was really cross and sulked.'

Her partner persuaded her to send an email offering to help out. She started volunteering, writing a strategy paper, and in October 2015 joined the Women's Equality Party as Chief of Staff. 'It was my dream job. The rest is history.' She pauses. 'Or not. In fact, it's absolutely not history. It's not even near to being history yet,' she says.[3]

This chapter addresses a flurry of questions about women in politics – and about history. The United States has just rejected its first serious female candidate for the Presidency. What does this mean? Clinton had seemed poised to lead the charge of the 50-foot women. Instead history did that repeating-itself thing for which it's renowned. Women have often made strides only to fall back. One lesson could not be more clear or more urgent: We must fight not only to extend gender equality but to retain those rights and protections we have.

The causes of her defeat bear more detailed unpicking. Clinton appeared part of the establishment, and in some ways she was. She had already occupied the White House, though never in her own right or on her own terms. Her story illustrates the limits of privilege-by-association and the sting in its tale. She earned her stripes, and some valid criticisms, during a career in politics spanning stints in the Senate and as Secretary of State, yet never escaped the accusation that she got where she did because of her husband. Her achievements were her own and so were her mistakes, but she was only ever permitted to own the latter. Her use of a private email server for government business was a bad misstep but in no way equivalent to the cascade of scandals and allegations surrounding Donald Trump.

During the Democratic primaries and in the main campaign, she accepted the mantle of the continuity candidate, the safe choice, the *likely* choice, enabling two white men, first Bernie Sanders, then Trump – the very definition of a fat cat – to present themselves as insurgents. This wasn't just a tactical error on Clinton's part. It reflected a profound misreading of the American people and of her own situation. Voters didn't want continuity; they wanted change. She could have embodied that change. Certainly as a woman she was (excluding third-party candidates) the only real outsider in the race, for reasons already raised and explored here in greater detail.

She lost at least in part because she, and those around her, didn't recognise the extent to which her gender was a disadvantage – and because many white female voters did not recognise the extent to which any privilege they enjoyed was circumscribed in the same ways. The result, the Trump presidency, is bad news for women. He used his first televised interview to reiterate his pledge to appoint an anti-abortion judge to the US Supreme Court. What we cannot know is whether a Hillary Clinton presidency would have benefited women, other than by stopping Trump.

We cannot know, but we can draw conclusions, about Clinton and more widely about the impact of women in politics. The Women's Equality Party argues that increasing the overall participation of women is necessary if women are to advance and to hold on to that progress. WE also maintain that such a change wouldn't benefit only women, but everyone, by improving politics and the outcomes of the political system. What evidence underpins these arguments? If given a chance to head governments and fill half the seats in parliaments, might women run things not just differently but better? Does the answer depend on the individual women concerned, in the ways

Crenshaw and Ensler highlighted in their reply to Steinem, or might this also be a numbers game, as Hannah's vision of descriptive representation implies?

The next chapter tackles a huge question underlying this debate – whether what women are and how we behave is biologically hard-wired. First we'll look at some of the Titans and at the rare examples of gender-balanced legislatures to make an assessment about the ways in which women are already shaping the future.

Let's start with a reality check. When Theresa May took over from David Cameron, *Money* magazine got a little overexcited. 'Even with all the uncertainty around the UK's post-Brexit future, one thing is clear: Britain will soon be led by a woman, its first female prime minister since Margaret Thatcher left office in 1990,' an article on its website declared. 'Female heads of state have become common everywhere, it seems, but in the United States.'[4]

In reality, May added to a total of female world leaders – including elected heads of government, elected heads of state and women performing both roles – that for all their stature could still fit into a minibus. There are female leaders in Bangladesh, Chile, Croatia, Estonia, Germany, Liberia, Lithuania, Malta, Marshall Islands, Mauritius, Namibia, Nepal, Norway, Poland and the UK – that's just 15 out of the world's 144 full or partial democracies, or 16 if we include the estimable Nicola Sturgeon who heads Scotland's devolved government.

Female leaders are less common globally than natural redheads are in Sturgeon's own country; and redheads in Scotland, contrary to popular imagination, are not common at all, a flame-haired cohort amounting to around 13 per cent of the total population. Redheads and female leaders stand out, so we imagine their numbers to be much higher. Fifty-three democracies elect a president and a prime minister, and in all but nine of these nations, both roles are held by men. That means female leaders still comprise just 7.61 per cent of all world leaders, 8.12 per cent with Sturgeon.

The rarity of female leaders skews any gender ranking that includes female heads of state or government as a measure of equality. Consider the World Economic Forum's *Global Gender Gap Report*. The annual report seeks to judge the gulf between male and female citizens in each country surveyed by combining national performance scores attained in four categories: economic participation and opportunity, educational attainment, health and survival, and political empowerment. The health and survival category illustrates the wider danger of such rankings, taking into account just two sets of statistics: sex ratios at birth and healthy life expectancy. This provides useful information about divergent male and female health outcomes for diseases, but is a tool blunt to the point of inutility for assessing, for example, the level or impact of violence against women and girls. The last of the categories examines not only the make-ups of parliaments and governments but also 'the ratio of women to men in terms of years in executive office (prime minister or president) for the last 50 years'. This helps to explain how in 2016 the Republic of Ireland strutted its stuff in sixth place, behind the Nordic countries and Rwanda, an unlikely feat that provoked eye-rolls among Irish women.[5]

When Mary Robinson became Ireland's first female President in 1990, she saluted female voters 'who instead of rocking the cradle, rocked the system'. Seven years later Ireland elected a second female President, Mary McAleese. She served until 2011. Both women used the platform to promote gender equality, but Irish Presidents have severely limited executive powers and instead deploy what McAleese termed 'moral or pastoral' influence. The Irish system did get something of a rocking, though, and not just because of the Marys. Before Ireland's economic miracle proved a bubble, a wash of cheap money swept away some old features of the social and political landscape and lured back to the country a diaspora with expanded ambitions for women.

Even so, this shake-up was nowhere near fierce enough to fully dislodge the intertwined legacies of the Irish uprising and Catholicism.

Revolutions often follow a pattern. The French Revolution and the Arab Spring both offered hope to the women who helped to instigate them, but swiftly abandoned any goals of female emancipation. Ireland's revolution appeared to embrace the women who fought as equals alongside men, but went on to betray them. On Easter Monday 1916, rebel leader Patrick Pearse delivered a proclamation of independence on the steps of Dublin's post office, promising 'religious and civil liberty, equal rights and equal opportunities to all its citizens', and making explicit that these rights included suffrage for women. This vision shimmered for six days only. British forces quelled the Rising and executed Pearse. The remaining independence leaders focused ever more narrowly on the goal of ditching British rule, and doled out an earthly reward to the clergy who supported their efforts, enshrining 'the special position of the Holy Catholic Apostolic and Roman Church as the guardian of the Faith' in Ireland's 1937 constitution. As a result, Ireland didn't permit divorce until 1995 and has yet to legalise abortion except when the mother's life is in danger.

Ireland's female Presidents represented not change but the desire for change. The fact of a female leader is no guarantee that women are thriving, and that means the gender rankings that count them are fallible. Nevertheless, treated with caution and stripped of congratulatory messaging about how well women are doing – which we really are not – rankings still provide a useful guide.

The Nordic countries always ride high, and deserve to do so, on the basis of measures such as female educational attainment and participation in the workforce. Their record of putting women into top offices is indeed noteworthy – by comparison to the exceptionally poor record in other parts of the world. Women have led Denmark and Finland – if only once – while Iceland has voted in, at different times, a female President and female Prime Minister. Erna Solberg, Norway's current Prime Minister, is the nation's second woman in the role.

The unlikely outlier is Sweden. This apparently egalitarian and liberally minded Scandi society has yet to elect a female premier. Stability – the goal of most governments and a marked feature of Sweden since it pulled itself out of the financial crisis that roiled the early 1990s – must share some of the blame. It feels good to live in a stable society if you inhabit a comfortable corner of that society, but stability can also function as a drag on progress. If political parties keep performing to expectation, they tend to stick with existing leaders and leadership formulae. It is only when things go wrong that people consider more radical change or that change simply forces its way through. This rule applies at national level too. Developing countries often prove more porous for women than long-established democracies, and a significant proportion of the countries that now have female presidents or premiers have experienced profound political and social upheavals in their recent pasts.

When crises loom, women sometimes climb. Brexit brought Theresa May to power. Michelle Bachelet became Chile's first female President while memories of General Pinochet's dictatorship were still raw. Park Geun-hye, South Korea's first female President, won office after a spate of corruption scandals, dwindling growth rates and amid mounting tensions on the Korean Peninsula. She stood aside after the National Assembly voted to impeach her in December 2016 in the wake of a corruption scandal centred on a close female friend alleged to have leveraged their relationship for personal gain and caused, Park said, by her 'carelessness'. South Korea's constitutional court will decide the final outcome for Park. The outcome for female politicians in South Korea is already clear, as battalions of Park's critics hold her up as proof that women are unfit to lead.

The challenges facing any female leader when she reaches the summit are profound. Those who come to power amid turbulence, denied the protections of benign economic cycles and the diligent work of predecessors, struggling to control parties engaged in internecine warfare, are more vulnerable still. Sometimes the ink has not yet dried on their official stationery before the tumbrels arrive. This is the glass-cliff syndrome mentioned earlier.

In 11 countries, a woman led for less than a year. Female leaders in Austria, Ecuador and Madagascar broke records for the shortest tenure in top jobs, lasting just two days apiece. Canada may have a self-declared feminist at the helm in Justin Trudeau but the nation's only female Prime Minister, Kim Campbell, managed just four months in office before losing a general election. 'Gee,' she deadpanned, 'I'm glad I didn't sell my car.'

The female leadership minibus lost a passenger in 2016, when Brazil defenestrated its first female president. Dilma Rousseff had taken over as the economy began to stall after a period of heady growth attributed to her male predecessor but reliant on buoyant Chinese demand and rising oil prices. Her impeachment for alleged financial irregularities and involvement in a bribery scandal linked to the state oil company Petrobras was not, as its architects claimed, the appropriate response of democratic politics to corruption. China's slowdown and falling oil prices played a part. So did an inherent misogyny. Some of Dilma's opponents agitated for her dismissal by producing stickers with her head superimposed on a different female body, legs akimbo and a hole where the crotch should be. Affixed to cars with the hole aligned to the petrol cap, they created the illusion that motorists filling their tanks were penetrating Dilma.

After her downfall, her critics waved signs that read '*Tchau Querida*' – 'Goodbye, Dear'. The price to Brazil certainly was. The charges against Dilma never included lining her own pockets; investigators alleged she had turned a blind eye to kickbacks at Petrobras and had disguised budget deficits. The same investigation suspected substantial bribe-taking among some of the politicians who engineered her expulsion.

Brazil's legislature is 90 per cent male; around half of these men have themselves been indicted on corruption charges.[6] One hundred per cent of the Cabinet assembled by Dilma's white, male replacement, Michael

Temer – himself accused of breaking fiscal rules and, separately, of misuse of electoral funds – was white, a striking move in a country shaped by the diversity of its population. Brazil's black and mixed-race nationals are in the majority, and also make up a lion's share of the country's poor. Temer's Cabinet boasted another distinction: it was the first since 1979 not to include a single woman. 'We tried to seek women but for reasons that we don't need to bring up here, we discussed it and it was not possible,' said Temer's Chief of Staff, Eliseu Padilha.[7] The new government quickly set about dismantling programmes designed to narrow Brazil's overlapping wealth, race and gender gaps.

Some women manage to hold on, although holding on isn't, of itself, a good thing. Ellen Johnson Sirleaf became Africa's first female head of state when she triumphed in Liberia's 2005 elections, two years after the end of a bloody civil war that killed more than 250,000 people and displaced nearly a third of the country's population. She has declared she will not contest the presidential poll planned for October 2017. 'Our people would not take it. And my age wouldn't allow it. So that's out of the question,' she said.

Her decision – provided she remains true to it – distinguishes Johnson Sirleaf from a raft of male African leaders who cling to power long after any democratic mandate ebbs. The international community has already garlanded her with praise. In 2011 Johnson Sirleaf accepted a Nobel Peace Prize along with two other women, Leymah Gbowee, a fellow Liberian, also praised for helping to heal the country's rifts, and a Yemeni human rights activist, Tawakkul Karman. A year later, Gbowee resigned as head of Liberia's Peace and Reconciliation Commission, attacking Johnson Sirleaf's efforts to tackle poverty and criticising a record of nepotism that had seen three of the President's sons take up senior positions at, respectively, Liberia's state oil company, its National Security Agency and its Central Bank.[8]

Johnson Sirleaf may not after all represent quite the model of African leadership that the wealthy democracies of Europe and North America hope to see, but at least a few of the flaws of her leadership are rooted in the continent's history of exploitation by some of those same countries. Liberia, founded by freed slaves, free-born black Americans and Afro-Caribbean émigrés, is the only African country never to have officially been a colony. (Ethiopia was briefly annexed by Italy in 1936.) What Liberia did not escape was Western imperialism. In 1926 the US tire and rubber company Firestone leased one million Liberian acres for 99 years at the annual rate of six cents per acre, inserting a clause that gave the corporation rights over any gold, diamonds, or other minerals discovered on the land, and also tying Liberia to a loan at punitive rates.

Africa's oldest democracy, Botswana, has been holding elections only since 1966. Africa's newest country, South Sudan, came into being in 2011. Colonisation – the patriarchal rule of the White Master – and the struggles for liberation that speeded its end continue to make their mark. Borders drawn with no respect to tribal claims, local history or practicalities exacerbate conflicts and encourage a tendency, reinforced by those conflicts, to try to consolidate power, whether along tribal or party lines or among families. With power comes wealth. 'Politics is the avenue to the most fantastic wealth and so of course it's been very competitive and the men want that space,' says Ayisha Osori, a prominent journalist, lawyer and women's rights advocate, who stood in the 2014 primary elections for Nigeria's House of Representatives. 'They want to keep that space for themselves and so women have to be equally as ruthless and as determined as the men.'[9]

The tangles of post-imperialism play out in the country Johnson Sirleaf governs and the ways in which she governs it, but her record also illustrates the point that Osori makes and that enthusiasts for increased female representation sometimes gloss over: female leadership isn't necessarily free from the imperfections of the male variety.

The performance in office of another Nobel Peace Prize laureate, Aung San Suu Kyi, reinforces that lesson. She would be Myanmar's President if the military junta that kept her under house arrest for 15 years had not also drafted a constitution that excludes her from the highest office. Instead, Suu Kyi has become the nation's leader in all but name, holding a dual role as State Counsellor and Minister of Foreign Affairs. An icon of peaceful resistance, her lustre is dimming as she fails to use her power to grant rights or recognition to the Rohingya, Myanmar's marginalised Muslim population, or to curb human rights abuses by the army as it seeks to stem independence movements. When 50-foot women disappoint, they do so in a big way because our expectations of them are higher.

One name always crops up in discussions about what women bring to politics: Margaret Thatcher. Love her or loathe her – and the middle ground I occupy is noticeably underpopulated – she was one of the most successful politicians of the twentieth century. She won three successive general elections and left a party that, after ejecting her as leader for fear of electoral defeat, went on to win one more. She galvanised the UK and its moribund economy, at a cost that explains the enduring anger she still evokes, levied on traditional industry and every Briton on the sharp end of the history she was making. She speeded the end of the Cold War, recognising in Mikhail Gorbachev a different kind of Soviet leader. 'I like Mr Gorbachev. We can do business together,' she said. They did.

She showcased female potential. Yet her ghost is most often summoned to demonstrate that female leaders do not invariably promote female interests. 'I owe nothing to women's lib,' she said, and during 11 years in office she made sure that women's lib owed little directly to her. She rejected the idea that government should help mothers to return to work, telling the BBC she did not want Britain turned into 'a crèche society'. She appointed only one woman to any of her Cabinets. Baroness Young held a minor portfolio as Chancellor of the Duchy of Lancaster for two years, and came to the role with a sniggering nickname that spoke to the disquiet of men in Westminster and the media at seeing women rise: 'Old Tin Knickers'.

Young's boss inspired a more respectful variation on this theme, but one reflecting a similar unease about female power. 'The Iron Lady' lived up to the soubriquet, tempered to a steely obstinacy by years of fighting her way into rooms full of patronising, posh men, and then presiding at conference tables with more of the same. An essay by academic Rosabeth Moss Kanter, published in 1977, two years before Thatcher first entered Downing Street, foreshadowed Thatcher's leadership style. Kanter, now a professor at Harvard Business School, observed that 'tokens', members of minority groups in organisations, are made to feel uncomfortable about their differences and so try to conform. That might mean acting like the majority, or fitting in with the majority's expectations of minority behaviour. Such behavioural distortions only stop when minorities reach a critical mass.[10] Subsequent studies suggested that mass is reached at 30 per cent and above, but more recent research points to a greater complexity in the number and habits of minority behaviour.

What is clear is that token women frequently try to fit in by behaving like men – or, in Thatcher's case, by out-manning the men. A computer analysis of Hillary Clinton's interview and speech transcripts discovered that her language became more masculine – a parameter defined by linguistics experts – as she moved from being First Lady and up the ranks of electoral politics.[11] This transformation may have hindered rather than helped her. Women draw criticism and questions about their competence if they show emotion – a behaviour deemed feminine – yet any women who conduct themselves in ways judged masculine are punished too. Leaked emails written by former Secretary of State Colin Powell described Clinton as 'a friend I respect' but then went on to list supposed defects that included 'a long track record' and 'unbridled ambition'. Researchers at Yale investigating differing voter reactions to male and female candidates found that voters felt 'moral outrage' against women who seek power because 'power and power-seeking are central to the way masculinity is socially constructed and communality is central to the construction of femininity, [so] intentionally seeking power is broadly seen as anti-communal and inconsistent with the societal rules for women's behaviour.'[12] For many women in politics, this creates the catch-22 described by Ann Friedman in a piece about Clinton's travails: 'To succeed, she needs to be liked, but to be liked, she needs to temper her success.'

For Thatcher, downplaying her force of character or pretending to match any culturally generated ideals of femininity was never a serious option. Occasionally her advisers persuaded her to give interviews in which she awkwardly described a domesticity that was clearly inauthentic. She preferred to ignore her sex, but the men around her seemed unable to forget it. 'She has the eyes of Caligula and the mouth of Marilyn Monroe,' observed French President François Mitterrand, creepily. His successor Jacques Chirac whined about Thatcher during a confrontation at a summit: 'What more does that housewife want from me? My balls on a plate?'

Veteran Conservative MP and former Cabinet minister Ken Clarke, forgetting he was wearing a microphone ahead of a TV interview with another former Cabinet minister, Malcolm Rifkind, voiced a milder version of this sentiment in a discussion of Theresa May that he did not intend for broadcast. 'Theresa is a bloody difficult woman,' he said. Clarke's thought train continued to its obvious conclusion: 'But you and I worked for Margaret Thatcher.' Britain's first female Prime Minister is the model by which the second female Prime Minister, and all other female leaders, continue to be judged.

Facile though these comparisons are, female leaders, as a class, tend to resemble Thatcher in one respect. There is less show-offery. Women more often appear to thrive on the exercise of power than the attendant publicity. Think how Angela Merkel compares to Nicolas Sarkozy and Silvio Berlusconi, or Theresa May to her one-time leadership rival Boris Johnson, or Hillary to Bill or Donald. Thatcher never sought press coverage for its own sake.

There is one other commonality between Thatcher and two current leaders that is worthy of mention: a background in science. When Thatcher entered politics, she forged a new path. The elite of society imbued their sons with the expectation of leadership, and trades unions provided an alternative training ground for political talent. Family ties delivered the world's first female Prime Minister, Sri Lanka's Sirimavo Bandaranaike, to power and installed the world's longest-serving female leader, India's Indira Gandhi, in office. Political dynasties produced Aung San Suu Kyi, Sheikh Hasina, her predecessor Khaleda Zia, Pakistan's Benazir Bhutto, Indonesia's Megawati Sukarnoputri, Argentinian Presidents Isabel Martínez de Perón and Cristina Fernández de Kirchner, Cory Aquino of the Philippines, and South Korea's Park Geun-hye. Thatcher had no such advantages. She studied chemistry and went on to work in the field at the food manufacturer Lyons (where, legend has it, she helped to invent soft-scoop ice cream).

Angela Merkel found a calm berth in East Germany as a researcher in physical chemistry. Theresa May took a degree in science too. These parallels are noteworthy because the trio also gained a reputation for the kind of evidence-based decision-making more routinely associated with laboratories than parliaments. Even so, Thatcher and Merkel will be remembered for big, bold projects rooted in ideology and emotion rather than cold calculation. Thatcherism held, at its core, an instinctive and visceral moral certitude that branded opposing ideologies as not just wrong but malign. Merkel's pivot from cautious consensus-builder to passionate advocate of European engagement in solving the refugee crisis drew deep on her own experience. She too had been the wrong side of the barbed wire.

Germany's 2005 elections ended in deadlock. Neither Merkel's centre-right Christian Democrats nor Gerhard Schröder's left-leaning Social Democrats, could muster a workable majority. Merkel consulted, forged alliances, held her nerve until Schröder withdrew, leaving her to head a grand coalition. She was not only the first woman to occupy the Chancellery, but the first leader of reunited Germany raised behind the Iron Curtain. As *TIME* scrambled late at night to produce a cover story, international editor Michael Elliott composed a headline that almost went to print before we noticed its double meaning: '*Not Many Like Her*'.

There still aren't many – if any – like her, and these days you'd be forgiven for assuming that not many of her colleagues or compatriots like her either. Four successive state elections in 2016 saw the Christian Democrats lose votes, primarily to the hard-right Alternative für Deutschland. The AfD started as a protest party campaigning against German commitments to bail out floundering Eurozone countries, but found fresh purpose on 4 September 2015, when Merkel responded to the press of refugees from Syria stranded in Hungary by opening the border and issuing a welcome. '*Wir schaffen das*', she said: we will manage.[13] At first most Germans agreed, but since more than a million refugees and migrants sought to make new lives in Germany, that consensus has melted.

Mass assaults on women in Cologne during the final hours of 2015 tested German hospitality. There is still little clarity about the nature of these attacks: to what extent these were planned and whether most perpetrators were, as initially reported, foreigners. The authorities continue to pursue prosecutions but have admitted they do not expect to identify the majority of those responsible. If they did, bringing them to justice would be difficult. Germany's antiquated laws on sexual assault put the burden on women to show they had physically resisted their attackers.

A narrative about Merkel gained traction inside the country and out: she was a busted flush. Germany's first female Chancellor had broken Germany and, far from helping German womenfolk, had exposed them to danger.

Pretty much everything about that narrative was wrong, although Merkel did make one key miscalculation. Until the refugee crisis, the criticism routinely levelled against her was that she used her power too sparingly – that she had responded too slowly to the Eurozone crisis and with too much focus on German national interests at the expense of poorer countries such as Greece. She put a different gloss on her approach: she preferred to govern in 'many small steps', rather than big ones.[14] This fitted with the legacy of her early life, in a police state where she learned to achieve without attracting attention. It was also pragmatic: the German voting system creates coalitions rather than outright majorities, and deploys multiple checks and balances. German history warns against unfettered power. Even so, Merkel confronted the migrant crisis as Europe's strongest leader, the only one with political capital. In finally spending that capital, she sought to instill in other European leaders a sense of collective responsibility. This was, as she saw it, 'a historic test of globalisation'.

Merkel alone rose to it. She had overestimated Europe's capacity for solidarity. Her remarks at a press conference after her party's poor showing in the September 2016 Berlin state elections, widely misreported as a *mea culpa*, instead restated her convictions. She did regret the phrase 'we will manage', which 'makes many people feel provoked, though I meant it to be inspiring'.

However, she had followed a humanitarian imperative and a strategy that, despite flaws, had started to bear fruit. Signs of progress did nothing to quiet her critics, especially within the ranks of her Christian Democrats and their Bavarian sister party, the Christian Social Union (CSU). They had never really accepted her; now, with federal elections due between August and October 2017, they began to treat her as a liability. Her approval ratings had indeed plunged, from 67 per cent in September 2015 – an astonishingly lofty figure for a politician in her third term of office – to 45 per cent, higher than the scores of most world leaders or any potential rivals for her party's leadership. That popularity is international. When I posted the news on Twitter that she had decided to run for a fourth term, my timeline filled with 'phews' and 'thank gods' and 'thank fuck: we need an adult'.

In Germany, female voters are more likely than men to vote for left-of-centre parties. This pattern repeats in many parts of the world, including the US, where the majority of white women who voted for Trump was not as large as the majority of white men who backed him. You can see why that might be. Conservatism is inherently disposed towards maintaining the status quo, and some groups of female voters know this is not to their benefit, not least because of the right's fondness for downsizing the state at the potential costs of state-sector jobs that employ women and services that support women, plus a tolerance for a wide income spread in a system that relegates more women to the lower tiers. Merkel bucks this trend by appealing across party lines to Social Democrat voters – and to women. At the last election, 44 per cent of all female voters backed Merkel's party, compared to 24 per cent for the Social Democrats.

She has done so in part by being a woman and showing what women can be in a country that until relatively recently in its dominant Western states envisaged only three spheres of female activity: *Kinder*, *Küche*, *Kirche* – children, kitchen, church. Up until 1958, a West German husband could demand his wife's employer sack her if she neglected the housework. These attitudes were still reflected in the education system Merkel inherited, in which a majority of schools in the west ended at midday so pupils could return home for a cooked lunch. When Merkel first led the Christian Democrats into an election, opponents and colleagues alike asked '*Kann die das?*' Is *she* able to do this? 'With a negative touch,' says Ursula von der Leyen, Germany's first female Defence Minister. 'Nobody is asking any more.'

This does not mean Merkel's record on promoting gender equality is perfect. Like many female leaders, her instinct has been to shy away from gender politics. She was uncomfortable with her first portfolio in Helmut Kohl's government, as Minister of Women and Youth. Germany's sluggish birth rate rather than any feminist impulse prompted Merkel to introduce a wide range of measures to support working mothers, including the provision of parental leave paid up to 65 per cent of salaries for up to 14 months, guaranteed daycare for children aged one or above, and an expansion of all-day schools.[15] She only reluctantly gave in to deploying quotas to increase female representation on the boards of large German companies. 'It is pathetic that in more than 65 years of the Federal Republic of Germany, it was not possible for the Dax-30 companies to get a few more women on supervisory boards on a voluntary basis,' she said. 'But at some point there had been so many hollow promises that it was clear – this isn't working.'

German society has witnessed significant changes. Female participation in the German labour force rose by two percentage points in the decade ahead of Merkel's election and by eight points during her first ten years in government. It would be unwise to claim a direct correlation; many factors will have played a part. Nevertheless, there's no denying that German women have risen under Germany's first female leader.

Theresa May's elevation prompted crowing in Tory ranks. She is the Conservatives' second female Prime Minister while Labour has yet to choose a female party leader. May, Merkel and two other current female leaders in Europe, Norway's Erna Solberg, and Poland's Beata Szydło (and Szydło's immediate predecessor Ewa Kopacz) are all on the right. Kolinda Grabar-Kitarović belonged to the conservative Croatian Democratic Union party before her election as Croatia's President. This does not mean right-wing politics promotes better outcomes for women, rather that parties of the left are especially bad at promoting women.

The paradoxical explanation for this phenomenon is that parties of the left have historically championed gender equality. This means they are often too convinced of their own virtue to recognise their failings. Those failings loosely group into two categories. The first is one of precedence. In their desire to solve all structural inequalities, these parties get caught up in unhelpful binaries of the kind that disfigured the Democratic primaries in 2008 – ethnic minorities or women, class or gender, pensioners or underprivileged youth – reflexively assigning the lowest priority to women even though most forms of disadvantage intersect with being female. Far-left activists aim not to fix parts of the system, but to change the whole system, again stranding women in an endless waiting game. They also mistake optics for action. Amnesty International's 2015 report on Bolivia noted that the socialist government had set up a Gender Office and Unit for

Depatriarchalisation and created a Deputy Minister for Equal Opportunities within the Ministry of Justice and Fundamental Rights, responsible for the advancement of women. However, none of these new institutions had been allocated the resources necessary to be effective. The Equal Opportunities brief, for example, received just 5.3 per cent of the ministerial budget.[16] As the White Queen tells Alice, 'The rule is jam tomorrow and jam yesterday – but never jam today.'

The second category and reason for the ongoing failure to promote women sometimes still dares to speak its name in parties and organisations of the right: hostility towards women. In December 2016, Conservative MP Philip Davies won election to Parliament's cross-party Women and Equalities Committee after the Tories failed to put up any other candidates. He promptly proposed dropping the word 'women' from its title. A few days later, he tried unsuccessfully to derail a bill to ratify the Istanbul Convention, an international accord to tackle violence against women, by filibustering in the hope that the bill would run out of time. Earlier in the year he had given a speech that inadvertently boosted sales of baked goods. 'In this day and age the feminist zealots really do want women to have their cake and eat it,' he declared. Women responded by posting photographs of themselves munching cake.[17]

The left likes to imagine that it is exempt from such wrongheadedness. In reality, misogyny flourishes like knotweed, undermining foundations of parity and respect and periodically breaking into the open, rampant and destructive. The online abuse directed against female MPs who disagree with Jeremy Corbyn's leadership has been different in degree and content to anything experienced by male dissidents. The invective doesn't emanate exclusively from the MPs' left-wing opponents, but could less easily survive in a culture that made serious efforts to stamp out such abuse.

Labour is by no means the only offender. Bernie Sanders' campaign for the Democratic Presidential nomination unleashed toxic attacks on Hillary Clinton, not by Sanders but by a rump of his followers, so-called

Bernie Bros. Two British hard-left parties, the Workers' Revolutionary Party and the Socialist Workers' Party, both failed to curb sexual violence in their own ranks. The WRP disbanded after revelations that its leader Gerry Healy had sexually abused female members. The SWP responded to a rape allegation against a senior figure in the organisation by holding a kangaroo court that interrogated the complainant. Had she been drunk? Had she definitely said no?[18]

George Galloway, a former MP who set up the Respect Party after his expulsion from Labour, dismissed rape charges brought in Sweden against Julian Assange. The WikiLeaks founder was guilty, said Galloway, of 'personal sexual behaviour [that] is sordid, disgusting, and I condemn it'. This was, however, merely 'bad sexual etiquette'. 'Not everybody needs to be asked prior to each insertion,' Galloway added.[19] In 2016, he campaigned to be Mayor of London. The Women's Equality Party fielded a mayoral candidate at the same elections, party leader Sophie, together with a London-wide slate of candidates. WE attracted 343,547 votes – a 5.2 per cent vote share and a magnificent result for a first election. (The Green Party's first electoral outing, at the October 1974 general election, claimed just 0.01 per cent of the vote.) The cherry on our feminist zealots' cake was Sophie's performance against Galloway. He started with an advantage as a public figure, a political veteran and one-time star of reality TV show *Celebrity Big Brother*; he had also presented shows for Iran-backed Press TV and the Russian-funded RT network. Sophie had come to politics as WE's first leader, just ten months before election day. She outpolled him by almost 100,000 votes.

We celebrated Galloway's defeat but there is nothing to cheer in the implosion of the British left. Democracies need strong oppositions to hold governments to account. The biggest challenges to Theresa May now come from the Scottish Nationalists, led by Nicola Sturgeon, and from the populist right both within the Conservative party and outside it. To counter these challenges, and in the absence of a countervailing threat from the left, May is likely to tack further to the right.

This bodes ill for women, if not entirely for the reasons set out by traditional left-wing analyses. From the outset, Sandi and I conceived of the Women's Equality Party as non-partisan. We did so not just because of the serial failures of the left to match deeds to words. Three-quarters of British voters identify themselves as centrists or to the right of centre. We need a chunk of those votes to make change. We want to reach Equalia. We want jam today.

A good starting point is to test a common assumption about women in politics: that women are pragmatic and collaborate across party lines. Academic research supports this view. Analysis of the progress of bills proposed in the US House of Representatives between 1973 and 2008 showed that women in minority parties did better than their male colleagues at keeping their bills alive because they were more adept at garnering support across the aisle.[20] (The US Senate demonstrated another female strength in January 2016. After a blizzard in Washington DC, women showed up for work. No men slogged through the snow. 'As we convene this morning, you look around the chamber, the presiding officer is female. All of our parliamentarians are female. Our floor managers are female. All of our pages are female,' said Republican Senator Lisa Murkowski. 'Perhaps it speaks to the hardiness of women.')

My own experience of covering politics encouraged me to believe women might be less inclined to party tribalism. I had seen Westminster women from different parties not only forming alliances in recognition of common goals, but bonding and swapping tips about how to avoid being slapped down or touched up.

Women are diverse but there is always a reservoir of shared experience. The more privileged among us may never truly understand the harsh realities of being doubly or triply disadvantaged by the intersections of race or age or sexuality or gender identity or disability or poverty. We occupy different positions in the kyriarchy – a word coined to describe these inter-sections and acknowledge the ways in which they enable women to oppress other women – but all of us have found ourselves on the receiving end of the patriarchy. Women of the right may not recognise either expression and are more likely to believe patriarchal structures should be reformed rather than eradicated, but they can be seriously effective in bringing about such reforms as Angela Merkel has shown. Moreover, the impulses of the right increasingly align behind the promotion of women, as the market increasingly recognises the value of women. The later chapter on business explains why that is – and why that recognition isn't yet matched by equal representation in boardrooms or equal pay at any level.

May's own record on gender equality is at best a curate's egg. A first tasty morsel came in 2005 with her co-founding of Women2Win, an organisation dedicated to increasing female representation on the Conservative benches. As Home Secretary she introduced new powers to curb domestic abuse, in particular in cases of coercive and controlling behaviour, and then chivvied the police to use these powers. By contrast, her handling of Yarl's Wood, a detention centre holding women and children pending immigration hear-ings, was truly rotten. She extended the contract with the private company Serco that runs the facility, despite allegations of sexual violence and other abuses towards its inmates by Serco staff.[21]

Under her leadership, the Conservatives have already pulled further to the right in an attempt to appease dissidents and retrieve votes from UKIP. On the surface, the battles between centre right and harder right are about how to implement Brexit and further restrict immigration, but the hard right also feeds on regressive social conservatism, invoking a future that turns the clocks back: to an age of safety and certainty and homogeneity; to faith in strong leaders who take care of the big stuff.

Such worlds have, of course, never existed, but that makes their pull more potent – and more dangerous. Worlds-that-never-were operate according to laws-that-never-work. The hard right identifies real problems – the

competition for scant resources, the democratic deficits created by globalisation, and religious extremism and misogyny dressed up as 'cultural practice'
– but proposes responses that will make everything worse: xenophobia
and a retreat into isolation. Often the nostalgia invokes a natural order
threatened by the forces of social change – and that supposed natural order
never turns out well for women. Beata Szydło's Law and Justice Party in
Poland has cut state funding for IVF treatment, tightened the availability
of contraception and only backed away from a total ban on abortion, even
in cases of rape, after mass protests. Some hard rightists allow themselves
to imagine that a lack of contraception or access to abortion will encourage
young couples to marry. Some hard rightists seem to believe that hostility
towards homosexuality will make it go away.

The hard right also routinely mistakes feminism for the cause of bad relations between the sexes, rather than recognising feminism as a response and
solution to the conflict. Even so, increasing numbers of parties of the hard
right are led by women. Frauke Petry – like Merkel, a former chemist who
grew up in East Germany – leads the surging Alternativ für Deutschland
and suggested that German border guards should shoot anyone illegally
trying to cross from Austria into Germany. Pia Kjærsgaard, co-founder
and former leader of the Danish People's Party, is now the Speaker of
Denmark's Parliament and a prominent critic of multiculturalism. Siv Jensen
has brought Norway's Progress Party into government for the first time,
as a junior partner in coalition with Erna Solberg's Conservatives. Jensen,
who serves as Finance Minister, has moderated her anti-Islam rhetoric
since taking office but opposes her own coalition's agreement to expand
the numbers of Syrian refugees it accepts.

That women rise in such parties is a reflection of the fractious nature of
such groups – remember: crises create room for movement – but the hard
right has also got wise to the way a female face can lend an air of friendly
modernity to their movements. They draw inspiration from a prominent
role model. In 2011 Marine Le Pen took control of France's Front National

from its founder, her father Jean-Marie, and four years later oversaw his expulsion from the party after he downplayed the Holocaust as 'a detail of history'. Under her stewardship the party has flourished, successfully expanding its reach to voters who shied away from its original incarnation. Her slicker, friendlier Front National sublimates its racism into messaging linking immigration to Islamism and an increased threat of terrorism. She inveighs against globalisation and praises Brexit. 'The time of the nation state is back,' she declared, launching her bid for the French presidency. That election, divided into two rounds, takes place in April and May 2017. Regional elections at the end of 2015 saw the Front National come first in the opening round of voting with 28 per cent. Le Pen and her niece Marion Maréchal-Le Pen both won more than 40 per cent in their contests. Nobody is betting against Marine Le Pen making it to the finish line in the race for the Élysée Palace. Conventional wisdom says she won't win, but we live in a time of crumbling conventions.

Le Pen reinforces the warning against expecting of female leaders a more compassionate politics. Yet she also illustrates strong arguments for prising open political clubs to admit more women. For one thing, traditional politics has been weakened precisely because it operates clubs. If mainstream parties had kept closer touch with voters, they might have done a better job of answering the real concerns of those voters. Instead they've created space for demagogues to masquerade as truth-tellers and champions of the working man (if more rarely of the working woman).

Moreover, whatever you think of Le Pen's politics, she's gifted. Try this thought experiment. Look at the female leaders mentioned in this chapter not as idols with clay feet, 50-foot women who disappoint by failing to be everything we want women of public life to be. Consider, instead, their talent. Unless you believe men make better politicians than women, every male-dominated parliament is a parliament that is missing out on potential – and that means most parliaments miss out. Just 18 countries come close to gender parity in politics. Forty per cent or more of the lawmakers in the legislatures of Cuba, Ecuador, Finland, Iceland, Mexico, Mozambique, Namibia, Nicaragua, Norway, Senegal, Seychelles, South Africa, Spain and Sweden are women. In two countries, Bolivia and Rwanda, female parliamentarians slightly outnumber their male colleagues.

At these proportions – safely over the 30 per cent threshold identified as the minimum necessary to avoid tokenism – political cultures may not necessarily feminise but female representatives should be under less pressure to ape male behaviours or conform to male expectations. This appears to be the case in least a few of these countries, especially in Northern Europe. Finland, Iceland and Norway have pioneered progressive legislation to ensure gender equality. Sweden may not have got round to electing a female leader but laws drafted with a real understanding of the mechanisms holding back the female population make it one of the best countries in the world for women. Its female Foreign Minister, Margot Wallström, is also attempting to pilot a feminist foreign policy. Critics accused her of naivety after she criticised Saudi Arabia's treatment of women, and the Saudi government responded by cancelling an arms contract with Sweden. 'I don't think a feminist foreign policy is idealistic. It is the smartest policy you can have at the moment. Every peace agreement has a better chance to succeed if you involve women,' she replied.

The same is true of every transition that countries undertake. Women led protests against apartheid, but when the African National Congress was formed in 1912, women were excluded from its ranks. They finally gained access in 1943, and continued to play a pivotal role in the movement. In 1990, the ANC executive promised to strive for gender equality in the emerging South Africa. 'The experience of other societies has shown that the emancipation of women is not a by-product of a struggle for democracy, national liberation or socialism,' the statement read. 'It has to be addressed in its own right within our organisation, the mass democratic movement and in the society as a whole.'[22] The 1994 Constitution made good that pledge by outlawing discrimination on the grounds of sex, marital status or pregnancy. The scandal-hit presidency of Jacob Zuma, who served a prison sentence on Robben Island alongside Nelson Mandela, shows how far the ANC has drifted from its ideals.

Acquitted of rape in 2006, Zuma has condemned himself as an apologist for rape and sexual harassment. 'Under normal circumstances, if a woman is dressed in a skirt, she will sit properly with her legs together. But [the accuser] would cross her legs and wouldn't even mind if the skirt was raised very much,' he said during his trial. On another occasion, he reprimanded female journalists. 'When men compliment you innocently, you say it's harassment. You will miss out on good men and marriage.'[23]

Women hold 43 per cent of South Africa's Cabinet posts and 46 per cent of Deputy Ministerships. Female parliamentarians lost ground at the 2014 elections, to 41 per cent of the total from a previous peak of 44 per cent, but their numbers remain high enough that they might be expected to make an impact. There is some evidence that descriptive representation is working as it should – a greater slice of government spending has been directed towards education and targeted towards girls and women – but progress in many areas is slow or has stalled. Increased female representation can pay dividends but gender-balanced institutions operate within – and are circumscribed by – gender-imbalanced cultures.

There are other considerations too. The first country in the world to elect a female majority to its legislature, Rwanda, is no nascent Equalia, even though the World Economic Forum in 2016 ranked it the fifth most gender-equal country in the world. It is true that child mortality rates have declined, maternal health has improved and as many girls as boys go through education, and Unicef has praised female parliamentarians for being more attentive than male MPs to the plight of children and families following the 1994 genocide.[24]

Yet context is all. One reason so many women entered politics is that so many men had been killed. Seventy per cent of the surviving population was female. Even so, Rwanda's transitional parliament achieved female representation of just 25.7 per cent.

The Tutsi-led Rwandan Patriotic Front had emerged victorious from Rwanda's civil war, deposing the Hutu-dominated government primarily responsible for the genocide. (There is evidence that the RPF also carried out massacres.) Its leader Paul Kagame took office as President in 2000, won the first elections for the role in 2003 and returned to power in 2010. Five years into his second administration, he oversaw changes to the constitution to remove an interdict on presidents standing for more than two terms. He later announced his intention, unlike Ellen Johnson Sirleaf, to run again in 2017.

His rule is despotic, for all the show of an electoral process, restricting political opposition and the press freedoms vital to the exercise of democracy.[25] While Kagame has imposed peace at home, the United Nations accused Rwanda of fueling the conflict in neighbouring Democratic Republic of Congo that deploys sexual violence, including mass rape and mutilation, as a weapon of war, just as Rwanda's factions violated women and girls during the genocide. The UN's own peacekeepers, stationed in the DRC since 2014, are also implicated, accused not only of doing too little to protect victims but of themselves contributing to the epidemic of rape.[26] Rwanda's achievements must be weighed against this record.

Female representation is no guarantor of benign government or positive outcomes for women unless allied to other areas of progress. This is why the Women's Equality Party started with six core objectives rather than simply pressing for more women in political life. Yet, if equal representation is no panacea, it is, as this chapter has sought to demonstrate, vitally important. Moreover, the damage caused by unequal representation is easy to see. Countries that marginalise women do not prosper. Governments without female representation do a poor job of governing. This book will examine countries and governments that prove the patriarchy isn't only bad for women, but for men.

So the final question for this chapter is how to reach equal representation – and the answer is simple. Thirteen of the nations at or near gender parity in their legislatures have either introduced mandatory gender quotas or the main parties in their political systems have done so voluntarily.

The Women's Equality Party proposes a simple formula to increase representation of women in Westminster. For the next two election cycles we advocate that every party should ensure 66 per cent of its candidates for the seats of retiring MPs and 66 per cent of other candidates are women. Our submission to the Women and Equalities Committee in 2016 also included a recommendation for quotas to achieve other kinds of diversity.

Nobody flinches at the use of quotas to try to solve conflicts. Scarred countries from Iraq to Northern Ireland to Rwanda have brought in quotas to ensure a balance among former enemies.

Critics always protest that quotas promote mediocrity. This ignores the biggest quota system of all, the one that all over the world promotes ineffectual men over more talented women. 'Unlegislated quotas mean men have had an unfair institutional advantage for centuries,' says Sophie Walker. 'Millions of women, working class and black and minority ethnic people have switched off, and that hurts us all.'[27] Descriptive representation leads not only to better governments but to more engaged voters. This means not only achieving gender balance but embracing the diversity of gender.

Chapter Three: All womankind

SIMONE WILSON MADE the biggest decision of her life to avoid wasting a good manicure. Her nails, a deep French red, had survived the London Erotica show without chipping, a good run under any circumstances and especially after three days at the T-Girl bar, changing barrels and working a till. While her fellow barmaids channelled early Britney Spears, she leaned in like Sheryl Sandberg, low-key and business-like in a calf-length skirt worn with court shoes, bobbed hair and the immaculate nails. She'd taken the precaution of getting a gel manicure. Gels are more robust than polish but also harder to remove, so her beautician, anticipating she'd want to ditch them before returning to her day job as managing director of the water-fittings manufacturer Barber Wilsons & Co, gave her a special home removal kit.

It was Sue Henison, Company Secretary at Barber Wilsons, who suggested her boss should keep the nails for the Enigma Ball at Bletchley Park the following Saturday. The dress code for the annual shindig is 'stylish' with 'mad hats optional'. Wilson had decided on a blue evening gown with glamourous accessories. 'I did the weekend [at London Erotica], and I'm driving away on the Sunday with the biggest smile on my face, having had a wonderful time for three days. And I phoned Sue up and said, "You're right, I don't want to take the gels off ",' Wilson remembers. 'And Sue said, "Well, just work from home."'

The plan might have succeeded but Wilson is a hands-on manager, nail polish or no. On Tuesday a technical problem on the shop floor demanded her presence. So, she says, 'I just put on a standard boy suit and came to work, with red nails.' When she arrived, she hurried straight upstairs to her office. Henison came looking for her, admired those shiny red nails and then asked 'What are you going to do?'

'Ah, fuck it.' Wilson replied. 'This is it.'

'And so I went downstairs and I saw a couple of the key people and said, "You may have noticed that I've got painted nails today. I'm telling you now that outside of this place I live my life as a woman and these are beautifully painted nails and I didn't want to take them off just for you, boys." I said, "I'm coming in to work actually how I'd really love to come into work for the rest of my life."'

This decision, in 2011, followed a year-long crisis – a second marriage failing, the family firm struggling as the construction industry slowed. When Wilson sought counselling, distressed and wrestling with the impulse to jump from a bridge, her doctor referred her to the Nottingham Centre for Gender Dysphoria. Simon Wilson found sexual pleasure in the act of wearing female clothing. Simone Wilson does not. 'The more I did it, the more comfortable I felt,' she explains. 'It was no longer stimulating, because it didn't feel wrong.' In becoming Simone, Wilson felt, for the first time ever, right.

Barber Wilsons fittings aren't cheap, but they're durable. Wilson understands life as a series of similar trade-offs. Her father kept her on the sidelines until his death. His legacy of debt and strategic missteps left the company with no safety margin to weather the economic slowdown, so as the new managing director she took hard choices: layoffs, a refinancing package, a move. She sold the business to a Midlands-based firm and will stay on board until she turns 65. Then, she says, 'the world will be my oyster'.

She adapts not merely to survive but to thrive, yet she cannot ignore the nature of the contract. You get and you give. Her personal transition has brought inner peace and a chance at happiness, but sorely dented her status in the outside world.

It took only a few interactions with customers to ram this point home. 'Instantly I've got a female name, instantly I am deemed to be not competent to know my products,' says Wilson. 'First thing that happened, you know, "We'll put you through to our managing director, she'll help." But "Oh, haven't you got a man I can talk to?"'

Wilson is woman enough to be underestimated. She is woman enough to experience misogyny. She is woman enough to attract the unwanted attentions of men. She tells a story about a recent night out with a female friend. As they chatted over dinner in a pub, a man offered to buy them drinks, then called them names when they refused.

She has had surgery. She wanted to be able to go to a spa. 'The one thing I didn't want was to flash a willy in there. Even the slightest flash of willy and I would be hugely uncomfortable, the women who saw it would be hugely uncomfortable, and I didn't want to go there. It just completes it mentally. It finished me off. I am a woman. Period.'

The law agrees with her, but for one final step. 'I've got a female driving licence; I've got a female passport. The only thing I've yet to do is – and I've got all the paperwork now, all ready – I've just got to do my gender recognition certificate so my birth certificate will say "girl". And then,' Wilson says, 'the boy is buried.'[1]

For all that, Wilson is not woman enough for some people and never will be. Her appearance gives few clues to her recent journey but her voice, though soft, lingers in a low enough range to draw misplaced homophobia from occasional bigots and trigger wrangles in some quarters of the women's movement.

A starting point for most feminists is the understanding that gender is heavily shaped by social and cultural factors and that those factors can be changed. We like to believe it's possible to liberate all women not only from oppression and subordination, but also from our restrictive social conditioning. The great, unresolved question is what we would be capable of – *what we would be* – once freed from reductive notions of womanhood. How crucial a role does biological sex play? To what extent are gender differences biologically determined? Wilson's red nails took her right into the uncomfortable heart of that debate. Her existence alone is provocation to anyone who believes that a person who is born male can never understand what it is to be female, much less become female.

As soon as the Women's Equality Party opened a Twitter account, the messages started. 'Does the party accept trans women?' Yes, we'd reply, often pointing out that the party was open to everyone, men too. This response did nothing to mollify some critics.

Later in this book we will address a huge and real issue they raised: the male propensity for sexual violence. There have been instances of sexual assaults against women by trans women, but the numbers are small compared to the toll of violence by men who identify as men against women including trans women. Trans women of colour are particularly vulnerable.[2] In 2015, Laverne Cox, star of the TV series *Orange is the New Black*, declared 'a state of emergency' after the murder of Tamara Dominguez, the seventeenth trans woman – and fifteenth trans woman of colour – to die in a hate crime in the US during the first half of that year. 'We in the transgender community are reeling right now,' she said.

This chapter looks at the issue of sex and gender, the explicit concern of most angry tweets. These increased in volume after WE asked Simone Wilson to speak at a September 2015 fundraiser and published, the following month, our first policy document. It contains this statement: 'WE recognise that the binary words 'woman' and 'man' do not reflect the gender experience of everyone in our country, and support the right of all to define their sex or gender or to reject gendered divisions as they choose.'

The Women's Equality Party aims to make change by creating a unified mass movement for gender equality. In striving for intersectionality, we were forced to confront how divisive the concept of equality can be. The concept of gender is at least as controversial. 'Just because you lop off your dick and then wear a dress doesn't make you a fucking woman,' Germaine Greer told the BBC the same month we published our policy document. 'I've asked my doctor to give me long ears and liver spots and I'm going to wear a brown coat but that won't turn me into a fucking cocker spaniel.'[3]

Students at Cardiff University had launched a petition to cancel her planned lecture at the institution, accusing Greer of 'transmisogyny'. As its title suggests, her most famous book *The Female Eunuch* assumed there are fully realised versions of females and males, and lesser versions, whether neutered by surgery or society. 'I'm sick of being a transvestite,' Greer wrote. 'I refuse to be a female impersonator. I am a woman, not a castrate.'

First-wave feminists, fighting for basic human rights, argued that women were as competent as men. Second-wave feminists such as Greer worked to wrest the definition of women away from men and assert female forms of potency. Trans women, in her eyes, ape exactly those aspects of imposed femininity that she has long rejected. They are not joining the sisterhood; they are luxury travellers, swathed in male privilege and carrying male prescriptions for the ideal woman tucked into their handbags.

Her statement to the BBC – 45 years after publication of *The Female Eunuch* – ends with the acceptance that some people are born intersex 'and they deserve support in coming to terms with their gender. But,' she continues, gender reassignment 'is not the same thing. A man who gets his dick chopped off is actually inflicting an extraordinary act of violence on himself.'

Nobody challenges Greer's distinction between being intersex and transgender. Biological sex is determined by combinations of sex chromosomes – in the vast majority of cases XX for females, XY for males – and by other, complex mechanisms. Gonadal steroids (sex steroids), such as oestrogen and androgen, send instructions that decide whether a body develops along female or male lines. A person's phenotypic sex – determined by their internal and external genitalia and secondary sex characteristics, such as breasts and beards – will usually, but not always, align with chromosomal sex. Intersex conditions are rare and highly varied. All of them involve unusual combinations of the factors that determine sex. For example, someone with male XY chromosomes, the SRY gene that initiates male sex development, and SOX-9, the protein that can inhibit the development of female specific characteristics, will still appear female if there's a mutation in the receptor that detects testosterone. Most trans people start chromosomally male or female, and remain unchanged at a chromosomal level after they transition from one gender to another.

Wilson accepts some of the other premises of Greer's argument. Wilson retains privileges from her former life. Nobody ever questioned whether her old male self was suitable for jobs in industry and technology. Yet the hostility still touches her and the daily pressure to justify her decisions causes her more persistent pain than any of her surgical scars. She would like to sit down with Greer and hash everything out. 'I was born with a female brain,' she says. 'Now, that doesn't make me a woman, but it does make me female. So, where [Greer] has caused much controversy amongst the trans community with her "they're still bloody men in my eyes" attitude, that's true in biological terms because of the XY chromosome thing. But I would like to say to her, "Okay, so I accept that I am not a woman, but do you accept that I am female?" I present as a woman and I present female. I am female in my thinking and mostly in my actions.'

Huckleberry Finn, hero of Mark Twain's novel, disguises himself as a girl but is rumbled by one false move. Tricked into catching a ball while seated, he claps his knees together rather than spreading his legs and using his skirt as a net as a girl would have done. The trick is effective because Huck inhabits a society in which girls always wear skirts and boys wear trousers.

From the vantage point of a changed world in which trousers are no longer a mark of masculinity, it's easy to see that Huck's action is learned behaviour rather than proof of an innate sex difference. Such clarity is rare in the study of gender. Researchers in many different disciplines struggle to disentangle culturally imparted gender from biological imperatives, not least because culturally imparted views of gender cloud their perceptions. The starting point for most explorations of sex and gender is a desire to explain the known world – the world known to the researchers. That, of course, is a man's world. Human history is patriarchal, a near-continuum of male dominance as told by men and therefore underplaying the role of women.

Within that framework, schools of thought take hold and then cede to the challenges thrown up by scientific discoveries or societal shifts. Aristotle described females as 'deformed males'. For significant periods before the Enlightenment, male and female anatomies were treated as expressions of the same underlying sex, with the male genitalia inverted and internalised in females. There is controversy over why and how the notion that there were two distinct sexes came so strongly to the fore. The historian Thomas Laqueur argues that the late seventeenth century saw a questioning of old certainties and social structures that put pressure on those structures and sent people looking to physiology to explain the gender roles.[4] Laqueur's critics point to rapid advances in science throughout the ensuing century, and a greater understanding of physiology, as reasons for the change.

Those advances are continuing apace but rather than providing definitive answers they throw up new and deeper puzzles. Research into the female brain – the physiological brain and not the psychological brain Simone Wilson believes has been hers from birth – has established observable differences. A man's brain is, on average, 10 per cent larger than a woman's; a man's amygdala, the area associated with processing emotions including fear, is bigger too. The straight gyrus, a strip along the underside of the frontal lobe, is larger in a woman's brain. 'Over the past decade or so investigators have documented an astonishing array of structural, chemical and functional variations in the brains of males and females,' reported the magazine *Scientific American* in 2012.[5] Just three years later, a study of 1,400 brains, led by Daphna Joel, a behavioral neuroscientist at Tel Aviv University, demurred. 'Humans and human brains are comprised of unique "mosaics" of features, some more common in females compared with males, some more common in males compared with females, and some common in both females and males.' The study concluded, 'Our results demonstrate that regardless of the cause of observed sex/gender differences in brain and behavior (nature or nurture), human brains cannot be categorized into two distinct classes: male brain/female brain.'[6]

In place of clear dividing lines, the study found overlap and continuum. Not only that, but brains are astonishingly plastic. They are changed by experience. A brain might start with more features common in males and acquire more female features.

Dead brains can be dissected and living brains scanned by sophisticated technologies, but it's incredibly difficult to figure out what's actually going in people's heads. Humans cannot be subjected to laboratory testing free from cultural contamination. Parents will often remark with wonder and affection that their children showed distinctly male or female characteristics in the crib. They tell you they created gender-neutral environments, shunned blue and pink, and yet Marlon was a little bruiser from the beginning and Amy's first word was 'princess'. This seems to them proof positive of hard-wired difference. They are unaware of studies demonstrating the messaging the bruiser and the princess absorb from the moment of birth, the blue and pink binaries that infiltrate hospital wards, nurseries and their own thoughts. Experiments reveal that girl babies – and boy babies dressed as girls – will be coddled and cooed over more than babies thought to be boys. Boy babies are considered less needy and more able than girls, even by their mothers.[7]

To exclude the effects of human socialisation, researchers in two separate experiments looked for gendered behaviour in very young monkeys. The primates were given a choice of gendered toys in their enclosures. In both cases, the male monkeys appeared less interested than their female counterparts in toys that invited playing mother (a doll in one study, stuffed animals in the other). This could be proof that females are born with an inbuilt instinct to nurture. Cordelia Fine in her excellent book *Delusions of Gender* points to an alternative explanation: that monkey colonies may pass on gendered roles to their young as fast and effectively as humans do.

This ambiguity doesn't trouble the human primates who continue to insist that women are biologically destined to be dopey helpmeets and men to be muscular providers. These people couldn't be more strongly opposed to feminism, yet some feminists unwittingly draw from the same well in asserting uniquely female qualities.

That well is seemingly inexhaustible. In explaining autism as an expression of 'extreme male brain', the eminent Cambridge University psychologist Simon Baron-Cohen applied as much delicacy and nuance to the discussion of gender as his cousin Sacha brought to the film *Brüno*. 'The female brain is predominantly hard-wired for empathy. The male brain is predominantly hard-wired for understanding and building systems,' declared Baron-Cohen in his 2003 book *The Essential Difference*. Such theories may have impeded diagnosis for women and girls with autism, with later research pointing to many missed cases. Baron-Cohen himself moved away from assuming a gender split and looking more closely at the role of hormones. In the 2003 book, he did throw a bone to any readers who might be snarling at his definitions of male and female: he was referring, he said, to average men and average women, not to all men and women. 'So it should be some reassurance to you if you are male and going for a job interview in the caring professions, or if you are female and going for a job interview in the technical professions, that your interviewer should assume nothing about your skills for these jobs from your sex alone.'

This was hollow reassurance indeed given the bias – conscious and unconscious – that operates at every job interview, on both sides of the table. Interviewers appraise candidates through lenses crafted by their own upbringing and experiences. The candidates they see will already have self-selected according to similar criteria – men are more likely to have shied away from entry-level nursing positions and women to have ruled themselves out of jobs as coders years previously. Even then, applicants come burdened with ideas about intrinsic sex differences that are not always supported by science, even if they have been promoted by scientists.

That's not just because scientific complexity gets lost in translation to popular science, but because of the interlocking mechanisms that keep cultural memes alive long after science has moved on. These days most psychologists view Sigmund Freud as a man who needed to lie on his own couch and work through the neuroses that brought him to many of his conclusions, especially about women. 'How wise [are] our educators that they pester the beautiful sex so little with scientific knowledge,' he exclaimed.[8] He acknowledged his lack of understanding of women – a 'dark continent for psychology' – yet proceeded to formulate multiple theories about the female of the species.

He did not wonder why Austrian society of the late nineteenth and early twentieth centuries treated its women so poorly and granted them so few rights. He instead assumed deficiencies in the female sex and looked for explanations, alighting on anatomical difference. 'Here the feminist demand for equal rights for the sexes does not take us far, for the morphological distinction is bound to find expression in differences of psychical development,' he opined. '"Anatomy is Destiny", to vary a saying of Napoleon's. The little girl's clitoris behaves just like a penis to begin with; but, when she makes a comparison with a playfellow of the other sex, she perceives that she has "come off badly" and she feels this as a wrong done to her and as a ground for inferiority. For a while still she consoles herself with the expectation that later on, when she grows older, she will acquire just as big an appendage as the boy's ... The female child, however, does not understand her lack of a penis as being a sex character; she explains it by assuming that at some earlier date she had possessed an equally large organ and had then lost it by castration.'[9]

Freud's women are not eunuchs – they are less than eunuchs, and are subsumed by terrible jealousy and unhinged sexual impulses as a result. The theory of penis envy long ago deflated, but not before it had pushed its way into psychological discourse and penetrated wider consciousness. In seeking equality, women are still accused of wanting to be men. Many of the insults thrown at feminists damn us for supposedly masculine attributes – *You're hairy! You're ugly!* – while also reminding us of our anatomical differences – *Cunt! Hairy, ugly cunt!* Here's an example of the helpful advice I receive via Twitter: 'Shave your cooter you smelly hippy!'

Science hasn't abandoned the search for hard-wired gender differences, but it has got better at interrogating its own cultural prejudices. Researchers, seeing that more men and boys are diagnosed with autism than are women and girls, ask if this means men and boys are more prone to autism or whether women and girls might be better equipped by their socialisation to mask the signs. Women are twice as likely to suffer from depression and anxiety. This book lists any number of external reasons why that might be.

The more you know, the more you know you don't know. Robin Lovell-Badge is a Group Leader and Head of the Division of Stem Cell Biology and Developmental Genetics at the renowned Francis Crick Institute in London. His curriculum vitae is shiny with awards and accolades. He has spent his working life probing the mechanics of sex determination at cellular level and below, discovering with another scientist, Peter Goodfellow, the SRY gene on the Y chromosome and a whole family of genes called SOX. (One of the researchers in Lovell-Badge's laboratory inspired the name because of his habit of wearing odd socks.) The gonads in mammalian embryos have the potential to develop into testes or ovaries. The SRY gene can be expected to trigger the development of testes if another gene, SOX-9, is also present. In humans this probably happens about six weeks into the development of the embryo, but here, as on many points, there's some uncertainty.

A conversation with Lovell-Badge is simultaneously a tour of astonishing progress in understanding sex and gender and a window into the reasons we still lack definitive answers. He agrees that hormones are implicated in the behaviours associated with males and females but cautions that these impacts are dependent on a multiplicity of other factors. 'There is indeed evidence that exposure to androgens at particular points during foetal development in the womb can probably influence aspects of gender role, gender identity, gender preference,' he says. He gives an example, Congenital Adrenal Hyperplasia, an intersex condition in which a genetic mutation means the adrenal glands of an XX-female floods the embryo with testosterone. The babies are usually born with masculinised genitalia. 'In these cases, there's some evidence that the levels of androgens will masculinise gender roles to some extent. They will often have very tomboyish behaviour as kids. But of course social conditioning is important as well. If you have a child who is born with genitalia that are masculinised, it's quite possible that their family, at least for a while, treats them as if they were a boy.'[10]

Popular associations between hormones and gender outcomes can be wide of the mark too. The jutting horns of stags speak not to high levels of male hormones but of oestrogen. The linkage between testosterone and aggressive behaviour is born out in non-human mammals, and the strangest example of all is to be found in the dog-eat-dog world of hyenas. Survival depends on aggression, so the species has evolved what Lovell-Badge calls a 'ridiculous system': both male and female hyenas have phalluses ('mating is very difficult, as you can imagine'), and the first newborn of every female dies, strangled by the narrow birth canal. However, high levels of testosterone do not necessarily lead to aggression, and all aggression is not testosterone-fuelled.

More subtle prompts may be given by genes. 'There's a process called X-chromosome inactivation, or dosage compensation, the role of which is to sort of equalise the dosage of genes on the X chromosome between males and females,' he says. 'Men have one X, women have two, but one of these X-chromosomes and the majority of genes on it are silenced – meaning that women effectively only have one active copy, men only have one active copy. However, particularly in humans, there are quite a lot of genes on the X chromosome that escape this process of inactivation.'

How might these genes be shaping our personalities, instructing our behaviour, making us feel comfortable in our skins or trapped in the wrong body? 'It is very difficult to do the science behind this, certainly in humans, because it's politically charged.' Lovell-Badge grimaces. 'As you will know, there are people who think it is all a matter of choice, whether you're gay or trans or whatever. Whereas that's clearly not the case. And then there are members of the intersex community who are curious to know why they are the way they are. But then there are others in that community who think that if science finds an answer as to whether there's a particular gene that's involved, then there would then be pressure to 'cure' them; and so they're unwilling to participate. It is hard to get the funding to do the science; it is hard to get volunteers to participate; and you can't actually do any experiments – you can only observe, or try to observe, in a neutral way, and again that becomes difficult too.'

In the teeth of all these obstacles, scientific research continues to expand and deepen our understanding of these areas. One outcome is already clear, says Lovell-Badge. The old binary, male and female, is false. We are all 'on a spectrum,' he says. 'Most people are on one end or other of four spectrums: your anatomy or physiology, and then in terms of behaviour, gender identity, gender preference and gender role. Although there's probably some connections between all four, they can operate independently.'

The restaurant that Cat/Milo Bezark suggests for brunch is in the Arts District, a newly fashionable area of Downtown Los Angeles. We sit outside – this is California – but in a courtyard, shielded from the awkward realities of the neighbourhood. Homelessness in the city jumped 11 per cent over the past year and Skid Row is within walking distance. The waiting staff – all Hollywood-beautiful – bring supersized mugs of tea and dishes that could feed the 5,000 or at least some of the tent-dwellers up the road: eggs with avocado, exotic fruits, granola.

We talk too much to pay close attention to the food or the environment. We haven't spent quality time together for a few years and there's a lot of catching up to do. Facebook creates the illusion of staying in touch but really it has just allowed me to enjoy Cat/Milo's fashion choices from a distance: hair emerald one moment, frosted and quiffed the next, piercings, ensembles mixing styles generally considered polar opposites – feminine and masculine, daywear and evening wear, summer and winter. Anyone who fears that feminism threatens us with a future of colourless uniformity needs only to spend time with Cat/Milo to realise that mistake. Today Cat/Milo wears a jacket, shorts and no make-up apart from chipped turquoise nail polish. The night before, at a family gathering, deep purple lipstick drew comment from Cat/Milo's twin brother, Connor. 'What have you done to your lips?' he asked. 'They look nice.'

Cat/Milo started life with the same forename as me, and quite a few of the same genes. Cat/Milo's father is my first cousin, who claims to have named his child for me, but my suspicion is that he and Cat/Milo's mother just liked the name. Cat/Milo liked it too, but now prefers the shortened, feline version and sometimes also answers to 'Milo', because Cat/Milo, at 19, no longer identifies as female.

Cat/Milo is trans – in Cat/Milo's jaunty expression a 'trans kid'. The transition isn't from she to he, but from she to 'they', the preferred third-person singular pronoun for many non-binary people. Ancient Egyptians referred to all sexes as 'hm', though the hieroglyph can also mean someone deprived of sex, a eunuch. Many modern languages are constructed in ways that don't rely on gendered pronouns and offer gender-free alternatives.

Sweden adopted a gender-neutral pronoun, 'hen', coined in the 1960s and in official use since around 2012.

But English, which used to have equivalents ('ou' and 'a' among others), gradually lost this flexibility, retaining only the dehumanising 'it'. Attempts to revive old gender-neutral words or invent new ones have tended to gain traction only within circles already engaged in redefining gender, but there has been more movement recently. In 2016, new guidance issued by Britain's Boarding Schools' Association recommended teachers address children by their pronoun of choice, and listed the options 'zie' and 'they'.[11] The latter is Cat/Milo's pronoun, familiar if clunky in singular usage. Like the shift from 'Miss' and 'Mrs' to 'Ms', it doesn't really fix the problem of inherently discriminatory language. For as long as women are asked to select from all three honorifics, any of those choices gives away far more information than the generic 'Mr'. There's another option, the non-binary honorific, 'Mx', which in 2015 made it into the Oxford English Dictionary but still carries coded signals about the people whose names it prefixes. Anyone using it tends to be non-binary or alert to the non-binary world.

Many Mxs are, like Cat/Milo, fourth-wave feminists. They – Cat/Milo and other fourth-wavers – aim to tackle gender inequities by dismantling the ways in which we think about gender. Language is an obvious starting point. They have taken into everyday conversation terms that until recently remained on the margins. Women and men comfortable within the gender assigned to them at birth are 'cisgender'. ('Cis' is a Latin prefix meaning 'on this side of', the opposite of 'trans', 'on the far side of'.) The initials LGBT – already expanded from 'lesbian and gay' to include 'bisexual and transgender' – keep getting longer. LGBTQI recently added a letter, to become LGBTQIA. Q stands for 'queer' or 'questioning', I for intersex, and A for 'asexual', 'agender', 'aromantic', 'ace' or, according to the *New York Times* in an earnest piece of the kind that 20 years ago informed readers that cellular phones might be used not only for voice calls but also to send SMS messages, an 'ally, a friend of the cause'.[12]

At 16, Cat/Milo started thinking which of these letters might apply to them. As a child, Cat/Milo remembers having a pink room and Connor a blue room, but their closeness as twins leads Cat/Milo to speculate that 'maybe we queered each other up a bit … I very early became a tomboy and he very early became kind of a softie boy. He would play with my dolls and I would play with [older brother] John and his action men.' The definitions of gender and sexuality that seemed to work for their classmates didn't fit Cat/Milo or Cat/Milo's closest high-school friends.

'We started talking about these two binary genders of male and female,' Cat/Milo says. 'The male supposedly likes trucks and climbing trees and blue and fighting and fixing cars, and women supposedly like nail polish. But we figured out that those are just arbitrary groupings of different attributes. Who decided that if you like cars, you also like climbing trees and you also like the colour blue? That doesn't make sense. So, I initially started off my gender identity by feeling like "Fuck gender. I don't need gender." And this is before I understood that it could be a whole spectrum. I was just like "Neither of these make any sense, why did society form these two groupings of attributes and say that you have to fit into one of these things?"'

At first Cat/Milo concluded they must be agender. Later Cat/Milo refined that identity to genderqueer. 'The important thing about gender and queerness is that each person has to have their own definition of it, and each definition is just as valid as the next person's definition of it,' Cat/Milo explains. 'Because if you try to give a singular definition for any identity then you're going to exclude people, and that's not the point of queerness. What's important about queerness to me is that if you identify as queer, then you are queer.'

It's hard to square this doctrine of tolerance and acceptance with another feature of Cat/Milo's college-age cohort: a determination to shut out voices that challenge their views. This is the generation that sometimes prefers to no-platform Germaine Greer rather than debate her.

Critics point to the privileges that middle-class young feminists enjoy. They have the certainty of youth and take positions they may not realise are possible only because other people, including Greer, enabled them. First-wave feminists fought for the vote. Cat/Milo and their friends got to pick Bernie or Hillary – for whatever that choice was worth. (Most of them, Cat/Milo included, felt the Bern.) Second-wave feminists pushed for legislative and reproductive rights. Cat/Milo and their friends approach the discussion of children with the benefit of these rights (though these are under attack from conservative politicians everywhere and, since the US election, appear under greater threat than ever). Third-wave feminists made huge strides on identity, inclusivity and diversity. Cat/Milo and their friends are the heirs to all this.

But they are also dealing with challenges that their forerunners never imagined. Later in the book, we consider whether free speech can remain a sacred ideal in a world of digital abuse and pervasive, poisonous imagery. You too might want to shut out voices if all you could hear was a cacophony.

Choice, too, is confusing and in some respects illusive. The increasing acceptance of gender fluidity and the opportunity to browse a greater number of gender identities holds out the possibility that everyone can find out who they are, be comfortable in their skins, but it means only so much when most gender identities deliver similarly unsatisfactory outcomes in terms of status and opportunities. Go shopping in the Urban Radish, a hipster supermarket in the Arts District – 'a market and eatery rooted in the community' – and you'll find yourself choosing between multiple brands of organic granola. Some crunch better than others but they're still variations on oats.

Women, trans women, trans men, non-binary people are all at a disadvantage to cisgender men in global terms and specific ways. Intersectionality helps to explain why the picture doesn't always look that way – why there's a male cashier at the Urban Radish checkout bagging goods for a wealthy woman; how Cat/Milo and I come to be eating our brunch in a nice restaurant while outside a homeless man begs for cigarettes. It is less easy to explain why so many affluent white cisgender men feel not privileged but put upon, or simply unhappy. One reason, of course, is that definitions of manhood, like all definitions of gender, are increasingly fluid. In straining to reassert fraying ideas of masculinity, men hurt everyone, including themselves.

Chapter Four: Being a man

THE MEN OF H7 toiled not, but they had sinned. They weren't forced to mop floors or peel potatoes alongside the inmates the guards called 'ordinary decent criminals.' This was 1994 and anyone convicted of terror-related crimes demanded, and received, special treatment from the UK government. There were 502 such men at the Maze prison, jailed between them for 236 murders and 116 offences involving explosives or weaponry. They didn't seem like peace-makers but they had become players in the Northern Irish peace process, as proxies for their communities and conduits to terrorist cells still at large. In return for their involvement, they got to choose how to while away their days at Her Majesty's pleasure.

Each organisation appointed its own 'Officer Commanding' and had the run of an H-block or a discrete wing of one of the letter-shaped buildings. Members of the Provisional IRA read improving books, memoirs of revolutionaries, political tracts. They were preparing for power, however distant that prospect might seem. Loyalist factions, kept separate not just from Republicans but from each other because of deadly rivalries between their groups, lifted weights and gave themselves tattoos by needling mixtures of ash, toothpaste and baby oil under their skins. They were preparing for power too, the kind that marks out territories and patrols municipalities.

H7 – dubbed 'Jurassic Park' by warders – housed 88 members of the Ulster Volunteer Force, a gang renowned for its brutality. Adherents tortured, shot and bombed people with no links to Republican terror but simply for being Catholic, and more than once accidentally killed Protestants too. I had come to the Maze as a journalist, to try to understand the different perspectives informing the peace negotiations and whether men such as these could ever give up violence.

There was a hitch. The guards had planned for me to conduct any interviews with the UVF in the administrative hub of the prison. The last woman to enter H7, a social worker, re-emerged with a chunk bitten out of her throat. I found this out only later, together with the reason the authorities decided to send me into H7 despite the risks. The UVF were insisting that I visit them on their turf because they knew I'd already spent time in H5, the IRA's domain. If I did not accept the equivalent UVF hospitality, they would riot.

So the prison was on high alert, with guards poised to swoop in and rescue me if necessary, when Jackie Millar, the UVF's Officer Commanding, greeted me at the barred gates to H7 and led me to the cell he'd selected for our meeting. As we walked past the shower rooms, both of us caught sight of flaccid UVF members and their naked, muscle-bound owners. Millar was mortified and punctuated the rest of our conversation with apologies. No lady should ever be forced to see what I had seen.

He was still apologising when he escorted me back to the gates with the elaborate courtesy of a teenage boy returning his prom date to her parents. The guards, visibly relieved to see me in one piece, presented me with one of the enamelled pins they'd commissioned to honour survivors of the Maze's Jurassic Park. It depicted a grinning, green tyrannosaurus lounging against a yellow 7.

Dinosaurs no longer roamed the fields beyond the prison walls, but Northern Ireland hadn't yet made it to the modern era either. The Catholic civil rights movement had splintered into violent dissent. Nationalist politicians used democratic channels to press for the country to reunite with the rest of Ireland; Republican terrorists made the argument with Armalites and bombs. The Protestant population mirrored these strands. Unionist politicians insisted that Northern Ireland must remain in the United Kingdom; Loyalist terror groups scrawled this message in blood.

The conflict blocked the economic and social development that was transforming other parts of the UK and, to the South, the Irish Republic. Multinationals and high-street chains stayed away. Tourists, if they dared to come at all, generally headed straight for the Giant's Causeway in Antrim and straight home again. An occasional straggle of Van Morrison fans made pilgrimage to Cyprus Avenue. In Britain, the foodie culture was going mainstream, planting gastropubs on every high street, but Northern Irish restaurants had little competition or outside inspiration, and it showed. In Londonderry – 'Derry' to Nationalists – a Chinese restaurant in the historic city centre offered a 'three-course lunch': first course, tomato juice; second course, sweet-and-sour pork with chips; third course, coffee.

The menu of identities, lifestyles and opportunities on offer to Ulster's working and lower middle classes was similarly limited. Westminster legalised abortion in 1967 but the statute still does not extend to Northern Ireland. Sex between men, decriminalised in England and Wales the same year, continued to be a criminal offence in Northern Ireland until 1982. Churches on both sides of the sectarian divide preached fire, brimstone and the missionary position within heterosexual marriage.

Their congregations lived remarkably similar lives on opposite sides of the so-called peace walls built to keep them apart for their own protection. Unionists and Loyalists daubed the pavements red, white and blue, and decorated walls with murals of William of Orange. They named their sons for him too. Nationalists and Republicans marked out their territories in the orange, green and white of the Irish flag and painted portraits of fallen comrades on the buildings. The familiar faces included Bobby Sands, who had died on hunger strike in the Maze 13 years earlier, protesting the removal of the special status accorded to 'political prisoners' that would later be restored and extended.

Paramilitary organisations policed the neighbourhoods that birthed them, rewarding misdemeanours such as small-scale drug-dealing with severe reprisals including kneecapping and execution. Supposed defenders of the Crown and self-proclaimed Irish freedom fighters shot and beat up more than 500 children between 1990 and 2013. They did so as much to protect vested interests and banish competition as to keep order. The IRA relied on a steady stream of donations from sympathisers in the US and elsewhere, Loyalist groups at various times enjoyed the illicit support of the British state, and both sides derived much of their income from crime – drugs, fuel-laundering, extortion.

They sometimes defended their communities against outside enemies, but could not be relied on to act against the enemies within. Serious allegations of sex abuse in the Republican community by the IRA, and cover-ups by senior members of that organisation, remain untested by law, but one high-profile case centred on Sinn Fein did come to court. In 2013 Liam Adams, brother of Sinn Fein president Gerry Adams, was convicted of raping his own daughter more than three decades earlier. The party has now become a democratic force both sides of the Irish border, but during the Troubles was closely entwined with the IRA. In the witness box, Gerry Adams admitted he had known about his brother's abuse for nearly a decade but had not informed the police.[1]

Republicanism and Loyalism were closed, defensive cultures. For most born into them, the only option was to go with the flow or get away fast and as far as possible. The boys who stayed could choose between joining the paramilitaries or merely supporting them. The first of those choices conferred status and, more than that, brotherhood. 'Devoted actors adopt values they regard as sacred and non-negotiable, to be defended at all costs. Then, when they join a like-minded group of non-kin that feels like a family – a band of brothers – a collective sense of invincibility and special destiny overwhelms feelings of individuality. As members of a tightly bound group that perceives its sacred values under attack, devoted actors will kill and die for each other.'[2] This passage, from the journal *Science*, refers to recent research into the lure of ISIS, but could just as well explain why so many tender boys rushed to bloody themselves in the name of Republicanism or Loyalism.

Girls had even fewer choices. Republican ideology echoed other left-wing nationalist movements in seeing the plight of women as a function of imperialism. Some women, like Mairéad Farrell, took frontline positions in the IRA, but the push for gender equality always came a distant second to the main aim of Republicanism: a united Ireland. Farrell, who would eventually be shot dead by British special forces in Gibraltar in 1988, supported this hierarchy of priorities as did her sisters-in-arms. 'I am oppressed as a woman but I am also oppressed because I'm Irish,' she said. 'Everyone in this country is oppressed and we can't successfully end our oppression as women until we first end the oppression of our country.'[3]

The majority of young Republican women, like their Loyalist counterparts, looked forward to marriage, domesticity, tragedy and disruption. More than 3,600 people died during the 30 years up to the 1998 Good Friday Agreement and thousands more lost family to murder or prison, often leaving mothers, wives or sisters as the sole breadwinners of their households. This might have been expected to break down old stereotypes and increase understanding of female potential, but templates for masculinity and femininity remained as unyielding in these communities as the political hardliners who, long after the formal end of the Troubles, continued to fight the peace.

Northern Ireland's peace – scrappy and imperfect as it is – provides a compelling case study in the benefits of affirmative action and quotas. Since 1989, a programme of affirmative action reinforced by legislation has worked to ensure fair employment for Catholics and Protestants. Quotas and other mechanisms underpinned a decade of power-sharing in the Northern Ireland Assembly until a stumble early in 2017.

There are other reasons to look closely at Northern Ireland. In questioning where nature ends and nurture begins in defining gender, Republican and Loyalist communities provide some pointers. That they are drawn from Northern Ireland's small population (1.6 million in the last decade of the Troubles) and narrow gene pool makes it easier to discern the impact of nurture – though little about the rough cradling of Derry's Bogside or Belfast's Shankill or the Falls Road areas could be described as nurture.

Peace has opened the floodgates to the forces that conflict had held back. Property developers are at work on the high streets and in favoured neighbourhoods. Chefs are flocking to Belfast and Derry, and every kind of menu has expanded. Many see in this banquet an opportunity to try new things, but for others, and especially low-income, highly partisan sectors of society, the adjustment has been hard.

Post-conflict Northern Ireland is still divided by economics and religion. In the 2011 Census, 82.3 per cent of the population described themselves as Christian – that compares with 59.4 per cent in England, 53.8 per cent in Scotland and 57.6 percent in Wales. The poorest neighbourhoods tend to be the richest in sectarianism. Paramilitary organisations stoke old hatreds to justify their continued existence. The peace dividend reached some parts of the population but bypassed other demographics.

A 2013 article by Margaret Ward, the Director of Northern Ireland's Women's Resource and Development Agency, highlights the ways in which the peace is failing women. She criticises the political classes for attempting to shape the post-conflict nation without factoring in women's lives or experiences. She reports that a conference 'in order to consider contentious issues like parading and flags, had police, politicians and community representatives in attendance, and only three women out of more than 30 participants. Peace building is still seen as an activity that primarily involves men.'[4]

One inevitable consequence of this omission is that problems affecting women fester unchecked. Ward also cites evidence from a series of workshops with women from Republican and Loyalist communities. The women lay out the realities of life on estates run by paramilitaries: mothers are threatened and attacked for trying to protect their families; girls are at risk from sexual exploitation by the gangs who have diversified into prostitution; alcohol dependency and drug addiction are 'a huge and often hidden legacy of the conflict', not least among former prisoners. Domestic and sexual violence are increasing and the prohibition on reporting these crimes to the police, rather than to the paramilitaries who may themselves be the offenders, remains in place.

When women are on the receiving end of abuse from men, it's hard enough to think sympathetically about what is driving the abusers, much less to worry about the damage the abusers are doing to themselves. But the strangest, saddest legacy of the conflict shows with terrible clarity the toll on men of the narrow ways in which they have been permitted to define themselves. In the first 15 years after the 30-year Troubles, suicide rates in Northern Ireland more than doubled, killing nearly as many people as the entire conflict in half the time. Seventy-seven per cent of victims were men. The strongest spike occurred among those who came of age amid the bloodshed, but the pattern is repeating in generations born after the peace. 'The transition to peace means that externalised aggression is no longer socially approved. It becomes internalised instead,' one study concluded.[5]

Suicide rates vary across the world, and are highest in countries of the former Soviet Union, parts of the Far East and East Africa. Cultural differences are clearly at play. The Irish on both sides of the border more frequently take their own lives than Britons. Among all the variations and variables, one trend is constant. More women than men attempt to die by their own hands. More men succeed; some 15 in every 100,000 head of population globally for men compared to 8 in 100,000 for women. Men use violent and reliable methods – hanging, shooting. They do not cry for help. Fewer suicidal men confide in friends and family or seek counselling. Men are also more likely to perceive a stigma attaching to failed suicides.

These trends, though widely recognised, remain little understood. A paper co-authored by three psychologists at English universities, Viren Swami, Debbi Stanistreet and Sarah Payne, suggests that the confusion starts with the definitions of femininity and masculinity applied by researchers: 'One tradition that remains popular within the psychological sciences theorises gender as singular female or male "personalities" or "schemas" – what Kimmel (1986) described as "role containers". This view of gender suggests that there are male or female gender-stereotypic traits, and an "innate" need to fill appropriate roles. However, ... such a view is overly-simplistic and does not capture the multiple forms of masculinities and femininities that can be demonstrated, nor where the pressure to fulfil roles comes from.'[6]

The trio prefers a more nuanced approach, 'that gender, rather than being mere role containers, is something that is repeatedly and constantly "done".' The phrase comes from a study on gender that Swami, Stanistreet and Payne quote at length: 'Doing gender involves a complex set of socially guided perceptual, interactional, and micropolitical activities that cast particular pursuits as expressions of masculine and feminine 'natures'.'[7] They conclude: 'Certainly it is possible to identify, within particular societies or cultures, clusters of behaviour that are considered enactments of "dominant" masculinity or femininity ... The link seems obvious: if all behaviours are an expression of gender, perhaps "doing masculinity" puts men at higher risk for suicidal behaviours compared with women's "doing femininity".'

Sons of Northern Ireland's conflict do masculinity in ways that damage everyone, including themselves. Rigid beliefs and utter certainties – transmitted by church, community and domestic authorities – inform their notions of what they should be. If they are not strong, fearless defenders of their families, faiths and way of life, what are they? A society that sets so much store on outer shows of conformity and belonging – the painted curbs, the prison tattoos – has little tolerance of deeper difference. A society that uses violence to repel the Other – when that Other looks and speaks and thinks so much like its persecutors that insignia and tattoos are the only obvious signifiers of difference – has no room for doubt. To question anything is for every construct to unravel. To admit to weakness, to yearn for the soft and the gentle, is to be despised, by others and by yourself. For an unconscionable number, death seems a kinder option.

Men should push for gender equality not for what they can get out of it, but because it is the right thing to do. Men must be part of the movement in order to ensure that all of us, wherever we are on the gender spectrum, reach Equalia. It is not enough to be supportive – to be the man I met just after we set up the Women's Equality Party who said 'I agree with everything you're doing. I'd like to see my wife get more help with childcare.' (He did not mean that he'd like to see himself enabled to give her more help.) Men will have to pitch in, without overriding, and – vitally – must create space for women.

This is all true. Nevertheless, this book will also show that men would be the beneficiaries of the new settlement, that Equalia's peace dividend would be more evenly distributed than Northern Ireland's. Recent studies have spoken to the negative impact of stereotyped gender roles: men who are the sole breadwinners for their families suffer greater strains on their health and wellbeing. The reverse is also true. A large-scale statistical comparison discovered that men in more gender-equal Nordic countries are healthier and happier than their peers in more patriarchal cultures.[8] 'A lot of what we know about how gender plays out in marriage focuses on the ways in which women are disadvantaged,' Christin Munsch, the lead author of one of the studies and Assistant Professor of Sociology at the University of Connecticut, remarked. 'Our study contributes to a growing body of research that demonstrates the ways in which gendered expectations are harmful for men too.' Later we'll look at the economic boost and better outcomes in many areas of life from gender equality, but first we need to talk about male identity, male fragility, male violence and the benefit to men of addressing these things.

We need to talk about Kevin. He is the monstrous creation of Lionel Shriver in her 2003 novel of the same name. He is the son who commits incomprehensible atrocities. He is the personification of male violence. He maims and murders without the tattered excuse of the bigger causes the sons of the Irish conflict clutch to their chests like old comfort blankets. He may be – as a startling proportion of these conflict survivors and their sons are – suicidal. Many perpetrators of mass shootings aim to die at the scene. He is certainly unhappy and confused.

Psychologists are divided on the question of psychopathy much as they are on gender, and indeed they are divided on the question of gender and psychopathy. It is a spectrum disorder and distinguished from sociopathy by one fundamental. Sociopaths are created by social and environmental factors. Psychopaths – believed to be responsible for half of all serious crime as well as collateral damage to the people they manipulate and abuse – are thought to arrive in the world with the genetic seeds of the condition that blocks conscience and empathy.

Psychologists used to believe the condition affected more men than women. Some now argue that female psychopaths go under-diagnosed because the test is geared to men and the form that female psychopathy takes is different. 'In women, the tendency to run away, exhibit self-injurious behaviour, and manipulation, all characterise impulsiveness and behavioural problems,' says one recent study. 'Moreover, their criminal behaviour consists primarily of theft and fraud. In men, however, the criminal behaviour often includes violence.'[9]

It may not be possible to locate the precise borders between nature and nurture, but it is clear that people born with psychopathic tendencies take their behavioural directions from the societies in which they find themselves – and all of those societies place men at the top of the hierarchy, consigning women to lower tiers, often sexualised, objectified, de-humanised. There are links between the sex industry – the literal commodification of women – and sexual violence and misogyny. Later we examine these issues in depth but it is important in any discussion of male identity to acknowledge those links and to understand the bigger picture. Monster-men exist, psychopaths who in any culture would wreak havoc: Jimmy Savile; Ian Brady; Andrei Chikatilo; Ted Bundy; Yang Xinhai. Yet even these are subject to influence in terms of the ways their psychopathy expresses itself. Moreover, psychopathy is thought to affect only one per cent of the population. For the vast majority of men, socialisation shapes who they are and how they act within the vast range of possibilities afforded by the male biological entity.

A hapless 19-year-old student at Warwick University attracted mockery with an article that protested as 'the biggest insult' his invitation to attend campus workshops on sexual consent. George Lawlor expostulated: 'I don't have to be taught to not be a rapist. That much comes naturally to me, as I am sure it does to the overwhelming majority of people you and I know … I'm not denying there have been tragic cases of rape and abuse on campuses in the past, but do you really think the kind of people who lack empathy, respect and human decency to the point where they'd violate someone's body are really going to turn up to a consent lesson on a university campus?' He posted a picture of himself holding up a sign that read 'This is not what a rapist looks like.'

It was a silly gesture, but he was not alone in making that mistake. It is comforting to think of rapists as separate from the rest of society, easy to spot, monstrous. But monsters don't look like monsters and most rapists are not monsters. There are no reliable visual clues to potential rapists, apart from one. They don't have a particular skin colour or cast of feature and they don't necessarily wear hoodies. But they are more likely to be men, just as their victims are more likely to be women. Around 78,000 women are raped in England and Wales every year; about 9,000 men are raped in the same period.[10]

Women do commit rape, of other women and sometimes of men. Those crimes are almost certainly under-reported, because all sex crimes are under-reported by victims fearing a different kind of violation by the criminal justice system meant to help them but too often lacking the delicacy or determination to do so. Male victims may also try to rationalise the assaults as confirmation of their own manliness or feel shamed into silence. After all, real men don't get raped.

That messaging is pretty unambiguous in most parts of the world. Its concomitant message is far less clear: real men don't rape.

Lawlor was reaching towards a valid point: that he had been brought up to believe rape is wrong and that accepting and internalising the prohibition against rape diminishes the likelihood of becoming a rapist. But rape is a crime motivated not by lust but by anger and hatred. Men are not biologically programmed to be rapists, most are not by instinct or inclination rapists, but all men live in societies that give implicit and explicit permissions to treat women badly. When men break, straitjacketed by a male identity that simultaneously makes them vulnerable and stops them from seeking help, they may take out their rage against women.

Pavan Amara, herself a rape survivor, set up a London-based initiative to help women who have undergone assaults of this nature to regain sufficient confidence in their bodies to access medical services and to build relationships including sexual relationships. 'When I first told some of my male friends that I was going to do this, it was very interesting the different reactions that my female friends and my male friends had,' she remembers. 'My female friends were saying: "That's fantastic! We'll support you. Do you want me to do this or that?" My male friends, even though they're really good guys and very supportive personally for me – these were the people who had often heard me cry for hours when I was at my worst – they became so uncomfortable talking about it. For one of them, I asked him to read the original thirty interviews that I'd done [with other rape victims], just to check everything and get an extra pair of eyes on it. He said: "Yeah, I will", and he didn't, and he didn't, and he didn't. Eventually I said to him: "Why haven't you looked at this yet?" – he was usually very efficient – and he said: "It's because I sat there trying to read it and I just couldn't, because it was so upsetting for me.'"[11]

Men's inability to engage with the fact of sexual violence is certainly a contributory factor to it, says Amara. 'I thought that was a really interesting comment, because it was almost like he'd like to live in his world where this doesn't happen to a lot of women. But it does. And it shows you what a different world men and women are living in often – where they won't even open the door into the world, even look at the world, where a lot of women are actually living because it makes them uncomfortable to do that. Men often worry that they don't have the emotional resources to deal with what they're going to see, and so they pretend it doesn't exist.'

How should we help men to develop the resources to help us and help themselves? This question has gained urgency not only because of the scourge of structural violence. Seventy-two per cent of white male voters without college education voted for Donald Trump. In Rust Belt states, buffeted by globalisation, their numbers were particularly high.[12] Across the world, regressive political movements are drawing support from men with genuine cause for grievance. They are marginalised, and they believe the demagogues who tell them that immigrants and women are responsible.

We need a counter-narrative, and that is what the Women's Equality Party seeks to provide by laying out the benefits that would accrue to men through gender equality – not only in economic terms, but by creating kinder societies more at ease with themselves. The patriarchy may be the enemy of women; men are not.

Women and men are often allies, friends; we may be lovers or parents. Women want to understand men better, but men exclude women not only from good things, but also from their own pain and confusion. This is something many women know from direct experience: of partners, children, male friends and colleagues. We're also aware that there is some truth to the stereotype of male friendship as an inadequate support system, all banter and bluster, hilarity and mutual concealment. We rarely get to see the all-male environment for ourselves. The hard men of H7 softened and shrivelled under my gaze – a woman walking into a male enclave often feels she is re-enacting the scene in countless Westerns where a gunslinger enters a saloon and all customers freeze, Bourbon suspended halfway to mouths, cigars dangling. Our presence alters male behaviours.

How then should women observe and learn about male behaviour? Like the Republican prisoners in the Maze, we can seek out literature to prepare us for power-sharing, books about men and masculinity and male identity. We might read Ernest Hemingway who framed such definitions as 'pain does not matter to a man' or 'man is not made for defeat … A man can be destroyed but not defeated'. Or we can read those same quotes in *Manliness*, Harvey C. Mansfield's disquisition on the subject, which starts from the mistaken premises that a gender-neutral world is the goal of feminism and that gender equality is largely upon us. We can browse mgtow.com, the website for Men Going Their Own Way, abandoning relationships with women in favour of the man-only manosphere.

Occasionally women find ways to penetrate the world of men undetected. In 1959, a white American called John Howard Griffin passed himself off as a black man in the segregationist Deep South. The limitations of such a device are obvious: the experiences Griffin wrote up in the book *Black Like Me* are the experiences of a white man in blackface. What he learns is not how it feels to be black but what racism, and the instrumentalisation of black women by racists, looks like. Hitchhiking in Alabama, he takes a ride from someone who appears to be an amiable grandfather and pillar of the community. The illusion is shattered when the driver asks if Griffin's wife 'has ever had it from a white man.' Griffin's protests elicit a statement about power dynamics. 'I'll tell you how it is here. We'll do business with you people. We'll sure as hell screw your women. Other than that, you're just completely off the record as far as we're concerned.'

Nearly half a century later, in the spirit of Griffin's work and inspired by a cross-dressing reality TV show, a journalist called Norah Vincent embarked on a parallel exploration. She became Ned and, over a year and a half, made regular expeditions into the male world. 'My observations are full of my own prejudices and preconceptions, though I have tried as much as possible to qualify them accordingly,' she writes in *Self-Made Man*.[13] She joins an all-male bowling league, visits strip clubs, dates women, visits a monastery, goes on a male camping retreat. Her big takeaway is that assumed manhood – and, she assumes, manhood itself – is not the liberation she anticipated but is in some ways more limiting than the female experience. 'It wasn't being found out as a woman that I was really worried about. It was about being found out as less than a real man, and I suspect that this is something that a lot of men endure their whole lives, this constant scrutiny and self-scrutiny,' she observes. 'Somebody is always evaluating your manhood. Whether it's other men, other women, even children. And everybody is always on the lookout for your weakness and inadequacy, as if it's some kind of plague they're terrified of catching, or, more importantly, of other men catching. If you don't make the right move, put your eyes in the right place at any given moment, in the eyes of the culture at large that threatens the whole structure. Consequently, somebody has always got to be there kicking you under the table, redirecting, making or keeping you a real man.'

London's Garrick Club remains a male-only preserve after a vote in July 2015 failed to summon the two-thirds majority necessary to open membership to women. 'The arguments against letting in women were threadbare,' a member who had backed change complained to me in an email afterwards. 'Women can't remember jokes and there'd have to be a Ladies' loo built in one of the dining rooms.'

An opponent of gender-equal membership unpacked his concerns for the *Guardian*. 'Men behave differently if there are no women there. There is camaraderie, banter, the knowledge that you can say anything you want and have a jolly good discussion about anything in a completely egalitarian atmosphere in which no one is trying to impress anyone else. That's my main objection to having women members – it's not against women, but the idea that some men would not be able to resist showing off to impress the women, that is an innate male characteristic, whether you are a bird or an animal.'

Male hippopotami attract mates by urinating and defecating and twirling their tails in the mixture. Does that condemn anyone man enough to don the salmon-pink and cucumber-green Garrick ties to similar behaviours? There may be a kernel of truth to the idea that the natural world holds clues to what men and women would be if untainted by human civilisation, but as the experiments with monkeys and gendered toys demonstrated, those clues are difficult to decode. Humans are not the only animals that learn behaviours and construct societies.

It is possible to override instincts too. If it were not, my father, David Mayer, would not himself be a member of the Garrick Club. He is an American; he has the same Jewish-outsider mentality that inspired Groucho Marx to decline membership of any club that accepted him. This intensified when we moved to England and my father first encountered the intricate snobberies and stupidities of the classes that believe themselves better than the rest. The Garrick Club embodies everything he detests. It also has one of the most important theatre collections in the world, and he is a theatre historian.

He vigorously backed the vote to admit women to membership because he knows many female academics who would benefit from the same unfettered access to the collection that he enjoys. In the run-up to the vote, he invited Sandi and me to lunch at the Garrick (women are allowed to enter a few rooms of the establishment as guests of the male members). He hoped our presence, as co-founders of the Women's Equality Party, would be noticed, and it was, though not quite as anticipated.

After the meal, we paused at the foot of the grand staircase that until only a few years ago was barred to women, who would instead be directed to a shabby backstairs. Both sets of stairs converge on an entrance lobby, which Sandi faced.

I noticed her expression change suddenly, to bemusement, a slow-dawning comprehension and finally a shocked recognition. In front of us, hand outstretched, stood an elderly man, his pate as smooth and freckled as an egg. 'I just wanted to come over and congratulate you for what you're doing with the Women's Equality Party,' he said.

Only when I heard his voice did I realise this was Rupert Murdoch, media magnate, whose global empire stretches from television to film to internet to print, including the publisher of this book and, of course, the mass-market *Sun* with its famous topless 'lovelies' on Page Three. At the beginning of 2015, the tabloid appeared to yield to pressure by banishing the 44-year tradition. That pressure came not just from feminist campaign-ers, but from Murdoch himself. He had tweeted that he found the feature 'old fashioned', adding 'Aren't beautiful young women more attractive in at least some fashionable clothes? Your opinions please.' The Everyday Sexism Project feed, run by the estimable Laura Bates, replied immediately: '@rupertmurdoch or consider THIRD option? Report *news* on women's achievements not looks?'

In January 2015, Page Three vanished from the print edition, apart from a single, teasing reappearance – 'We've had a mammary lapse,' chortled the headline. A victory for women? Not so much. A sign of changing times? Absolutely. The parade of nipples migrated to the *Sun*'s online edition and has become more explicit.

London's *Evening Standard* reported our Garrick Club encounter. 'Who knew Rupe was a feminist?' it wondered.

Chapter Five: Home economics

IT WASN'T THE easiest of mornings, even before the call from her husband. Anne's elder daughters, aged six and five, had stayed home from school, and the harsh Wisconsin winter meant she couldn't send them and their two-year-old sister into the garden to play. Even the family's basset hound refused to go outside. All of them careered around the house instead.

At least the neighbours wouldn't scoff at the mess. Frost etched lace curtains onto every window, obscuring scenes of devastation, puddles of milky cereal congealing on the Formica kitchen table, toys scattered across a parquet floor that had lost its sheen to muddy paw prints and dog hair. Icicles serrated the eves of the suburban houses set back from a street that almost merged into front yards. Only improvised flags suspended from car aerials marked the curbside that day. In this part of the world, snows fell so deep that it was vital to mark the location of parked vehicles so that the snow ploughs didn't simply roll over them.

Seven years earlier, Anne had abandoned her degree in history and art history at Smith College, one of America's top universities for women, in pursuit of a goal that had seemed to her more urgent: domesticity and children – this domesticity, these children.

At first, campus life had daunted her and she spent lunchtimes alone by the shores of Paradise Pond. There, another student, also struggling to adjust, befriended her. Sylvia Plath roomed in a different dormitory during Anne's first year, then took time out for a breakdown she would later describe in her autobiographical novel *The Bell Jar*. On her return, Plath was allocated lodgings on the same corridor as Anne, in Haven House, and in June 1955 obtained her Bachelor of Arts with the highest honours. Anne should have graduated at the same time, but had left college the previous Christmas to marry, just six months shy of getting her degree. Perhaps she wanted to recreate the family she had lost. When she was 12, her father died unexpectedly from heart failure; her younger brother Kenny perished in a lightning strike months later. However, at least some of the pressures were external. 'Women of my generation were largely educated at university level to be better wives and mothers,' Anne explains. 'Few avenues were open for career-minded ladies and those fell to the ones who, sadly, didn't get a ring on their fingers by graduation. No one considered putting off marriage to pursue a career in my experience. If you were, say, Sylvia Plath, you could be married and write poetry but look how that ended.'

She expands on that idea, as she lists the lessons she has learned over 82 years: 'not to beat myself up about what I have or have not achieved or in what order, to be proficient in my work and utterly loyal to my friends and clients, and neither to sell myself short nor to have an exaggerated notion of what my life has achieved. To be happy in my own body and soul but to be able to reflect that I would have had a very different life if I had been born one or two generations later. I have been thinking of all this a lot because I have been talking to Frieda Hughes about her mother. Sylvia was Icarus and I the plodder, but I am the one who is still here.'[1]

In the estimation of her professors, Anne also had the potential to soar. One of her tutors, Phyllis Williams Lehmann, thought so highly of Anne that she selected her to assist on archaeological excavations in Samothrace that had already reunited the Winged Victory, the marble statue of the goddess Nike on display in the Louvre, with two of her fingers. The dig would have been Anne's first job as a graduate. Nike's head has never been retrieved and Anne, miserable and lonely in Wisconsin, wondered if she would ever get to use hers again. On that bitter winter's day when her husband rang to announce he would be bringing a distinguished colleague back for dinner, she searched in vain for anything to concoct into edibility, then went to clean the floors, planning to visit the supermarket later in the day. 'I took out the cylinder shaped vacuum and it was so full of dog hair it refused to work,' she recalls.

'A blind anger I had never experienced before or since' enveloped her. She bundled her three children into the station wagon and drove to the university where her husband taught. He stopped mid-sentence as she marched down the central aisle of the lecture theatre, trailed by three small figures in snowsuits with dangling mittens, to deposit the broken hoover on the lectern. 'You get this fixed. I have had enough,' she shouted, turning on her heel.

Looking back across decades, she sees a crossroads, a path not taken. 'If only I fully believed that at the time, our lives would have been very different. He didn't fix the hoover but he took the distinguished guest out to dinner.'

Anne finally finished her degree, years later, at Northwestern University in Chicago, and later still began a career she pursues to this day. She had taken contemporary dance classes in Wisconsin and after her husband transplanted the family to London to research a book, she trained in Martha Graham technique. When Robin Howard, the grandson of Prime Minister Stanley Baldwin and a decorated veteran who had lost both legs in World War II, founded The Place as a home for a new Graham-inspired company, London Contemporary Dance Theatre, he hired Anne as the venture's first publicist. She had no previous experience. 'The fact that I turned out to be rather good at it was fortuitous for him and for me,' she emails. 'The fact that work saved my life was only to be expected. With a first class brain and education, bringing up three children was never going to occupy my entire intellectual and emotional life, although — and this is very important — it has always been CENTRAL to my life and much more important than anything else I have achieved. Once I started working I never stopped. Nor will.'

As children, my sisters and I knew our mother Anne was unhappy. She suspected my grandmother would have preferred her to die and Kenny to survive. As a teenager she had starved herself until she looked as boyish as the brother she mourned. As an adult she ate little and cared less about preparing meals, though she did internalise one rule of cooking she picked up from a women's magazine: never put two foods of the same colour on the same plate. She argued with our father and, though brilliant and funny, had a short fuse. We realised early on that the marriage wasn't strong, that my father wasn't faithful and that my mother had given up trying to enforce monogamy and followed his lead. None of this damaged our bond with either of them and we remain closer than many families, but it wasn't until I read Betty Friedan that I could understand my mother's unhappiness as the expression and symptom of the malaise that smothered her generation of white, middle-class American women.

Betty Friedan dubbed this malaise 'The Problem That Has No Name' and used her first, ground-breaking book, *The Feminine Mystique*, to delineate it. 'The problem lay buried, unspoken, for many years in the minds of American women. It was a strange stirring, a sense of dissatisfaction, a yearning that women suffered in the middle of the twentieth century. Each suburban wife struggled with it alone. As she made the beds, shopped for groceries, matched slipcover material, ate peanut butter sandwiches with her children, chauffeured Cub Scouts and Brownies, lay beside her husband at night – she was afraid to ask even of herself the silent question, "Is this all?"'[2]

Like my mother, Friedan attended Smith College, graduating in 1942. Friedan and her contemporaries were lively, ambitious, career-minded. By the time Friedan returned to Smith for a week's research in 1957, two years after my mother should have graduated, the author found a student body preoccupied not with their studies but the marriage market. 'The civilised women of the present century, with a few exceptions, are only anxious to inspire love, when they ought to cherish a nobler ambition, and by their abilities and virtues exact respect,' wrote Mary Wollstonecraft in her celebrated 1792 tract *A Vindication of the Rights of Women*. More than one and a half centuries later, Friedan observed the same distemper afflicting her successors at Smith. She asked a senior which subjects were most popular. 'Girls don't get excited about things like that anymore ... I guess everybody wants to graduate with a diamond ring on her finger,' the student replied.

Friedan noted that these undergraduates didn't truly believe in the happy ever after and already showed signs of frustration at their narrowing horizons. She found explanations for their docility in a range of vested interests that had aligned to turn the clocks back. When men went off to fight World War II, women joined the labour market in unprecedented numbers, mostly in low-paid jobs. Female employment dipped briefly after troops returned, but by 1954 had again climbed to wartime highs and kept climbing, in the US and in Europe. Men worried they risked losing out to newly assertive females, professionally and privately. Churches and conservative organisations stoked their fears. Businesses peddled a dream of the perfect homemaker, the perfect wife, the perfect mother, the perfect woman, all the better to sell the accoutrements they proclaimed necessary for perfection.

After publishing *The Feminine Mystique*, Friedan turned to activism, becoming a leader of second-wave feminism, founding NOW, the National Organization for Women, and with other women, including another Smith graduate, Gloria Steinem, the National Women's Political Caucus. She organised the 1970 Women's Strike for Equality and campaigned for the Equal Rights Amendment to the US Constitution: 'Equality of rights under the law shall not be denied or abridged by the United States or by any state on account of sex.' The ERA came close to ratification, but was halted in its tracks by a conservative activist called Phyllis Schlafly who successfully mounted a counter-campaign, claiming that the housewives Friedan sought to liberate would be damaged by the bill, losing benefits and exemption from the draft. Schlafly also raised the spectre that women might be forced to use mixed-sex toilets. The US still does not guarantee equal rights for women at a national level and the federal system has created a patchwork of laws relating to discrimination and reproductive rights.

As recently as 2014, toilets again emerged as a battleground for gender equality. The Alliance Defending Freedom, a richly funded conservative Christian group based in Arizona, focused on bathrooms as part of its campaign to roll back progressive laws and rules introduced by some states. As Schlafly had done, the Alliance presented its argument as a defence of women's rights. 'Policies permitting access to restrooms, locker rooms, changing rooms, and other private spaces based on a person's gender identity, rather than their biological sex, are being enacted across the country as part of an effort to push a political agenda,' its online petition states. 'But this political agenda not only disregards common sense and basic privacy concerns, it also ignores safety concerns, including a large group of unintended victims: sex abuse survivors.' Like-minded pressure groups including the Family Research Council picked up the baton and several states followed up by proposing laws to make it a crime for people to enter single-sex bathrooms that did not match their chromosomal sex.

There is no evidence of an increased risk to women from gender-neutral bathrooms. Single-sex bathrooms are hardly impregnable, and indeed make obvious hunting grounds. As a student in Germany I fled from a serial sex attacker who staked out the women's toilets on campus. Trans women, forced to use male bathrooms, would of course face significantly elevated risks of assault. The underlying goal of the campaign and of a flurry of related initiatives to restrict provision of birth control or limit abortion was to reassert a fading vision of a binary world that contains only two gender identities and acceptable behaviour sets. America's Christian right sees heterosexual marriage, and reproduction within that form of marriage, as the bedrock of society. Conservatives urge those who do not naturally fit this pattern to deny their sexuality or gender identity. They exhort women to submit to the authority of God and husband even at the expense of sanity.

This dogma, and the arguments summoned in its favour, reinforce damaging political polarities. Substantial segments of the population feel themselves encircled, like Custer's troops, by hostile forces. Under the current administration, the 81 per cent of white evangelicals who backed Trump see an opportunity to reassert their world-view. These defenders of untruths, injustice and the American way are right about one thing: That worldview is threatened and single-sex bathrooms really are a symptom of that threat.

Moves to create gender-neutral bathrooms reflect wider and deeper societal shifts – our improving understanding of the gender spectrum and of the value of female labour, paid and unpaid. Women in industrialised countries lose hours of their lives to queues for toilets and that's not good for anyone. Baby-changing facilities are often located within female bathrooms, but there is increasing pushback against the idea that the dirty business of nappies is women's work alone. These debates have gained traction in many countries, because the model that conservatives so ardently seek to uphold – a nuclear family in which men provide for deferential wives and grateful children – doesn't work for many people. It never did.

Early humans were egalitarian and the hunter-gatherer societies that still exist in some parts of the world share out the duties of work and child-care and the benefits of food and security within extended communities. Narrower family structures emerged with the development of agriculture and became increasingly detached from wider support networks as industrialisation took hold, establishing patterns of childcare still in existence. Factory workers struggled with long hours, often leaving elder siblings in charge of younger sisters and brothers. Children were expected to start paying their keep as soon as possible. Affluent mothers outsourced childcare duties to poorer women.

No matter what a woman's social standing, her choices were limited – and her lifespan often shortened – by numerous pregnancies. Societies through history have understood the fundamental importance of a woman's right to choose. Ancient Egyptian women placed lint, honey and acacia leaves in their vaginas ahead of sex to prevent conception. Followers of Islam in the late ninth and early tenth centuries deployed elephant dung, pitch and cabbages. Onanism, now more commonly understood to mean masturbation, originally referred to coitus interruptus, named for Onan, a character in the Book of Genesis who during sex with his sister-in-law 'would waste the semen on the ground, so as not to give offspring to his brother.' When such methods failed, herbs, abdominal massage and other, more brutal interventions were used to induce abortions.

It wasn't until the nineteenth century that governments began to outlaw terminations. They did so for a variety of reasons. The death toll from abortions was high, and male doctors, fighting a turf war with female midwives, sought to control all aspects of reproductive medicine. Industrial societies increasingly relied on cheap, docile female labour, and vested interests correctly spotted that allowing women to decide whether or not to have children would help to emancipate them. In the US, critics of rising immigration stoked fears of 'race suicide', urging white, middle-class women to have more children to counter the influx.[3] As Europe slid into two World Wars, its leaders called on women to do their bit by producing families as large as private armies. In France, the President still awards the gold Médaille d'Honneur de la Famille Française to married mothers with eight or more children. Nazi Germany introduced a similar incentive scheme.

Margaret Sanger resisted this ethos, though she had dodgy ideas too; she believed in eugenics – selective breeding to improve the human race – to boost public health and not, as often claimed, to eliminate the black population. She opened her first birth-control clinic in Brooklyn in 1916.

More than three decades later, she met the endocrinologist Gregory Pincus and triggered the push to develop the Pill. At the time, around one million American women every year underwent backstreet abortions; more than 1,000 died. The new miracle drug gained the approval of the US Food and Drug Administration in 1960, and within five years 6.5 million women were happily swallowing it with their morning cornflakes. Critics screeched that the Pill undermined public morality by encouraging sex outside marriage, despite the fact that doctors prescribed it predominantly to married women. By the time my generation of women became sexually active, the Pill was indeed easily available, as were many of us.

Coming of age in the 1970s, sandwiched between hippy notions of free love and the advent of HIV/AIDS, we were slow to suspect that sexual licence may not always be an expression and instrument of women's liberation, but sometimes risked subverting the struggle for equality into a male fantasy of the ever-ready female. At least we could now have sex without getting pregnant. Or, if we slipped up, there were, in some countries, clinics that could deal with that too. The globe even now roughly divides into two halves. In the Southern hemisphere – in particular South America and Africa – abortion remains prohibited or allowed only in cases where the woman's life is deemed at risk. In the Northern hemisphere, Ireland – the Republic and Northern Ireland – are, apart from Andorra and Malta, the last remaining hold outs against abortion. In 2012 Savita Halappanavar, a 31-year-old dentist, died miscarrying in a hospital in the Irish Republic after doctors hesitated to intervene for fear of prosecution. Every day as many as 12 women leave the Republic to travel abroad for terminations, primarily to the UK but also to the Netherlands and other European destinations. In 2016, a pregnant woman and her friend tweeted their journey from Ireland to the UK to procure an abortion under the Twitter handle @twowomentravel. One of them later gave an anonymous interview to explain their decision to publicise the trip. 'What's the alternative? Silence? Silence is breaking 12 Irish hearts a day ... Silence has the blood of Savita on its hands.' In the same year a Belfast court handed down a suspended sentence to a 21-year-old woman shopped by her flatmates for using abortion pills bought on the internet.

Reproductive rights in the US look more fragile than ever. Ever since the Supreme Court's landmark 1973 judgment that Jane Roe, an unmarried pregnant woman from Texas, had a constitutional right under the Fourteenth Amendment to terminate her pregnancy, anti-abortionists have sought to dismantle the nationwide guarantee of reproductive rights. Planned Parenthood is the largest family planning and abortion provider in the US, and active in 12 other countries. It is under constant onslaught, from lawmakers and the protesters they stir up in a campaign to take away the public funding it uses for basic health care such as safe-sex counselling, and breast and pelvic exams. The current government backs such a move.

During his presidential campaign, Donald Trump suggested that women having illegal abortions should face 'some form of punishment'. He retracted the sentiment, but such punishments are already being handed down.[4] Indiana is a case in point. In February 2015 an Indiana court sentenced Purvi Patel to 30 years in prison, with ten years suspended. The prosecution alleged she had procured an abortion by swallowing pills bought over the internet. In a Kafkaesque twist, the authorities found her guilty of two crimes that are mutually exclusive – foeticide, the killing of the foetus in the womb, and child neglect, the failure to tend to a live baby. Patel, an unmarried woman living with her observant Hindu parents, had gone to hospital in 2013 bleeding after what she claimed was a stillbirth. The state appeals court overturned the foeticide conviction and reduced the child-neglect felony, but accepted the criminality of Patel's actions and the need to jail her, even though abortion is legal in the state up to 20 weeks.

Indiana bans all abortions after that threshold and forces women seeking terminations to undergo invasive medical procedures. A judge suspended legislation passed by the state to remove the right to abort a foetus with a disability but the fight is far from over. The Indiana Governor who presided over the attempt to tighten the laws was Mike Pence – 'a Christian, a conservative and a Republican, in that order' – and now Vice President of the United States.

Mary Wollstonecraft argued for equality within the sexes as well as between them, but her own life reflected the difficulties of achieving either state. 'All power inebriates weak man; and its abuse proves that the more equality there is established among men, the more virtue and happiness will reign in society,' she remarked in 1792. She knew how much damage weak men could do. Her sister Eliza fled an abusive marriage but was forced to surrender custody of her baby daughter to her husband. Six months later, the baby died.

Coverture, a doctrine enshrined in English common law and generously shared around the world, treated wives and children as the property of husbands. (Some of its tenets, such as the prohibition against women controlling bank accounts without their husbands' permission, remained effective well into the twentieth century.) Wollstonecraft avoided falling into the clutches of coverture until relatively late in life, instead earning her way with jobs as a lady's companion and governess, and scandalising polite society by producing her first baby, Frances, out of wedlock. By this time she had embarked on a career as a writer and pamphleteer and employed two maids to help her look after her child so she could work.

Childcare was a boon to Wollstonecraft. The question of who should look after the children in a gender-equal world continues to baffle feminists. Bee Rowlatt, in her entertaining Wollstonecraft-inspired travelogue-cum-examination-of-motherhood, *In Search of Mary*, suffers twinges about relying – as her heroine did – on paid female help. Her feminism means Rowlatt believes every woman should be able to have it all, but the reality is that she can only manage career and motherhood if someone else shoulders some of the household drudgery. Domestic labourers tend to be female and to earn little. A recent study of au pairs in the UK found some of them working for as little as £2 an hour for 50-hour weeks. Rowlatt employs a nanny to look after her four children, an easier option for a feminist conscience at an average of £8.65 per hour, but prohibitively expensive for many households. She doesn't go into the details of how much she pays or how eagerly her husband shares domestic duties, but he works too, in a job that involves frequent travel. Even enlightened men tend to spend far less time than women on housework and caregiving, as successive surveys demonstrate. A longitudinal study of British households saw almost no change in this uneven division of chores between 1994 and 2012.[5] A documentary on Jeremy Corbyn's reign as Labour's most left-wing leader since the 1980s featured an interview with his wife, Laura Alvarez. She told the team shadowing her husband that he was 'not very good at housework.'

Rowlatt's journey takes her briefly into the ambit of women in inner-city Leeds for whom having it all is unimaginable. The feminist movement, in its white, middle-class incarnations, looks irrelevant. Yet it is precisely the women she meets and others in similar situations that feminism most needs to assist. They are most vulnerable and least represented. If they're in work, it is often on contracts offering little security and less money. They have no resources of their own to bridge the gap between government support for newborns and their parents, and the start of free pre-schools. In our first policy document, the Women's Equality Party proposed government-funded childcare for all children from nine months old, with the first 15 hours free and all extra time available at £1 per hour.

We did this to draw attention to a hole in childcare provision, hoping that magpie entrepreneurs and politicians might pick up the shiny policy and build it into their plans. We also pointed to fresh evidence of skills shortages in the UK labour market, knowing that crises rather than crises of conscience more reliably spur business and government to action. Tech companies including Facebook, Google, Netflix and Yahoo responded to the haemorrhage of talent to competitors by offering extensive parental leave and daycare facilities. Demographic worries often prove the catalyst for government initiatives.

Betty Friedan might have found a more receptive audience for her advocacy if the US had not been in the final, fertile throes of the baby boom. Friedan was right to warn that The Problem That Has No Name would filter through into a declining appetite for motherhood, but it wasn't until five years after *The Feminine Mystique* that American mothers slowed the production line to fewer than three babies per adult woman, dropping again in the 1970s to fewer than two – below population replacement levels – and proving her point.

She also over-estimated the transformative powers of the policies she pushed as an antidote: maternity leave and childcare. Her mistake would be easier to spot if Washington had let itself be persuaded by her lobbying. Instead the US remains one of only three countries out of 185 surveyed by the International Labour Organisation not to compel employers to offer paid maternity leave. The other holdouts are Lesotho and Papua New Guinea. American exceptionalism muddies waters that in countries with mandatory leave run stark and clear. Such leave is essential to women's progress, but it cannot by itself create equality at work or at home.

The UK, for example, passed two laws in 1975, the Sex Discrimination Act and the Employment Protection Act, that together offered new rights in the workplace, including protection against dismissal for pregnancy and entitlement to paid maternity leave. The 1970 Equal Pay Act had already asserted the principle that women should be paid the same as male colleagues for the same job. These laws have been expanded and improved over the intervening decades, though they are far from perfect, erratically applied and easily sidestepped. In 2003, British fathers got paternity leave for the first time. From 2015, new rules enabled parents to share paid leave, a policy first enacted by Sweden back in 1974. Mothers must take the first two weeks. After that couples can choose which parent stays home for up to 37 weeks, recompensed at £139.58 a week or 90 per cent of an employee's average weekly earnings, whichever is lower. An additional 13 weeks' unpaid leave is also on offer.

In many professions, young women in the UK now keep pace with their male colleagues. Yet pay and promotion gaps open up as soon as female workers have children. Up to 50,000 women are sacked or forced out every year just for getting pregnant.[6] More are sidelined. A study by the Equality and Human Rights Commission found that 77 per cent of mothers reported negative or possibly discriminatory experiences during pregnancy, maternity leave or on return to work.[7] Another study found that full-time working mothers can expect a wage penalty, earning about 11 per cent less than their childless female colleagues. Women still can expect to earn £300,000 less than men over their working lives.

In recasting maternity leave as shared parental leave, the UK has followed the Nordic countries along a path that at least heads in the direction of Equalia by recognising childcare not as an issue only for mothers but for parents. It doesn't go far enough to eliminate the maternity penalty altogether. For one thing, shared leave is of no use to the UK's two million single parents. Ninety per cent of these are women.

For another, two-parent households are resistant to change. Only when Sweden stopped giving parents free choice about how to divide up leave, instead designating a chunk exclusively for fathers, did the uptake among men increase, from nine per cent up to 47 per cent of those eligible. Use-it-or-lose-it rules in other Nordic countries have boosted uptake too, but mothers still take longer periods of leave.

Men are reluctant to stay at home to take care of their children because of the gender pay gap that survives in part because of their reluctance to stay at home and take care of their children. They earn on average more than their female partners and so feel themselves obligated to keep earning, even though many – 48 per cent of US fathers, for example – say they would rather tend their kids.[8]

The barriers to realising this ambition are not all structural. Cultural biases also act as a deterrent. Many of us are brought up to the idea that fathers are breadwinners. This is the only possible explanation for the paternity bonus that sees fathers paid more than men without children by around 21 per cent.[9] Think too about how often a man caring for his own children is deemed to be 'babysitting', as if such care is short-term and negotiable. And one of the biggest barriers to change is our understanding of maternity. Many women nurse the idea that without children they cannot experience the fullness of womanhood. Church, conservatives and the media enthusiastically promote this linkage.

Kristin Cavallari, a former regular on two reality TV shows, takes a traditional approach to mothering, at least within the terms set by celebrity culture. She has diligently shared the progress of each of her three pregnancies – and her exercise regime to regain her pre-baby weight – on social media and with journalists.

She has three children – Camden, Jaxon and Saylor – with her husband Jay Cutler, a quarterback for the Chicago Bears. Ahead of Saylor's birth, Cavallari took to Instagram. 'It's hard to believe I will be a mom of 3 in just a few short weeks. I owe so much to my babies,' she posted. 'They have changed me in so many ways for the better.' *E! News*, reporting her social media updates, added: 'The savvy mom-to-be also plugged her upcoming book.'

Books and babies are both marketable commodities within the celebrity universe, but only one of these commodities imparts wisdom without the brow-furrowing effort of reading. There is nothing new about the notion that mothers know things other mortals cannot: the meaning of selfless love, the instinctual investment in the future.

For centuries, male-led institutions have enthusiastically propagated the idea of motherhood as a holy – and wholly transfiguring – experience, to the detriment of fatherhood, which is rated a second-class form of parenting and too often lives down to that billing. The media focus on pregnancy is a newer expression of this phenomenon. 'We live in an age when women are supposed to perform pregnancy,' remarked the Nigerian novelist and essayist, Chimamanda Ngozi Adichie. 'We don't expect fathers to perform fatherhood.'

In casting maternity as a higher form of parenting – a club that self-evidently only women can join – mothers are granted apparent ownership and control. Some mothers – maybe all mothers – reading this will say that I, as a childless woman, cannot understand the profundity and specificity of mother love. They may be right, but I worry that the mystification of motherhood dupes women into accepting the maternity penalty as the price of entry to the club.

'Misery loves company,' a close friend told me back in the days when her children were young, I was still fertile and she thought she might persuade me to follow suit in starting a family. She never seriously regretted her choice any more than I have ever regretted mine, but those early years would have been easier for her if I hadn't been in her line of sight, exercising the freedoms of childlessness.

For one thing, the implicit promise of all those celebrity confessionals – that motherhood confers social status on women – proved hollow for her as it does for so many women. A strand of psychology called Terror Management Theory recognises much human activity as a mechanism to distract from fear of death. Research in this field has established a key difference between the impact of parenthood on men and women. Fatherhood gives men social standing and so, according to studies, helps ward off fears of death. Maternity confers no similar benefits. In interview after interview conducted by the psychologists, women said they expected motherhood to raise and augment them. Instead, they often felt diminished, no matter that they passionately loved their children. Mummy/Mommy blogs have become one of the fastest growing forms of self-expression on the internet by documenting the isolation and exhaustion of the new mother, and the loss of identity. 'Talk to me, friend, and tell me all the dark shit in your brain.

I've been there. I've fucking been there. I've regretted having children. I've thought they would go away. I've tried to run. I've thought "I hate motherhood".'[10]

The deification of motherhood as an act of completion makes it harder for women to reconcile the experience with expectations. The failure must be theirs. It also explains how easily mothers themselves subscribe to the idea that childless women lack essential insights.

When Conservative MP Andrea Leadsom launched her brief and unsuccessful bid to become leader of her party and British Prime Minister, she suggested that her rival Theresa May might not share her dedication to public service. 'I don't know Theresa very well but I'm sure she'll be very, very sad that she doesn't have children,' Leadsom mused. 'But genuinely being a mum means you have a very real stake in the future of our country. A tangible stake. I mean she possibly has nieces, nephews, lots of people, but I have children who are going to have children, who will directly be a part of what happens next.' Leadsom later apologised to May but the incident was far from isolated. Any woman without children is liable to find herself stigmatised as emotionally stunted, selfish and incomplete, but the childless female politician suffers additional slurs. She lacks the necessary insights to represent women because she hasn't been completed as a woman and she isn't invested in the future. The reality is demonstrably different. Angela Merkel and Nicola Sturgeon are brilliant politicians who have created opportunities for all women, including mothers, without recourse to the direct experience of motherhood. It's unlikely that Julia Gillard could have done more for women as Australian Prime Minister if she had been a mother, but she'd definitely have escaped a barrage of taunts that painted her as 'one-dimensional' and 'deliberately barren.'

After years of enduring similar criticisms, Sturgeon revealed in 2016 that she had miscarried a baby. She did so 'in the hope that it might challenge some of the assumptions and judgments that are still made about women – especially in politics – who don't have children.' She said she did not know whether a child might have deflected her from leadership, acknowledging that it is easier for women to rise if they are not also caring for children. 'Some of us simply don't want to [have children]; some of us worry about the impact on our career – and there is still so much to do, through better childcare, more progressive working practices and more enlightened attitudes, to make sure we don't feel we have to choose.'

Women fought for choice. Now choice itself has become oppressive, because the choices are always between imperfect solutions.

Louise Brown, the world's first baby conceived in a laboratory, was born in 1978, the year I headed to university. In 1986 I wrote my first freelance piece for the *Guardian*. It charted the rise in the number of working women who had given up on finding suitable mates and were instead wielding turkey basters with a view to becoming single parents.

More advanced technology seems to offer yet another lifestyle option: deferring decisions about children. 'At the last IVF conference, somebody said: "One day there will be someone who jokes that they had their baby the old fashioned way: we had sex",' says Helen O'Neill, a geneticist at the Embryology, IVF and Reproductive Genetics Group of the Institute for Women's Health at University College London. 'It's quite true. So many people are now needing assisted reproduction or IVF, and this is only going to become more commonplace – our lifestyle choices mean we delay in having children, very often until it is too late. Technology now allows us to freeze eggs, sperm and ovarian tissue. Even uterine transplants and ovarian tissue transplantation have been successfully carried out and resulted in babies born to these advances.'[11]

Sigmund Freud argued that anatomy was destiny. In *The Dialectic of Sex*, published in 1970, Shulamith Firestone laid out a future in which technology redrew that destiny by permitting babies to be grown outside the womb. Scientists haven't developed that capacity but, in O'Neill's words, 'We're already bending biology.' She warns, however, that the available technologies are far from fail-safe. She also points out that despite widespread beliefs to the contrary, men, as well as women, lose fertility rapidly with age.

These facts, unheeded, have already played out in my age group and are trashing the life plans of generations below ours who discover in their 30s and 40s that their fertility has diminished. IVF doesn't always work and adoption agencies give preference to younger couples, no matter that the media keeps churning out stories of celebrities becoming first-time mothers in their 50s or adopting children as lightly as they acquire the latest designer clothes. In 2015, the same year that the Central Committee of the Chinese Communist Party scrapped its 35-year-old proscription on couples having more than one child – 'an active response to an ageing population' according to state news agency Xinhua – Britain's Office for National Statistics revealed that one-child households now represented 47 per cent of all UK families. Women across the industrialised world have implemented the one-child policy China discarded. Some do so intentionally, planning to stop after one baby; some realise too late that biology has made the choice for them.

The same miscalculation helps to explain the record and spiralling numbers of childless women. The reality of involuntary childlessness does little to spike the guns of media defenders of motherhood. This genuine *Daily Mail* headline – possibly the most concentratedly essence-of-*Daily-Mail* headline ever written – is a prime example of a recurrent meme about the selfishness of the unproductive: 'How the rise of childless women could change the face of Britain: Rampant infidelity. A struggling economy. Meltdown for the NHS. And shorter life expectancies.'[12]

The article makes no compelling case for any of these outcomes, but the equation of childlessness with selfishness is a perennial for the *Mail* and other media outlets. So too is the idea of childlessness as a curse. The actor-producer-director Jennifer Aniston in her late forties still finds herself the focus of frenzied pregnancy speculation if the photographers encamped on her doorstep perceive the slightest changes to her bodyweight. During a particularly torrid bout of stalking in July 2016, she felt moved to write an article calling out the assumptions that underlie the avidity of the long lenses. 'The sheer amount of resources being spent right now by press trying to simply uncover whether or not I am pregnant (for the bajillionth time ... but who's counting) points to the perpetuation of this notion that women are somehow incomplete, unsuccessful, or unhappy if they're not married with children.'[13]

Many women consciously choose not to have children, for a variety of reasons, economic and social. The spectre of The Problem That Has No Name still lingers. True choice – and true gender equality – will be possible only when women can become mothers without paying a higher price than men, whether financial or social, at work or in the home.

Lawmakers, civil society, individuals and enlightened media can all contribute to positive change. Science is also raising tantalising possibilities about how the world might reorder itself, which I'll address when we reach Equalia.

After all, as Helen O'Neill points out, we're already bending biology. Human reproduction has been possible without sex since 1978. Of course, this doesn't just have implications for the future of maternity. Sex has lost its exclusive utility. So what is it even for, and how is the way we do it shaped by the world's largest and least regulated business, the sex trade?

Chapter Six: What really shocks me

A WOMAN WITH a camera strapped to her head squirms, squeals and literally barks when not sucking the penis of a portly gentleman. He too wears a headcam, accessorised by an erection he works with his free hand. The other hand wields a riding crop. Fifty shades of neigh or maybe just a case of nominative determinism? The film is prominently displayed on Make Love Not Porn, a website founded by the evocatively named Cindy Gallop in 2009 to distribute such movies and to spread the word about the critical differences between what she terms Real World and Porn World.

The two worlds are moving into dangerous alignment as reality increasingly takes its cues from pornography. Betty Friedan's housewives spent hours waxing – tables, chairs, sideboards. Real World women of today make time to wax upper lips, underarms, mons pubis and often the labia majora and perineum. According to a study published in a specialist journal of urology, 'partial or complete pubic hair removal has been reported by upward of 70 per cent to 88 per cent of young women in the United States. Similar findings have been reported from both Australia and the United Kingdom.' Does that matter? Well, urologists are dealing with increasing numbers of injuries caused by hair removal, but the deeper concern is why the fashion has gained so many adherents so fast and what other attitudes might come packaged with it. The phenomenon started in Porn World, where women flaunt pudenda as bald as Vin Diesel's head, climax without so much of a touch to the clitoris and appear to take pleasure in sexual practices that in reality hurt, cause permanent damage or simply annoy.

Gallop was inspired to set up her site because her younger male lovers had picked up bad bedroom habits from blue movies. She launched the project at a TED talk.[1] Sex education in schools was inadequate, she told her audience. She knew from direct experience what filled the learning gap: porn.

MakeLoveNotPorn.com aims to deconstruct myths and to provide films showing consensual sex, uploaded not by pornographers but enthusiastic practitioners who earn 50 per cent of any profit from rentals. Before Gallop's foray into ethical erotica, she set up the Singapore and New York branches of the agency Bartle Bogle Hegarty, part of the giant Publicis Groupe, and founded an eponymous consultancy. Her success belied the unconscious bias, discrimination and harassment that blocks women from rising in the advertising industry. Across the globe women make 85 per cent of all purchasing decisions, yet comprise only 11 per cent of creative directors.

In March 2016 Gustavo Martinez, chairman and CEO of the communications multinational WPP, resigned amid accusations of racism and sexism. He denied the allegations; a video later surfaced showing him joking about rape during a company event.[2] Maurice Lévy, chief executive officer of Publicis Groupe, quickly declared this 'a one-time mistake ... not a fair representation of the industry.'[3] Cindy Gallop disagreed. She posted on Facebook that the imbroglio was in fact 'the tip of the fucking iceberg'.

Advertising works by constructing a message and then spreading it, vigorously. If the industry had set out to design a campaign communicating the scale and nature of its disrespect for women, it could hardly do better. Four months after Martinez' resignation, Kevin Roberts, the worldwide chairman of Saatchi & Saatchi, one of the agencies owned by Publicis, swiped at Gallop in an interview. 'I think she's making up a lot of the stuff to create a profile, and to take applause, and to get on a soap[box],' he said, adding that 'the fucking debate [on gender] is all over'. Publicis acted swiftly, placing Roberts on leave and issuing a statement: 'Diversity and inclusion are business imperatives on which Publicis Groupe will not negotiate.' Lévy, it seemed, might have learned a lesson.

The wider industry shows little sign of that educative process. An email to prospective guests of an event at the 2016 Cannes Lions advertising festival sponsored by digital agency VaynerMedia and media company Thrillist Media Group landed on the desks of some of the women who had made it to senior levels of the business despite the obstacles. 'Thank you for your interest in attending!! Please be aware that this specific list is for *attractive females and models only*.'

The sponsors apologised; a third party had sent the email. There is always someone lower down the food chain to carry the can, and there are always convenient dinosaurs – close cousins to the useful idiot – whose views are sufficiently extreme to reassure everyone else that the dinosauria, and not they, are the problem. Yet advertising is a top-down culture. It fails its clients and its shareholders by doing too little to connect with the 85 per cent of consumers making purchasing decisions. It fails everyone by rendering its 50-foot billboard women prostrate and pornified.

Let's imagine agencies made faster progress on getting women into their upper echelons. How should those women speak as equals with male colleagues whose insidious thoughts about women – thoughts the men themselves often do not recognise or acknowledge – spurt out of every part of the advertising industry? How should any woman at work or at home or in school or in daily interactions with men meet their gaze knowing these men have imbibed some of the teachings of Porn World? This isn't just about bad sexual etiquette but something much more harmful: the idea that any woman can be bought and sold, as a whole body or a collection of parts and holes. These questions came up during a meeting convened in September 2015 to discuss proposals for the first policy document of the Women's Equality Party.

They prompted in me a Damascene conversion. I went into the room an instinctive and passionate liberal, a defender of free speech at any ugly cost and a proponent of legalising and regulating pornography and prostitution. I emerged with doubts and dilemmas I have yet to fully resolve. This chapter traces my grapplings with policy – which at times have been as clumsy as any coupling in a homemade porn movie – and attempts to explain why feminists so often make war not love when debating the sex industry. How might we resolve these differences to reach Equalia? The following chapter looks at the ways all branches of the media, including advertising, most often hinder but sometimes help our progress.

Pavan Amara, as already discussed in an earlier chapter, is one of the one in five women in the UK to have suffered sexual assault. Eleven years ago, when she was 17, a stranger raped her. That she didn't know him is much more unusual than the headline crime itself. Ninety per cent of attackers have some acquaintance with their targets. There were some other uncommon features to the case. Amara became one of just 15 per cent of victims to report such an attack to the police, and the case itself had a rarity value, one of only 5.7 per cent of reported rapes to result in a conviction.[4]

The trauma might have silenced her or made her retreat into herself. Instead she has grown tall, as an activist and the founder in 2015 of an organisation providing specialist medical services and counselling to rape victims. Her work makes her keenly aware of the apparently contradictory strains that cloud attitudes to sexual violence and its survivors. She lives in a culture that appears to have few boundaries and fewer inhibitions, yet says recovery from rape is compounded by widespread inhibitions about discussing women's enjoyment of sex or the reality of sexual violence. 'Magazines are happy to put "orgasm tips" on the cover, but if you want to have an honest conversation, people still don't really want to. And then when it comes to sexual violence, again, people want to come across as if they're open-minded enough to talk about it being a problem, but in practice they don't want to talk.'

Her clinic offers cervical screening, STI testing and contraceptive fitting and advice to women who have experienced sexual assault; in 2016 a specialist maternity clinic started up. The reason these services are needed, Amara explains, is contained in the name she chose for her organisation: My Body Back Project. 'It's all very well to say to women after they've been raped that "your body belongs to you and you're in control of it". But if you don't show women that, if every single experience that they have after that tells them the opposite …' The sentence trails off. 'After being raped they have to go for forensic testing where their body doesn't belong to them; then they have to have a jury look at photos of injuries or their body, which again makes them feel their body doesn't belong to them. Then you have your personal life often completely invaded by the court and the police. Again you're given this message that you don't belong to you. You go for clinical appointments and somebody just wants you in and out of the room, very quickly, you're told again that you don't belong to you.'[5]

Amara's own odyssey inspired and informs the initiative but she started by interviewing 30 other rape survivors to find out how universal her experiences were. A third of the women said that being raped had affected their use or choice of contraception. Over half said that they hadn't attended any cervical screenings since their attack and that they couldn't envisage that they would in the future. Seven hadn't been for STI testing since, even though they suspected they may have caught something from their assailant. Four, including three with serious conditions such as asthma and diabetes, were no longer registered with a GP. They feared being quizzed about their histories, forced to revisit details of the attack. During examinations doctors sometimes asked them to assume the same positions the rapists had. Doctors sometimes gave orders, as the rapists had.

The staff in My Body Back clinics are specially trained to understand these dynamics and avoid triggering flashbacks. The patients, rather than the doctors, issue instructions about how the consultation should run. Amara and other rape survivors seek to regain control, and from there, some level of normality. It is especially difficult to rebuild a sex life and re-establish a confident sexuality. 'Sex had been used as a weapon before, and then you're just expected to just get on with it?'

Amara set up discussion sessions to help assault victims 'learn about loving their bodies after violence.' Many of the women attending the sessions find it difficult to become aroused. They would turn to pornography and then find themselves watching scenes of violent misogyny, simulated rape, rape itself.

Amara's response was to create a new section on the My Body Back website, the Clit List, a pre-screened list of erotica including long and short movies that show consensual sex and are ethically made. The MakeLoveNotPorn site is one of Amara's recommendations. 'There's nothing wrong with wanting to watch people have sex, really. It's the way that it's done that's so wrong. There's this monopoly on visual sexual stimulation being just for men, rather than also accepting that women also want to be visually stimulated sometimes. We need that sometimes just as much as men.' Amara shakes her head. 'These days the words "porn", "exploitation", and "misogyny" are synonymous. But they shouldn't be. They don't have to be.'

Her assertion goes straight to the crux of a series of difficult debates, about sexuality in a world shot through with pornographic imagery and riddled with sexual violence. These phenomena are related. Part of the answer for Amara, as for Gallop, is to reclaim pornography as ethical erotica. Others still question whether there is any place for commercial sex in a gender-equal society.

Halla Gunnarsdóttir co-chaired the working group on ending violence against women and girls. There were six such working groups, each looking for ways to bring about one of the Women's Equality Party's core objectives.

They drew on the views of party members, the findings of community events and on the wisdom of experts already active in the relevant fields. WE had no desire to reinvent wheels that campaigners had spent years designing, polishing and perfecting and for this first document and in subsequent policy development consulted key organisations, including Daughters of Eve, Eaves, Equality Now, EVAW (End Violence Against Women Coalition), Everyday Victim Blaming, Imkaan, OBJECT, Rape Crisis, Sisters for Change, Southall Black Sisters, Standing Together, UK Feminista, Women's Aid and Women's Networking Hub, all focused on different aspects of gender-based violence and victim support; as well as equality champions the Fawcett Society and the Women's Resource Centre, Gingerbread (which helps single parents), Sisters of Frida (a collective of disabled women), Women in Journalism and even Girlguiding UK.

Halla had spoken at the original Royal Festival Hall meeting to discuss founding WE, immediately joined the steering committee and later became WE's first head of policy, guiding the development of manifestos for the May 2016 elections in London, Scotland and Wales and formalising policy-making structures within WE. Before that, she had served as a political advisor in the health and justice ministries in Iceland and then worked for McAllister Olivarius, a law firm with a strong track record in fighting cases involving harassment, unequal treatment in pay, promotion and inclusion, sex abuse and revenge pornography. She had researched the sex industry over many years and witnessed its toll in the searing testimonies of the women it chews up and spits out.

Just as video didn't actually kill the radio star, the internet hasn't, as many prophesied, fatally wounded the pornography business but merely changed the distribution model. There is an ever greater abundance of free-to-view content, but many of the platforms providing the content are owned and operated by pornographers who monetise the sites by selling advertising and cookies – digital information collected from anyone who visits the sites – and charging for premium content. Mainstream product is getting rougher and nastier in the competition for clicks and to serve an audience increasingly desensitised by porn and pornified culture. Australian researcher Maree Crabbe analysed the porn movies attracting the highest online traffic and discovered 88 per cent of scenes included physical aggression such as gagging, choking and slapping. For her documentary *Love and Sex in the Age of Porn*, she interviewed a male porn actor based in Los Angeles and working under the name of Anthony Hardwood. 'You know when I started it was like very lovey-dovey sex,' he told her. 'After three years they wanted to get more energy, more rough, they do, like, one girl with you know like four guys, and they just take over and destroy her.'

Ann Olivarius, a founding partner of McAllister Olivarius, described in a blog post another emergent trend: 'One of our clients, a porn actress, approached us the day after she was released from hospital, where she had her rectum sutured after the filming of a brutal scene. She was going to be out of work for a while and wondered what job protections might exist for her. They were very few. She had been in the business for three years, which is about as long as most women I have met ever last. She had no pension, had never heard the word "promotion", and she had no idea how to proceed. The industry had taken three years of her life and left her with nothing but a rectum prolapse, which by the way is something the porn industry takes pride in producing (there is a growing market for "rosebud" in porn films – that is, when the inner walls of an actress's rectum collapse and the red internal tissue "blooms" out of the anus).'

Much pornography is a filmed record of sexual coercion – whether economic or physical or both – and, increasingly, of violence, but academics disagree on whether porn directly increases viewers' predilection to commit sexual assaults. A 2016 meta-analysis of 22 studies from seven countries suggested that it does, especially if the pornography is brutal: 'Consumption was associated with sexual aggression in the United States and internationally, among males and females, and in cross-sectional and longitudinal studies. Associations were stronger for verbal than physical sexual aggression, although both were significant. The general pattern of results suggested that violent content may be an exacerbating factor.' A decade earlier a law professor called Anthony D'Amato took a diametrically opposite view, suggesting porn potentially reduces rape by providing an alternative outlet for sexual appetites that might otherwise remain pent up: 'Some people watching pornography may "get it out of their system" and thus have no further desire to go out and actually try it.' D'Amato's analysis ignores one fact on which serious research aligns: that rape is never a simple expression of sexual desire but of anger or control or entitlement or some combination of all three.

The financial transactions involved in making pornographic movies almost always follow a familiar pattern: a man purchases the consent of a woman who would otherwise not agree to sex. This is the same transaction as prostitution. Many actors arrive on movie sets by the same routes – trafficking, abuse, drug addiction. These are realities that the Women's Equality Party has to change in order not only to end violence against women but to realise any of our objectives. While women are routinely commodified and objectified, exploited, terrorised and forced into dependencies, gender equality remains illusory. That was the point that Halla eloquently set out in recommending WE adopt the Nordic Model, which legalises the selling of sex but criminalises its purchase.

During her time in government in Iceland, she had worked on developing policies to stem the pipelines into the sex industry and close down its distribution mechanisms. In 2009, Iceland became the third country in the world to introduce the Nordic Model on prostitution, devised in Sweden in 1999 and adopted by Norway just months ahead of Iceland. A majority of my colleagues agreed with Halla that this should be our policy too. Sandi was in favour. I could not, at that first meeting, raise my hand in support. I still do so with serious reservations.

For one thing, as I've just explained, it's hard to disentangle prostitution and pornography. The arguments against them are pretty much identical: they exploit, they abuse, they perpetuate the dehumanising idea of women as a collection of saleable body parts.

We weren't at this stage debating a ban on pornography but this seemed to me the logical next step. Because of its easy availability, bad pornography – and that's the vast majority of pornography – does more harm than ever before, to people in the industry, all the kids growing up watching it, to women, everyone. Yet I agree with Pavan Amara and Cindy Gallop that watching people have sex isn't inherently damaging.

The feminist writer and poet Audre Lorde warned that women risked denying our sexuality in our efforts to resist the ways in which sex is weaponised against us. She wrote:

'In order to perpetuate itself, every oppression must corrupt or distort those various sources of power within the culture of the oppressed that can provide energy for change. For women, this has meant a suppression of the erotic as a considered source of power and information within our lives. We have been taught to suspect this resource, vilified, abused, and devalued within Western society. On the one hand, the superficially erotic has been encouraged as a sign of female inferiority; on the other hand, women have been made to suffer and to feel both contemptible and suspect by virtue of its existence. It is a short step from there to the false belief that only by the suppression of the erotic within our lives and consciousness can women be truly strong. But that strength is illusory, for it is fashioned within the context of male models of power.'[6]

Moreover, as a journalist and writer, I feared the implications for free speech and free expression of a pornography ban. In 2014 I had attended a protest in Westminster. The organisers predicted crowds of 500, but disgruntled media easily outnumbered the demonstrators. The photographers brightened briefly as a group of figures in giant heels and fetish gear tottered into view. 'Blimey,' said one snapper, 'you don't get that outside the White House.' Tourists who had come to see Big Ben posed for selfies with a man dressed as Santa Claus and wielding a placard emblazoned with an invitation to sit on Santa's face.

If there was confusion around the purpose of the event, that was a fair reflection of the subject area it intended to highlight: Britain's laws relating to pornography. The government, in trying to iron out an anomaly that meant online pornographic films produced or consumed in the UK had been less tightly regulated than DVDs sold in British shops, imposed the same rules on both categories of porn, potentially creating fresh inconsistencies. Campaigners claimed guidelines banning potentially 'life-threatening' acts and 'strong physical and verbal abuse' established a list of sexual activities that could no longer legally be filmed or distributed in the UK. These included female ejaculation, primarily a feature of lesbian porn, and light spanking, a practice so ingrained in British culture that it is known in France as '*le vice anglais*'. The British Board of Film Classification (BBFC), the body that determines and applies the guidelines, rejected this interpretation. Catherine Anderson, head of communications for BBFC, emailed: 'There is no such list. Nor could there be given the importance of context in BBFC classification decisions.'

Even so, the restrictions 'inadvertently declared a trade war against foreign jurisdictions,' Myles Jackman, a lawyer specialising in issues around obscenity, told me. The authorities 'have managed to get financial institutions to block payments on debit and credit cards for payments in this country buying pornography from foreign websites. Were you in this country to use your debit or credit card to purchase pornography from certain US websites you would get an error message, even if the material was in compliance with regulations because the site might not be.' The end result he said, in a separate interview with the *Independent*, could impact far more than pornography. 'Pornography is the canary in the coalmine of free speech: it is the first freedom to die. If this assault on liberty is allowed to go unchallenged, other freedoms will fall as a consequence.'[7]

A standard definition of pornography is that it is material designed to stimulate arousal. Works of art periodically test that definition: for example, the 1954 novel about submission, *Story of O*, and the 1976 Franco-Japanese movie, *Ai no corrida – In the Realm of the Senses*, an earnest art-house movie that includes scenes of real (not simulated) sex, and sadomasochism and death.

More often works of censorship test the definitions of stupidity. Whether human editors or algorithms created by humans caused Facebook to remove photographs showing women breastfeeding isn't clear. The social media company also ended up in litigation with a teacher called Frédéric Durand-Baissas, who posted Gustave Courbet's 1866 painting '*L'Origine du monde*'. The origin of the world that the picture shows is a vagina, framed by luxuriant pubic hair. Facebook censored the image and blocked Durand-Baissas' account. Durand-Baissas sued. 'I felt like they were indirectly treating me like a pornographer whereas this is a French painting hanging in a museum,' he said.

When we were children, my sister Lise introduced me to books that at various times were banned as pornography. She had discovered in my parents' shelves a number of volumes containing vivid descriptions of sexual activity and read out from these as part of a self-appointed mission in sex education: John Cleland's *Fanny Hill*; D. H. Lawrence's *Lady Chatterley's Lover* and Germaine Greer's *The Female Eunuch*, among others.

Greer's book hadn't attracted censors but the passage Lise chose was an extended quotation from a short story in Hubert Selby, Jr.'s 1964 collection, *Last Exit to Brooklyn*, describing the gang-rape and murder of a prostitute called Tralala. Selby was aiming not to titillate but to shock. In 1967, after the book had already sold 14,000 copies in the UK, a nine-day obscenity trial, launched at the behest of a Conservative MP against Selby's publishers – and featuring an all-male jury to protect female jurors against distress

– found the defendants guilty of a breach of the Obscene Publications Act, in particular a clause prohibiting 'possessing an obscene article for gain.' The publishers appealed and this time won, and the law was amended.

This marked progress but, as discussed throughout this book, progress is always fragile and subject to reversals and backlash. Although I have reluctantly come to the view that legislative measures are necessary to restrict and ultimately eliminate damaging pornography, I cannot shake the fear that laws badly drafted – or worse yet, drafted by social conservatives to attack anything that offends their belief system – will be deployed to stifle artistic endeavour and free speech. The UK does too little to protect the latter – the US has the First Amendment guaranteeing freedom of speech but the UK has no constitutional guarantees apart from the European Convention incorporated into domestic law under the Human Rights Act, which a significant number of politicians on the government benches would like to see repealed. British courts are quick to suppress news and opinions, through laws against incitement to hatred and terrorism, against breaches of the peace and defamation, and by slapping on injunctions or super-injunctions that shroud not only the information injuncted but the fact of the injunctions themselves.

The internet unpicks such injunctions within hours and undermines efforts by authoritarian regimes to silence dissidents. Those regimes respond by trying to control or close the internet. China blocks Facebook, Tumblr and Twitter, and searches about Tiananmen Square or the Dalai Lama come up blank. ISIS has built a violent dictatorship and disabled the internet in areas it controls. Donald Trump suggested shutting down the internet in conflict zones, even though this would potentially torpedo sites operating in opposition to ISIS.

Online trolls smother opinion in a different way, with relentless campaigns to shame and silence. Men are called names, women are subjected to sexual harassment, threats and stalking. Young women are especially vulnerable. They 'experience certain severe types of harassment at disproportionately high levels', according to a 2014 survey by Pew Research Center.[8] A 2016 Australian study found 76 per cent of women under 30 had been abused online, one in four had been threatened with violence, and one in ten had been targeted for revenge porn, the sharing of intimate pictures without consent.

In many countries the rising generations that might be expected most vigorously to object to a thickening smog of censorship instead add to it, seeking to ban or no-platform people whose views may cause offence, or refusing to share a platform with them. Their apparent delicacy has earned them a contemptuous nickname, 'Generation Snowflake', but many of the critics who bandy about that term have never weathered the relentless onslaught of trolls. Others turn from trolled to trolls, glorying in their ability to dish out insults and treating each online interaction as a Nietzschean test of strength. In truth there is nothing empowering about enduring abuse. Many women self-censor or abandon social media to protect themselves.

In August 2013, I reported a bomb threat to the police, delivered via Twitter. They immediately advised me to give up social media. I was a journalist; you may as well tell a chef to avoid knives. The threats, delivered to at least eight women, were too cartoonish to be frightening, but their context was unsettling, part of a blizzard of rape threats directed at campaigner Caroline Criado-Perez after she started a campaign to retain a woman other than the Queen on British banknotes. Winston Churchill stood poised to elbow aside the prison reformer Elizabeth Fry on the five-pound note. Criado-Perez launched a petition on Change.org and kept pushing despite the intimidation, until the Bank of England responded and announced Jane Austen as the new face of the ten-pound note. 'The bank obviously made the right decision, but without the power of the internet, who knows what would have happened?' mused Criado-Perez. 'Early on, I'd felt like just one person taking on a leviathan, but social media turned out to have a wonderful galvanising power.'

Getting the word out is essential to create change. Channels of communication must be protected, even if those channels are used for ill as well as good. This perspective is not shared by the 3,000 students at Cardiff University who petitioned, ultimately unsuccessfully, to stop Germaine Greer from giving a lecture because of her views on trans women. Cat/ Milo Bezark, my 19-year-old cousin, defends such actions. Calling in – engaging with someone to bring them to the desired viewpoint – might be the ideal, but 'calling in takes a lot more time than calling out does. It takes a lot more patience, and how many people are going to get hurt in the process of you trying to call someone in, before that person changes their actions or behaviours, or language?'[9] Cat/Milo's cohort believes older generations have not done enough to protect oppressed minorities or the oppressed majority of women. They are absolutely right, but I worry that declaring discussion-free safe spaces and sprinkling trigger warnings across content risks retarding progress rather than speeding it. 'It's so easy to talk about the politics of language, and trigger warnings; it's really easy just to slap on trigger warnings,' says Pavan Amara. 'It's really easy to criticise people for not using the right language. I think because that's so easy to do, it often overlooks the real issues that are affecting women's lives. For example, you've got a lot of talk about whether you should use the term [rape] "victim" or "survivor", and yet until recently you didn't even have a bloody health service for rape survivors, or a maternity unit, and you've got rape crisis centres losing their funding.'

The Facebook group Cuntry Living, originally founded as a feminist discussion forum for Oxford University students, now more widely subscribed, bills itself as 'an intersectional, anti-racist, sex-positive online space in which we can challenge the patriarchy and other structures of oppression.' Participants are warned that it 'is intended to be as safe a space as possible. Healthy debate is welcomed, but we do not want members of the group to feel threatened and/or marginalised and/or shouted down by people who do not have an understanding of oppression … If you are knowingly ignoring/talking over individuals with first-hand experience of oppression, and/or espousing harmful and oppressive views (or if you like harmful and oppressive posts and comments), you will be removed from the group.' The administrators have not been slow to carry out that sanction. A regular participant called Becky Butler protested after a male friend she described as a feminist was excluded for having 'policed reactions to oppression'. 'Education should be a function of the platform,' wrote Butler. 'A refusal to elucidate feminist issues only strengthens the patriarchy. Obliviousness is the perfect tool for the preservation of existing structures … There is a terrible irony in Cuntry Living, our "safe space", frightening its members into silence.'[10]

Feminism needs robust and open debates in order to challenge our assumptions, sharpen our thinking, resolve any differences and move forward. Greer should be heard – and criticised. It's harder to make that case for Roosh V, an American blogger who claims his proposal to eradicate rape by legalising it was meant satirically – hold my aching sides – but whose books, websites and meetings promote dumb misogyny. In 2016 he cancelled appearances in Australia and the UK amid protests. Eighty thousand people signed a petition calling on the British government to ban him from entering the country. The government did not do so but welcomed his decision to stay away. Karen Bradley, then a Home Office minister, told the House of Commons, 'The government condemns in the strongest terms anyone who condones rape and sexual violence. We should ridicule, we should show contempt, we should show that these are the most ridiculous views.' I agree with Bradley, though my preference would have been to ignore the sad little gobshite in the first place.

Roosh V is the perfect example of a convenient dinosaur. Some men are attracted to his inchoate teachings. Many more find him embarrassing, but in treating him as a yardstick for sexism and misogyny they may permit themselves the illusion that they have no such problems. The reality is that most of us, of all genders, carry prejudices inculcated from birth. For much of the time we bumble along just fine without examining these prejudices or interrogating our own behaviour and only occasionally catch ourselves out. A friend tells us she's been to the doctor. 'Oh,' we reply. 'What did he say?' Another friend, male, has been to the doctor. 'Man flu,' we surmise. A female celebrity appears with a taut face or a new pair of breasts and we criticise the person rather than the pressures that put her on the operating table.

The Women's Equality Party was always conceived as a party for everyone and for the benefit of everyone. We want men to be involved, and not just because we need men's votes to win. We can only reach Equalia if men work towards that goal, and much of that work involves looking at themselves and the cultures they inhabit. One reason I felt reluctant to tackle the sex industry before the party was better known was that I worried we'd dent our ability to build a broad movement. Men might presume we were wagging accusatory fingers, rather than inviting them into a collaborative process of reflection and change.

I would not anyway have been in a position to take the moral high ground. I have watched a great deal of pornography. I never liked violent porn but always preferred porn without the frills and furbelows of silly plot-lines or synthetic romance that clog up many attempts at women-friendly erotica. German porn – group sex involving men with large bellies and cropped-hair women with tattoos – *nein danke*; I'm as much of a body fascist as the next *Daily Mail* journalist if the bodies are humping. Porn actors get through filming by detaching from proceedings. I dissociated for many years from the implications of viewing this sort of porn, pretending it was a subversive thing to do and insisting, like Cindy Gallop, that sex movies could be recast as vehicles of education and empowerment. (I still believe the second point to be true but am less certain it's possible to create ethical products that raise more than a snort of laughter or derision in anyone like me whose sexuality has been formed – or malformed – by existing cultures.)

That dissociative process is familiar to psychologists treating patients complaining of addiction to online pornography. Men interviewed for this book about using porn or paying for sex also displayed distancing techniques. They persuaded themselves they weren't doing anything harmful. The films already existed, whether or not they watched them. The women were already prostituted and at least they had treated them with courtesy and paid in full. One interviewee talked about his regular trips to the Far East. 'I wouldn't go to Soho,' he told me. 'You think the women there have probably been trafficked. They all seem to be Romanians or Bulgarians and they're obviously unhappy. But Thailand is different.' How so? 'It's part of the culture there. The girls tell me they like the work and it has status. They send money to their families.'

I knew what he meant. I had once visited a sex show in Bangkok, and found myself, as the only Western woman in the club, the subject of much curiosity. The show hadn't yet started and the performers clustered around me, asking questions about life in Britain. Several of them hoped to find husbands among a crowd whose sunburned necks and baggy t-shirts suggested a high quotient of UK nationals. The women themselves were slender, smooth-skinned, looked healthy and did indeed seem cheerful. One of them told me she had come to the city two years earlier to help fund her family in the rural north of Thailand. 'How old are you?' she asked me, in broken English. 'Forty,' I told her. 'Me too,' she chirruped. 'I'm 14 too.' As I stared at her, frozen with the realisation she had started her life in the sex clubs of Patpong at the age of 12, she said something I thought I had misheard: 'I must go smoke now.' Minutes later she lay spread-eagled on a chair, at eye level to the audience, with two lit cigarettes protruding from her vagina, blowing smoke rings.

Activists promoting the legalisation of the sex industry describe what she was doing as 'sex work' and themselves as 'sex workers'. It may not be easy to see dignity in this kind of labour, but that is clearly not for the observer to decide. 'I really, really did love the work,' Meg Muñoz told the annual

West Coast conference of Amnesty International in 2015. She started out as an escort, and added to the pay by having sex with clients. When she moved into her own apartment, she needed money to pay bills and to save up to go to college. 'I was moving toward a goal, and sex work helped me do that.'[11]

Her problems started when an ex-boyfriend started to blackmail her. What she was doing carried criminal penalties under US law, making her vulnerable to his threats. Her ex also used violence to turn himself into her pimp. The argument Muñoz laid out at the Amnesty conference was that she would have enjoyed far greater protection from this abuse if prostitution were legal.

Amnesty agrees and since 2016 has demanded the decriminalisation of prostitution. Amnesty's policy asserts that 'to protect the rights of sex workers, it is necessary not only to repeal laws which criminalise the sale of sex, but also to repeal those which make the buying of sex from consenting adults or the organisation of sex work (such as prohibitions on renting premises for sex work) a criminal offence. Such laws force sex workers to operate covertly in ways that compromise their safety, prohibit actions that sex workers take to maximise their safety, and serve to deny sex workers support or protection from government officials. They therefore undermine a range of sex workers' human rights, including their rights to security of person, housing and health.'[12]

A fair array of organisations have adopted similar approaches to Amnesty: the World Health Organisation, the Joint United Nations Programme on HIV/AIDS (UNAIDS), the International Labour Organisation, the Global Alliance Against Trafficking in Women, the Global Network of Sex Work Projects, the Global Commission on HIV and the Law, Human Rights Watch, the Open Society Foundations and Anti-Slavery International. They might be said to carry more weight than the starry signatories of a letter opposing Amnesty's move – Lena Dunham, Anne Hathaway, Meryl Streep and Kate Winslet. Another signatory, Gloria Steinem, has a long history of opposing the re-christening of prostitution as sex work. In the 1970s, 'sex positive' feminists argued that prostitution could be a radical, and feminist, act. Steinem demurred. This was not the world's oldest profession but 'the world's oldest oppression'.[13] She has not wavered from that position. 'Prostitution involves body invasion and so it is not like any other work. So how can you call it sex work? Prostitution is the only word you should use,' she said during a 2014 visit to India. Local advocacy groups such as the Indian collective Durbar Mahila Samanwaya Committee (formed in 1992 in Sonagachi, a red-light district of Kolkata in West Bengal, with 65,000 members), demanding 'recognition of sex work as work and, of sex workers as workers', disagree and have logged impressive results in restricting the transmission of HIV/AIDS and other sexually transmitted diseases with programmes encouraging condom use.

The achievements of Durbar and similar collectives elsewhere in India reinforced my instinct to support decriminalisation. Yet the world's biggest experiment in decriminalisation has been a failure. In 2001, Germany passed a law aimed at protecting women in the sex industry from violence, ill health, low status and commercial exploitation. Pimping and brothel-keeping would be legalised and carefully regulated. Prostitutes would be enabled, like any other workers, to join health, unemployment and pension insurance schemes and to claim for unpaid wages. The outcome has proved quite different. As Kat Banyard, the founder of campaign group UKFeminista, points out in *Pimp State*, her 2016 treatise against decriminalisation, 'Any would-be brothel-keeper can just open up shop and then register their new enterprise at the trade licensing office ... Basic workplace health and safety rules don't even apply to most women in Germany's legal brothels. Why? Because for them to apply an individual has to be an employee. And it is up to individual brothels whether or not they employ women or simply host them as "independent contractors". Overwhelmingly they've opted for the latter.'[14] Banyard musters depressing statistics: by 2014 only 44 people had registered their trade as prostitution to join the national insurance scheme, and 99 per cent of prostitutes did not have an employment contract.

Instead Germany has become a magnet for sex tourism. Traffickers lure impoverished migrants from Eastern Europe and further afield to meet demand. Many of the estimated 400,000 women working in the sex trade cannot appeal to the authorities for help for fear of deportation. They live in poverty while the owners of brothel chains and mega-brothels grow rich. When the Pussy Club opened in Fellbach, near Stuttgart in 2009, 1,700 would-be customers flocked to the opening weekend, tempted by a special offer: 'Sex with all women as long as you want, as often as you want and the way you want. Sex. Anal sex. Oral sex without a condom. Three-ways. Group sex. Gang bangs.' All this came at a flat rate of 70 euros per day or 100 euros at night. Branches opened in Berlin, Heidelberg and Wuppertal.

Customers were not always impressed. 'One thing I was pretty sure about was that the girls were on some sort of drugs or something,' complained one unhappy client on the website InternationalSexGuide.info, relating in detail his experiences in the Berlin branch: 'The Russian girl did not give that great a blow job but just the same monotonous sucking although the tall Brazilian girl did use her tongue to do some licking and flicking … After a couple of blow job sessions from both of them I worked myself up by hand until I was on the point of coming and I then asked the Russian girl to suck me. She zombie-like lowered her head and carried on sucking even when my dick twitched and I could feel the cum flowing out.'

Another reviewer, reporting on the same establishment, is indignant: 'I noticed this mid-30's Latina woman. She looked somewhat attractive, and since I usually do well with Latinas, I cocked my head and smiled at her. she told me to lie down, just before she went into a coughing fit, and then blew her nose noisily. what a mood setter, love sounds. when she proceeded to give me a hj, I asked for her to use her mouth but she said that she's sick and wouldn't kiss or do bbbj. I began to move down her body, but she wouldn't allow me to remove her skirt or panties and instead moved back to giving me a hj. i asked her if that's all that we were going to do and she said yes.

So I got up, and left the cubby, pissed as hell. What the f*ck was she doing working in a pt, wasting my time?'

The use of the star in the word 'fuck' seems a tiny but illuminating detail. Puritanism often underlies the world-view that divides women into Madonnas and whores, and regards both, in different ways, as less than human.

In 2012, the founder of Pussy Club and his accomplices were sent to prison for 'severe human trafficking for the purposes of sexual exploitation, in part including pimping, as well as withholding and embezzlement of wages totalling millions.' The chief witnesses for the prosecution during the 72-day trial were young Romanian women, who had been drawn to Germany by job adverts promising other kinds of work and then forced into prostitution. A 16-year-old arrived expecting work in the restaurant business. Instead she was forced to service up to 60 clients a day in the Fellbach Pussy Club.

The court case marked a rare move against bordello owners and pimps. It is difficult to prove exploitation. There were only 32 prosecutions of pimps in 2011, down from 151 a decade earlier.[15] Meanwhile every year more than a million sex tourists travel to Germany contributing to a trade worth up to $18 billion, compared to an estimated $14.6 billion in the US and $1 billion in the UK.

The Nordic Model starts from the same premise as decriminalisation, that the best way to protect people selling sex is to allow them to do so legally. It instead shifts the penalties to people who exploit others by trafficking and pimping them, or buying sex from them, while providing support and exit services to assist workers who choose to stay in the industry, and help for others to transition out of it. Sweden's experience looks encouraging. Street prostitution declined after it pioneered the law. Critics highlight a rise in online advertising for sex as a sign that prostitution has not diminished but gone underground, increasing the dangers for women.

Banyard rejects this interpretation. 'What is inconvenient for groups want-ing governments to enshrine brothel-keeping and pimping as legitimate jobs is that the effects of the [Nordic Model] have so clearly exposed the fallacy of fatalism surrounding prostitution.' Her book makes a persuasive argument against that fatalism, the notion that prostitution has always been and will always be: 'Street prostitution in Sweden halved between 1999 and 2009, with the law's official evaluation finding no evidence it had merely been displaced. Anonymous surveys conducted in 1996 and 2008 revealed that the proportion of men who pay for sex dropped from 12.7 to 7.6 per cent. Added to which, in 2011 it was reported that the number of people involved in prostitution in Sweden – the country's "prostitution population" – was approximately a tenth of Denmark's, where buying sex is legal. This was despite Sweden having 3.8 million more inhabitants than Denmark.'

A study on the links between trafficking and prostitution blamed Denmark's move to decriminalisation in 1999 for the beginning of a boom in prostitution, which 'rose by 40 per cent in a seven-year period after the law was changed. But the numbers of voluntary prostitutes cannot match the rapid growth of consumers. Consequently, pimps resort to sex trafficking to keep their customers supplied with unrestricted sex,' the authors reported.[16]

Decriminalisation has worked better in some countries and cultures than in Germany and Denmark. New Zealand, which decriminalised the sex industry in 2003, and the Australian state of New South Wales, where prostitution has been legal since 1988, have seen little appreciable increase in the volume of the business and may have achieved improved health out-comes for women selling sex. Nevada, the only state in America to legalise the selling and buying of sex within brothels, offers some protections to the workforce. The brothels are restricted to areas with low populations, and their remote locations mean that many of the brothels are losing money. Dennis Hof, patron of seven establishments, has fought back by diversifying into entertainment, taking advantage of the media's twin fetishes for reality

TV and pornified content by getting his Moonlite BunnyRanch featured on the HBO series *Cathouse*.

Geography and culture clearly play a role in determining how different legislative models work. Versions of the Nordic Model are now operating in Sweden, Norway, Iceland, Northern Ireland and Canada. France voted in favour in April 2016. 'The goal is to diminish [prostitution], protect those prostitutes who want to quit, and change mentalities,' said Maud Olivier, the politician who steered the bill through parliament.

It is this final aspiration that has swayed me in the direction of the Nordic Model, despite my concerns about its imperfections and unintended consequences. The idea that prostitution is a necessary outlet for male sexuality is not backed by science or history. It is part of the same thinking that casts rape as the expression of uncontrollable sexual urges, or encourages men to have as much sex as possible while denigrating women for their sexuality. It perpetuates that thinking.

Nor do I buy into the idea of The Happy Hooker. The autobiography of the same name, by Xaviera Hollander, a former call girl and madam, was another text my sister Lise read aloud to me. I remembered it as a cheery romp. Rereading it as research for this book, I discovered a much sadder story of abuse, particularly by the double-dealing, violent fiancé who persuades Hollander to follow him to the US. But it is the other women in Hollander's story, unnoticed when I was a child, who really stand out – the women not working as call girls but as street walkers. 'In the hooker hierarchy, we were the aristocrats, they were the serfs,' Hollander writes. Such divisions still exist. The women and girls trafficked into prostitution have less agency than serfs; they are slaves. The black streetwalkers Hollander shrinks away from in a New York police holding cell are not, as she claims to be, sexually empowered or empowered in any sense. A late 1990s study found that more than a quarter of New York City prostitutes were homeless and addicted to drugs; 90 per cent had surrendered a child to child protective services.[17] In the same decade, the death rate for women selling sex in the US was 204 out of every 100,000, compared to 129 out of every 100,000 for the physically dangerous job of commercial fishing. The top causes of death were murder, drugs and alcohol. Women suffered non-lethal assaults every month. Most vulnerable of all were, and remain, transgender women. Murder rates for all transgender people hit historic highs in the US in 2015. Almost all victims were transgender women of colour and 34 per cent of them were engaged 'in sex or survival work'.[18]

One key danger in trying to legislate away prostitution is that the people hit hardest are those for whom selling sex is survival work. Laws can never work in isolation. We need to address the inequalities underpinning the sex industry, and perpetuated by it. In the short term, no attempts to restrict the sex industry should proceed without adequate planning for support and exit strategies for its workforce.

The UK has not decriminalised. Only Northern Ireland has introduced the Nordic Model. Everywhere else is a muddle of contradictory rules in which it's legal to sell sex but not to solicit in a public place. Kerb-crawling is illegal, meaning sex buyers are targeted in their cars but not on the street. 'The current laws do not work,' as the final wording of the Women's Equality Party's policy document pointed out. 'There has been an increase in sex trafficking and many women are forced into situations comparable to slavery. The sex industry is closely associated with organised crime, poverty, drugs, sexual violence and child abuse. Women who sell sex are vulnerable to violent crimes, including assault, rape and murder, as well as sexually transmitted diseases which may pose a risk to their lives. They also experience barriers to accessing sexual health services.'

The party did not reach a final position on policy at the policy group meeting or for some weeks afterwards. We debated and researched and debated some more. In the end, we decided to recommend the Nordic Model but recognised that some of our members would support decriminalisation instead. We therefore called for a national debate 'that raises awareness of the realities of the sex trade so that anyone buying sex understands the likelihood that women who sell sex may well have been trafficked, forced or abused, and understands how the expectation that women and girls can be bought and sold feeds into wider misogyny.' The document concludes: 'the status quo cannot prevail.' In December 2016, Home Secretary Amber Rudd launched a research project to establish a 'robust evidence base' before considering policy changes. The report is due in June 2017.

Chapter Seven: Frozen out

THIRTY SECONDS IS a substantial chunk of cinema – and a long time to contemplate a bottom. This bottom remains idle for ten seconds, then stirs, shifts and settles again under the camera's steady gaze. Another 20 seconds pass until the opening credits roll … *Lost in Translation*.

Sofia Coppola's second feature as director exposed 18-year-old Scarlett Johansson, already a veteran of ten movies, to a new kind of attention. This was Johansson's breakout role. She starred opposite Bill Murray, who celebrated his fifty-second birthday during the 27-day shoot in Tokyo. The film handsomely recouped its $4 million production budget, grossing $119,723,856 worldwide and picking up an Oscar, three Golden Globes and a host of lesser awards. Japanese critics weren't quite so impressed – 'The depiction of Japanese people is terrible,' complained one. The Western press plumbed gushing reservoirs of superlatives. '*Lost in Translation* is found gold,' rhapsodised Peter Travers in *Rolling Stone*. 'Funny how a wisp of a movie from a wisp of a girl can wipe you out.'[1]

To many enthusiasts, the film demonstrated female potential, a wake-up call to male studio executives, male investors and male critics that wispy girls might be towering talents. Yet at least one admirer spotted a more problematic phenomenon. 'I have a theory that the most successful women directors are the ones who imitate the male gaze the best in their work,' says a writer-director. She speaks on condition of anonymity because

Hollywood has little tolerance for dissidence and an infinite capacity for bearing grudges. 'I'm a fan of these women; I like their work very much,' she continues. 'But Sofia Coppola opens up *Lost in Translation* on a close-up of Scarlett Johansson's butt in see-through pink panties. I don't think that's an accident. Or you look at Kathryn Bigelow, who's the first woman (and only woman) to ever win the Oscar for directing. The film *Hurt Locker*, which she won for, is about a lone-wolf army guy who defuses bombs. There's one woman in the entire movie and she's his wife back home. The system, the Academy, the Guilds, the reviewers, who are all male dominated, recognise films by women that feel like films by men, and for men.'[2]

The writer-director has gained some prominence and critical attention. She has filmed stories about women and has more stories she wants to tell, but funding for these projects continues to prove elusive. Her first feature to secure financing had a male lead. Perhaps her female-driven stories are less engaging? Maybe she just isn't good enough? These concerns plague her – like many women she is susceptible to imposter syndrome and veterans of the business, including some women, feel the fault lies not with the system but with women who complain.

Lynda Obst, for example, whose curriculum vitae as a producer stretches back to *Flashdance* and encompasses the giant rom-com hit *Sleepless in Seattle* and two space operas 17 years apart, *Contact* and *Interstellar*, gives such complaints short shrift. She thinks women in Hollywood never had it so good, and her hair-raising tales of her early days in the business certainly speak to progress. She remembers the industry as 'one big frat party with cocaine. It was almost a compliment when guys patted you on the butt; you had to really swallow your revulsion.'[3] But, she says, the business has been good to her and 'it has rewarded talented women consistently.' She adds that she is 'often baffled by the attitude of the very unhappy women of today, who think it's all an unbelievable, rigged conspiracy to keep women directors from working.'[3] Her view is that women do too little to assert themselves.

A host of recent studies analysing the film industry indicate deep-seated inequities, whatever the underlying reasons. Geena Davis, already something of a feminist icon since her turn as Thelma in *Thelma and Louise*, established an institute to study gender in the media in 2007. Among its revelations: only 23 per cent of films feature a female protagonist but those women are twice as likely as men to get – like the 50-foot woman – naked or semi-naked during the film. Analysis of crowd scenes produced another startling fact – just 17 per cent of the unnamed characters milling about at the edge of our consciousness are female and not the fifty-fifty-ish split of real-world throngs.

A separate study of the gender divide in speaking roles revealed that female characters are assigned far less dialogue than male characters, even if they're the female leads. The male dragon in Disney's *Mulan* spouts twice the number of words given to the titular female heroine.[4] Animated movies – able to create their characters rather than cast them – might be expected to score highly on all kinds of diversity, but they don't, unless you count talking dragons and donkeys as diverse. ('I'm not bad,' breathes the pneumatic Jessica Rabbit in *Who Framed Roger Rabbit*. 'I'm just drawn that way.') Few films, animated or otherwise, easily pass the Bechdel test, the criterion originally set by cartoonist Alison Bechdel that a work of fiction should include at least two women talking about something other than men. Women do not hold up half the roseate sky of the movie industry. The world it sees and projects skews male.

That's a pretty accurate reflection of many film sets. A report called *The Celluloid Ceiling* logged a two percentage point increase from the previous year in the number of female directors of the top 250 grossing films of 2015 – up to nine percent (the same figure as for 1998). Women elbowed their way into pivotal behind-the-scenes roles on those movies, but not in large numbers. Twenty-six per cent of producers were women, 22 per cent of editors, 20 per cent of executive producers, 11 per cent of writers, and six per cent of cinematographers. A third of the productions employed only one woman or no women at all in any of these roles.[5]

The UK did slightly better that year – women directed 11.5 per cent of films. Movies with some public funding employed a higher proportion of female directors – 21.7 per cent. However British movies with budgets of £30 million and over remained a largely male preserve, with only 3.3 per cent helmed by women.[6]

'You see the numbers and you're like "Oh, this is systemic. This is an epidemic. This is not just my narrow experience. This is happening …" ,' sighs the writer-director.

The interplay between public attitudes and media is complex. Does the public get what it wants, want what it gets? Or does the public take its cues on what it wants from the media? The question addressed in this chapter is valid for all the myriad forms of media and entertainment, mass communication and culture.

In advertising, the transaction is overt. Betty Friedan in *The Feminine Mystique* charts a deliberate campaign in the postwar era to return American women to domesticity in order to sell them white goods, cake mixes, beauty products and a social order that had been steadily losing its grip. Advertisers serve existing markets or help businesses – and entities such as political parties – to tap and even create new markets.

Other types of media are more likely to hide behind the idea that they are the servants and not the masters of public tastes and attitudes. Many academic studies say otherwise. Media exerts long-term influences and effects immediate behavioural changes.

It can plant unconscious bias and reward and reinforce conscious bias, but it is also the lifeblood of democracy, a mechanism for distributing news and knowledge and, sometimes, a force for beneficial change. Hollywood, the dream factory, is and does all of these things. To understand why, a good starting point is to look at the processes by which films get made, directors and writers employed, actors cast and stories told – and why some films don't get made, why some directors, writers and actors work less than you'd expect, and why stories directed by or written about women frequently struggle for recognition and studio support.

The drama in any movie starts with bringing it to screen. Turning the concept for a feature into a finished piece of cinema, on average 130 minutes long, is akin to starting a corporation – or a political party – from scratch. Unless the process happens quickly, it may not happen at all.

A producer hustles for investment and distribution deals based on the names attached to the project and the excitement around the property, which ideally should lend itself to a two-minute elevator pitch.

Fasten your seatbelts for a remake of the cult classic Attack of the 50 Ft. Woman. California, 1958. Cars with curves, women with curves. Troubled Nancy is driving alone when a spaceship forces her off the road. We're thinking Scarlett Johansson for Nancy but we'll have to scare off the rival talent with cattle prods. This is the biggest chick role in Hollywood. Literally, right? Nancy's no-good husband Harry – Bradley Cooper or Channing Tatum – doesn't believe her story until he sees the alien and runs away, leaving Nancy begging for her life. Now Nancy will be alien hors d'oeuvres on toast! That means Harry can keep her money and marry his girlfriend Honey aka Miley Cyrus. Miley – how hot would that casting be? But then Nancy turns up alive after all, so Harry creeps into the bedroom to poison her. Except Nancy has changed! Alien radiation has turned her into a giant! She wakes up and boy is she crazy! It's like Beyoncé with the baseball bat in Lemonade, *but with fewer clothes and lots of blood!*

Projects live or die on casting, and the starting point for many casting directors, working closely with the director, will be to nail down a star and then work around her other commitments or, more often, his. 'A typical film, even a television pilot, takes ten weeks to cast,' says Debra Zane, who has assembled the actors for many big movies, including *American Beauty*, and also launched Jennifer Lawrence in the role of *The Hunger Games'* Katniss Everdeen. 'Sometimes, like on a Marvel movie, they'll put the casting people on a year in advance. You start from the top. Sometimes an actor becomes attached to a project, and so you know Tom Hanks is going to play that part, or Leonardo DiCaprio is going to play that part, or Will Smith is going to be that guy, or it's going to be Charlize Theron.'[7]

At the time of our conversation in her Los Angeles office, Zane is figuring out the line-up for an all-female *Ocean's Eight* with Sandra Bullock in the role originally inhabited by George Clooney, and an all-female *Ghostbusters* reboot is about to premiere. This looks like a female-friendly trend, but the anonymous writer-director again harbours reservations. She's excited to see *Ghostbusters*, but questions whether simply swapping women into roles originally written for men addresses Hollywood's underlying problems with women. These are still male stories in format and conception and in many, especially the crop of action movies spawned by the success of *The Hunger Games*, the narrative follows the classic arc of the hero's journey, where the unwilling protagonist is bounced by circumstances into heroic action. The writer-director thinks female storytelling is less linear, more layered. For the female leads of these action movies, says the writer-director, 'you have to be fuckable first and then you can be a woman who rescues girls from the post-apocalyptic desert, or then you can be a girl who saves her sister from the war games in the near-future, then you can be the woman who saves the whole planet from aliens.'

The Hunger Games came to Zane to cast with no stars attached but a fan base that guaranteed the franchise would be greenlit. The trilogy of novels by US writer Suzanne Collins had topped bestseller lists the world over. There was no need for Hollywood to perform any gender reassignments. Collins had already borrowed from the action tradition to create kick-ass female characters. Katniss Everdeen, in Collins' own words, is 'a female protagonist in a gladiator story, which traditionally features a male'. Zane describes casting as the most exhausting assignment she's undertaken. 'We saw everybody. We saw everybody you can imagine. Every young actress you can imagine within that age range wanted to play Katniss,' she says.

A few months before our conversation, Hollywood's feeble record on casting actors of colour had played out in a glaringly and exclusively white

Academy Awards nomination list, spawning the hashtag #OscarsSoWhite. The UK broadcaster Channel 4 had also recently launched its latest diversity report in London. 'I'm not here to talk about black people; I'm here to talk about diversity,' said Idris Elba, the keynote speaker at the event in the Houses of Parliament. 'Diversity in the modern world is more than just skin colour. It's gender, age, disability, sexual orientation, social background, and – most important of all, as far as I'm concerned – diversity of thought. Because if you have genuine diversity of thought among people making TV and film, then you won't accidentally shut out any of the groups I just mentioned.'

I ask Zane whether 'everybody you can imagine' for the role of Katniss included women of colour. Yes, she says, and goes on to tell a story that illustrates why Hollywood remains wary of diverse casting – and why it needs to do more of it. 'When I read the book and the screenplay—I'm not sure which I read first—I automatically thought that Lenny Kravitz seemed like Cinna, Katniss's confidante and stylist. That doesn't always happen to me when I read; I like to read the story first and then work. But I just thought "That seems kind of cool". He got the part. There was a lot of backlash about him being black. A lot of people wrote horrible things on the internet.'

Trolls also targeted the all-female *Ghostbusters*, in particular its black star Leslie Jones, with a hail of racist and sexist abuse. The casting of Noma Dumezweni, a black actress, as Hermione in J. K. Rowling's play *Harry Potter and the Cursed Child*, unleashed a similar torrent.

The best way to stretch imaginations is to stretch imaginations. Directors sometimes come to Zane with fixed ideas about what sex or ethnicity or age of actor will suit a role. Does she ever push back? 'We read the script and we list out the characters. So, depending on so many things – like my relationship with the director – sometimes you don't feel free enough to say: "Do you think that this could be a woman?" or "It says that this is a white man but could we also show you some black men?"' But, says Zane, 'casting directors do try, because we also know that it's not terribly interesting any more to have just a lot of white men.'

Even when the cameras are ready to roll, a last-minute hitch can hobble a project or kill it off. In 2004, Britain's Labour government suddenly suspended a tax break created to stimulate the domestic film industry. The move endangered as many as 40 films. The biggest casualty was *Tulip Fever*, a movie based on Deborah Moggach's novel set in seventeenth-century Holland. Its producer, Alison Owen, had commissioned the planting of acres of tulip bulbs timed to push through the soil at precisely the right moment to form the floral backdrop for the love story set at the centre of the world's first economic bubble, tulip mania. She had also contracted two bankable British stars to play the lovers, Keira Knightley and Jude Law, and recruited a behind-the-camera team of more than 80 people, including director John Madden, winner of the Best Picture Oscar for *Shakespeare in Love*, and the celebrated playwright, Tom Stoppard, who adapted the book into a script. Then the UK Treasury closed its incentive scheme and overnight a funding gap of more than £6 million yawned. The tulips blossomed and withered. Knightley and Law committed to other roles. The crew dispersed. The project disappeared into Development Hell, the undiscovered country from where movies only rarely return.

Owen, producer of the awards-garlanded 1998 movie *Elizabeth*, starring Cate Blanchett, and 2003's *Sylvia*, with Gwyneth Paltrow in the title role of poet Sylvia Plath, moved on too. Her production company, Ruby Films, was one of the UK's most successful independents. In the years after the disappointment with *Tulip*, the company produced 24 films and major TV series including *Brick Lane*, *The Other Boleyn Girl* with Natalie Portman and Scarlett Johansson, *Temple Grandin*, *Tamara Drewe*, *Jane Eyre*, *Dancing on the Edge* and *Saving Mr Banks*, the Emma Thompson and Tom Hanks film about the making of *Mary Poppins* that dropped into cinemas in 2013. For ten years and more, Owen also worked every contact to drum up funding for another project, a feature film about the fight to enfranchise British women.

It may seem incredible that *Suffragette*, which finally came out in 2015, is the first movie to approach this story, hugely significant as this slice of history is, resonant and full of compelling characters and narratives. It may startle that a film scripted by Abi Morgan (*Shame* and *The Iron Lady*), directed by Sarah Gavron (*Brick Lane*, *This Little Life*) and with a cast including Carey Mulligan, Helena Bonham Carter and Meryl Streep, should meet with any scepticism among potential investors and distributors. For Owen this was no surprise at all.

'My passion at the moment is to do the Roe versus Wade story,' she says. The legal battle that led to the US Supreme Court declaring abortion a constitutional right – a right the current US administration aims to dismantle – is, Owen, adds, 'a fucking great story, full of suspense and great characters. But when you set out doing it you know you're setting out on a hard road.'

What does that road look like? She grimaces. 'First of all you tell the story to people and they're like "Oh my god, that's amazing! Why has that story never been made before?" And you're like "Duh, because it's about women". And [Roe v Wade] still won't be told anytime soon because I've got to fight for five years at least to get it made, because the people you're trying to raise the money from have preconceived beliefs about what works and what doesn't work and you have to break those things down one at a time.'[8]

Some films and film-makers are challenging those preconceptions. Owen cites one example that heartens her: the raucous 2011 comedy *Bridesmaids*, written by women and starring six women, which 'made back six times its $26.2 million opening (or $159 million) at a production cost of $33 million,' according to the online industry publication *IndieWire*. The figures refer to its domestic box office, and that's great business but, as the same article points out, the movie didn't perform as well as equivalent movies aimed at mixed or male audiences. *Bridesmaids* 'isn't going to outstrip

There's Something About Mary ($176.5 million), another summer comedy which lured both sexes and spurred the gross-out comedy trend, nor will it topple the highest-grossing romantic comedy of all time, *My Big Fat Greek Wedding* ($241.4 million) ... Clearly, the next step for any R-rated *Bridesmaids* wannabe is to pull in more males in order to gain entry into the $200-million testosterone tentpole club, taking a seat next to *The Hangover* ($277.3 million) or *Beverly Hills Cop* ($234.8 million).'

Some 35 per cent of ticket buyers on *Bridesmaids*' opening weekend were men – the average male audience for a so-called women's picture is only 20 per cent – which is why it did well, but it struggled to attract the older women that flocked to *Greek Wedding*. By contrast, lad humour such as *The Hangover*, written by men and starring three men, draws crowds that are upwards of 40 per cent female. '*Greek Wedding* proves that a female-driven comedy with an unknown cast has the potential to deliver busloads of older women to the multiplex and two century ticket sales – but only if it isn't raunchy and rated PG,' *IndieWire* concluded. 'If a bawdy female comedy is going to play to greater heights than *Bridesmaids*, it may have to water down its filthy hijinks or up the ante for the guys.'

IndieWire doesn't attempt to explain why this is so, and it's true that many of the reasons appear self-evident. Women are interested in stories by or about men, even if older women are squeamish about lad culture. Men aren't particularly interested in stories by or about women. Then again, why would they be? Almost everything in their life experience teaches them that women, clothed, aren't particularly worthy of attention. Women are rarely at the centre of the action and we supposedly have half as much to say.

Men run the news. A recent US study showed that 65 per cent of political news stories were authored by men while 68 per cent of onscreen news reports were delivered by men. These figures had been slowly improving but cutbacks in newsrooms are witnessing a depressing phenomenon: even if applied equally across genders – and there is anecdotal evidence that women are more often targeted and more often volunteer for redundancies – the survivors are more likely to be white and male because of the pre-existing inequities. A global survey of news in 114 countries revealed that just 24 per cent of the people seen, heard or read about in the media are women. Male editors focus on male narratives and worry that women lack the gravitas to do justice to these narratives, even if they are framed in comedic terms. Sandi was considered and then rejected as the host for the BBC's comedy news quiz *Have I Got News for You* on the grounds, she remembers, 'We couldn't possibly have a woman in charge of the news.'

There are a few corners of media in which women equal or outstrip men in numbers. Public relations is one. 'Having a bit of a "people-pleaser" gene probably attracts and/or makes it easier for women to excel in the PR environment,' Jennifer Hellickson, director of marketing at SweatGuru, told a journalist from the *Atlantic* investigating the phenomenon. The book publishing industry also hires more women than men. In 2010, editor-turned-agent Jason Pinter responded to a survey of the industry showing 85 per cent of its new intake was female. 'I hope it doesn't get worse,' he said. Yes, worse.

'If 85 per cent, it's hard to think that acquisitions aren't in some way affected by that,' he added.[9] He of course needn't have worried. After all, women in publishing as in every other profession fall behind or drop out from their 30s onwards. A 2016 survey of US publishers found 78 per cent of staff were female, but only 40 per cent of executives were and the closer to the top, the higher the concentration of men. The same survey uncovered an absence of other kinds of diversity. Only 10 per cent were non-white. Just eight per cent were differently abled.

Pinter was right about one thing: an industry that exists to find and tell stories has too narrow a gaze in deciding what those stories should be. J. K. Rowling's decision to use initials rather than her name, Joanne, 'was the publisher's idea,' she said. 'They could have called me Enid Snodgrass. I just wanted [the book] published.' She later launched a series of detective novels as Robert Galbraith. Her male editor exclaimed 'I never would have thought a woman wrote that.'

The same thing has been said of my work more than once, and meant, by the men who said it, as a compliment. I already had profile as a journalist when I wrote my first book, so it was too late to choose a gender-neutral pseudonym. Industry insiders instead advised me to collect endorsements from male public figures for the cover to offset the toxicity of my female byline.

You can see why the publishing business might think that way. In 2015 the online magazine *Slate* examined the subjects and authorship of popular histories and biographies published in the US in the previous 12 months. My biography of Prince Charles was one of these, but it was an outlier. More than three-quarters of the books had been written by men, 71.1 per cent of biographies had male subjects, and 87 per cent of the biographers were men. Only six per cent of male biographers attempted female subjects.[10]

Charles performed well, despite the disadvantage of my sex. Publishers were impressed. Top executives from publishing houses plied me with fancy lunches and told me they'd like to publish my next book, which they assumed would be another biography. They asked me if I had another subject in mind. Yes, I told them. I'd like to write about Angela Merkel. There was as yet no major English-language portrait of the German Chancellor, an anomalous position for a world leader of her stature. I had studied in Germany, spoke German, spent 11 years writing for the German news magazine *FOCUS*, covered Germany for *TIME* and had interviewed Merkel, one of few non-Germans ever to do so. At the last German elections, I followed her around on the campaign trail and trekked to her childhood town in Eastern Germany. I had good contacts and an analysis that differed in significant and potentially newsworthy ways from the mainstream view. Her pivotal role in Europe meant that the gap in understanding played out in poor negotiations and poorer guesses about what she might do next and why. Also, and most importantly, she is utterly fascinating.

One publishing magnate looked like he was choking, but I knew a restaurant of that calibre would have thoroughly pinboned his John Dory. 'Merkel's boring,' he said. 'What about a rock star? You're married to a musician. It's a natural fit.' A second publisher came back with an offer. It amounted to just nine per cent of the advance I'd received for Prince Charles. He was keen to do the book but the projected sales figures meant he couldn't go higher, the publisher told me with obvious regret. Key women in publishing subsequently disagreed with the analysis, but by that time I had already embarked on this book, signed by a female commissioning editor.

As it happens, I don't doubt that a book on Merkel might have to fight harder for readership than some other political biographies. As already discussed, she governed cautiously until the refugee crisis, and at other times has appeared dull because she wanted to do so. Her East German childhood taught her to fly below the radar.

That makes her a tougher sell, but would also make a biography a more rewarding and revelatory read. If she were male, the cost–benefit analysis would look more encouraging to the sales and marketing departments that help commissioning editors to decide whether to make offers and how much to stump up. In worrying about the high proportion of women infiltrating publishers, Jason Pinter forgot to take into account the wider context that keeps the world focused on manly things. Stories about women remain undervalued because women remain undervalued.

The Women's Social and Political Union (WSPU) was founded in 1903 by Emmeline Pankhurst and other women who concluded that the state could not and would not hear female voices. The WSPU's slogan, 'deeds, not words', reflected its strategy of civil disobedience and disruption – violent if necessary – to further the cause of women's suffrage. In the movie *Suffragette*, the slogan becomes a mantra of defiance, transmitted from woman to woman and crossing social and economic barriers. Towards the end of the film, its main protagonist, Maud Watts, played by Carey Mulligan, inscribes the phrase on a prison wall. It is a poignant scene. Watts, a factory worker, has sacrificed what little she had to the fight – her child, her husband, her job, her home, her reputation and her health – but the audience knows she is on the right side of history. We also realise, in that moment, that the slogan is wrong. Twin instruments are set to win the vote for women: deeds *and* words. The slogan has a potency of its own.

Deeds and words, activism and advocacy: these are also the drivers of the Women's Equality Party. That advocacy takes place on doorsteps, through speeches and meetings and the media. One reason WE did so well in the May 2016 elections was because of the party's exceptional marketing and advertising support. Four months before polling day, Suki Thompson, CEO and co-founder of the marketing consultancy, Oystercatchers, invited me to participate in a panel about the lack of diversity in the advertising industry. During the debate, I talked about Betty Friedan's analysis of the role of advertising in creating the regressive mythology she dubbed the Feminine Mystique. Advertising had the potential to empower as well as to contain and control, I observed. At the end of the event, Thompson spontaneously asked the audience of invited guests if any of them would like to assist WE. People from high-profile agencies and consultancies immediately put up their hands.

WE already benefited from pro bono design work by Kate Barker and her company Dekko Advertising, and now could go into the campaign with a range of promotional tools at its disposal, from clever little digital GIFs for online sharing to billboard advertisements and campaign films. The party's head of communications, Catherine Riley, oversaw all of this and over one crazed weekend also produced our first TV spot, punctuating the 48-hour shoot with imprecations to her colleagues: 'I need a film editor!' and, more startlingly, 'I need a baby!'

Another series of films, made by the UK arm of the agency Cheil, helped to convey several complex messages in an engaging way. We had to get voters to understand the party's non-partisan approach and that we were asking for only two of their four votes in the London election, one for the city-wide ballot and one for London mayor. We were keen to showcase the diversity of our existing support base to banish any misapprehensions among voters that we were just a party for women or for a particular type of women, and to encourage the continuing development of that diversity.

The solution came in the form of a tagline: 'Give half your votes to equality. WE think that's fair.' Cheil interviewed supporters – some famous, others not – and asked them to explain their composite identities ('Hi, I'm Hugh Quarshie, half actor, half director, half Ghanaian, half British, mostly a parent') and why they would be giving half their votes to us.

In a departure for political advertising, some interviewees also revealed their support for other parties. 'Hi, I'm Lily Allen,' said the singer. 'I'm half mother, half pint-sized plucky pop princess. I'm giving half of my vote to the Labour Party and the other half to the Women's Equality Party because I'd like to see a stop to harassment and stalking.' WE had worked with Allen and the anti-stalking organisation Paladin Service to highlight the systemic failures that led to a stalker breaking into her bedroom in October 2015 after a seven-year campaign of harassment that the authorities by turns ignored and mishandled.

The stalker, Alex Gray, needed help too. After his conviction the following April, he was indefinitely detained under the Mental Health Act. He told police he had intended to stick a knife in Allen's face. If the police had looked at the accumulating evidence of the threat he posed and not, according to Allen, discarded or lost some of that evidence, then they might have spared her a terrifying ordeal and helped Gray into treatment sooner.[11] Instead, officers responding to Allen's calls sometimes appeared to shrug off her accounts of menacing messages and apparitions. That they did so is not uncommon. One in two domestic stalkers and one in ten 'stranger stalkers' act on the threats they issue, yet the response of the authorities is often sluggish, with only one per cent of reported cases ending in prosecution.

Allen took on private security and hired lawyers to push for a trial. She decided to go public about her experience because the majority of stalking victims – 80 per cent of whom are women – do not have these options. Her celebrity gave her resources but it also exacerbated widespread confusion about the nature of stalking. There is little awareness of the real dangers or the oppressive impact of stalking. It appears to many people just one of those things, the price of being a woman and in particular the price of being a woman in the public eye. Who wouldn't trade a little discomfort for the benefits of fame?

In that spirit, female celebrities routinely endure online abuse and another kind of stalking – by photographers, many unattached to news organisations. The images they snatch fetch higher fees for the worse the celebrity looks, the more compromising her situation, the more grief-stricken, the more vulnerable. She will never be the right weight or the right age. Every photograph feeds into the discourse that women exist to be looked at and appraised, and that stalking is simply the over-enthusiastic exercise of that right.

Allen first came under scrutiny with the success of her 2006 debut album, *Alright, Still*, which sold more than two million copies. She raised hopes that the music industry might be changing. She spoke her mind, styled herself in dresses with clumpy boots, and wrote her own witty material. Predictably she drew negative commentary and more insidious attention, the kind that appears to compliment a woman for having the courage of her convictions in not losing weight, and the unblinking stare of long lenses.

Forced to look at themselves through those merciless eyes, often juxtaposed with women who more closely conform to conventional ideals, females often literally shrink. Strapping amazons become wraiths, Diana Spencers and Kate Middletons become pallid princesses. Singer Park Boram underwent four years of training by her Korean record company to become one of the stars of the nation's K-pop scene. Her chirpy debut single, 'I Became Pretty', tells the story of a transformation that involved her dropping nearly 40 kilos by existing on a daily diet of a single egg and a single banana.

Let's talk about records – the music industry's records of treating female artists badly and excluding women from its top ranks. Singer-songwriter Melissa Etheridge remembers only one female executive at any of the record companies when she was looking for a deal. The industry, she says, was 'a patriarchal pyramid of corporate business.' She smiles wryly at the instructions she received: she was to surround herself on stage with male musicians to mitigate the unfortunate fact of being a woman and to hide her sexuality. 'Don't tell anybody you're a lesbian. Okay. Whatever.' Her lyrics on the first records were, as she puts it, 'gender neutral'; the lovers she depicted might have been men. She is excited by what she sees as the feminisation of the industry. 'The most famous artists – pop artists – are all women: Beyoncé, Taylor Swift, Rihanna. Humongous! Adele! They're the largest selling artists right now. And you go into country music: it's women, women, women. You can't get away from it nowadays, you can't. The time has come.'

Perhaps, but those women artists face different pressures to male artists, and the numbers in all areas of the business are still terrible. Etheridge herself has started a campaign to push Hollywood to use more female composers. Despite having picked up a Best Original Song Oscar in 2007 for 'I Need to Wake Up', the theme to the documentary *An Inconvenient Truth*, and providing songs for several other movies, she hasn't been able to break into scoring films and sees other women being turned away. In 2015, women scored only two per cent of films. The same year, the *Guardian* audited the UK's 12 largest music festivals and found that 86 per cent of performers were male. After an injury to Dave Grohl forced his band Foo Fighters to cancel an appearance at Glastonbury in 2015, Florence + the Machine stepped in, becoming the first female-fronted band this century to headline at Glastonbury, and, up to that point, only the sixth female-fronted band or female performer to get a top slot at any time during the festival's 45-year history. In 2016, the music festival Lollapalooza achieved a mediocre best among the big US festivals by fielding female artists at 37 per cent of the total of performers, compared to ten per cent at Ultra. And in August 2016, a piece about the disappearance of women from the country music charts noted that only seven artists in the top 50 playlist for US country radio that month were women. Even as the internet chips away at their revenues, record companies remain patriarchal pyramids, dominated by men with definite ideas about what will sell and how women should present themselves to sell it.

'Being told how to look is about being a product, and I don't want to be a product,' said the singer Adele. Her intransigence in maintaining a normal body weight hasn't stopped her from racking up hit after hit. Two of her albums are among the UK's bestselling records of all time. Beyoncé has seized control of her own image and created space for black women to define themselves in their own terms and with their own aesthetics. She hasn't done so without attracting criticism, whether of the can-she-be-a-feminist-when-she-dances-in-her-knickers variety, or more cerebral attacks, such as the response of legendary American feminist bell hooks to Beyoncé's 2016 visual album *Lemonade*. This wasn't, said hooks, about liberation, it was about commodification: 'From slavery to the present day, black female bodies, clothed and unclothed, have been bought and sold.'[12] Beyoncé's supporters rallied. 'For centuries, black women's bodies and the corresponding images were placed in service to white supremacy... So even if *Lemonade*'s employment of black women's bodies to sell a product is, as hooks declares, "certainly not radical or revolutionary", the concept of producing such images for the benefit of other black women is,' replied the writer and blogger LaSha.[13]

Lily Allen too sought to define herself rather than letting the media and music industry define her. She sustained injuries in the process. Aged 22, she posted on Myspace. She had seen photographs of herself next to the model Kate Moss, the singer Cheryl Cole had called her a 'chick with a dick', and now she felt 'fat and ugly' and tempted to investigate cosmetic surgery. The next day she recanted: 'I know it's a silly way to feel and I am incredibly proud of myself and my achievements over the past year. There are so many good things about my life. I really am incredibly lucky. I guess it shows how much of an effect the media can have on us young ladies.'[14] The paparazzi continued to document her body through the birth of two children and fluctuating body shape. An unintended irony of her video for the 2014 single 'Hard Out Here', which satirises this experience, is that Allen has become thinner and therefore closer to the approved ideal.

The video opens with the singer on an operating table, as cosmetic surgeons drain away stomach fat under the direction of her oafish manager. He later joins her as she twerks with six backing dancers, four of them black. The camera, echoing the start of *Lost in Translation*, frames a disembodied set of buttocks, this time in furious motion. It's angry and funny like much of Allen's output. Lena Dunham, actor-writer-producer and creator of the US TV comedy *Girls*, loved the video, tweeting: 'Aw hell yeah @lilyallen give 'em the business <3.' Caitlin Moran, feminist and author of *How to Be a Woman*, took to Twitter to declare its dig at Robin Thicke's '*Blurred Lines*' – the catchy little ballad questioning the need for sexual consent that had topped charts in 25 countries a few months earlier – 'pretty much the bad-assedest thing to happen in pop this year'.

But not everyone shared their enthusiasm. 'It is meant to be a critique of popular culture and consumerism but employs and denigrates black female bodies to do so and elevate her status as a white woman,' a blogger called Mikael Owunna declared. Columnists expressed similar views. Allen responded with a statement entitled *Privilege, Superiority and Misconceptions*, provided in full in this footnote.[15] She had not requested black dancers and would hardly have sent them home for being black. 'The video is meant to be a lighthearted satirical video that deals with objectification of women within modern pop culture,' she wrote. 'It has nothing to do with race.'

This defence did little to defuse the controversy. Her critics jumped on the implicit notion that a white person could decide the validity of the experience of racism. The debate was further complicated by the conflicted reactions of feminism to rap music. In the words of the writer and cultural critic Ayesha A. Siddiqi, rap 'owns a unique history soundtracking the triumph of financial success in a country that long barred black Americans from that success.'[16]

It's hard out here for sure. The debate that followed the release of the film *Suffragette* was similarly tangled – and there's an irony there, or more accurately, an echo, because producer Alison Owen is Allen's mother. Owen and the film-making team she assembled focused on the British fight for the vote and the class divisions that complicated it. They knew they were tackling a history that hadn't been told at all, but the film-makers couldn't redress the imbalance in telling female stories with one film. They had to make choices, and some critics questioned those choices. Perhaps the film-makers should have rated diversity as highly as historical accuracy. The creative industries often reject calls to implement diversity quotas as a restriction on creativity, but Owen is a proponent of such measures. Real figures such as Princess Sophia Duleep Singh, daughter of the exiled Maharaja of Punjab and the subject of a detailed biography by Anita Anand, and other women of South Asian descent who joined the fray, might have been written into the script. Otherwise, the women's movement in Britain, like the wider population, was largely white – in 1841, just 0.25 per cent of the population was foreign-born, rising to 2.6 per cent by 1931 – and it was also infused with mixed messages around race.

On the other side of the Atlantic, the debate around race within the women's movement was overt and urgent. The battles for civil rights and women's rights sometimes marched in lockstep, at other times descended into infighting. Harriet Tubman, born into slavery and an ardent abolitionist who undertook daring missions to rescue others in slavery, became a leading advocate for women's suffrage. Sojourner Truth, whose life followed a similar trajectory, in 1851 delivered a speech at the Ohio Women's Rights

Convention pointing out the inadequacy of arguments that painted women as too fragile to vote. White women might be helped into coaches. Black women could expect no help at all. 'Look at me! Look at my arm! I have ploughed and planted, and gathered into barns, and no man could head me! And ain't I a woman? I could work as much and eat as much as a man – when I could get it – and bear the lash as well! And ain't I a woman? I have borne thirteen children, and seen most all sold off to slavery, and when I cried out with my mother's grief, none but Jesus heard me! And ain't I a woman?'[17]

Perhaps the most inglorious passage in the history of the women's movement saw white suffragists in northern states attempting to appeal to white women in the segregationist South. 'White supremacy will be strengthened, not weakened, by women's suffrage,' said Carrie Chapman Catt, president of the National American Woman Suffrage Association, and founder of the League of Women Voters and the International Alliance of Women.[18]

In the UK, speaking to a population riven by different divisions, Emmeline Pankhurst often invoked the vocabulary of US politics, most famously in a 1913 speech. 'Know that women, once convinced that they are doing what is right, that their rebellion is just, will go on, no matter what the difficulties, no matter what the dangers, so long as there is a woman alive to hold up the flag of rebellion,' she said. 'I would rather be a rebel than a slave.'

That sentiment was challenged by erstwhile supporters during her own lifetime after she joined the Conservative Party in 1926, motivated, according to her daughter Christabel, by her belief in Empire. When, 102 years after the speech, the phrase, truncated, made its way onto T-shirts worn by *Suffragette*'s leading actors during a promotional photoshoot for the London listings magazine, *Time Out*, many white British eyes read it as the liberationist statement Pankhurst intended. But for some, especially in America, there was a different and disturbing resonance. The population and troops of the pro-slavery Confederacy were known as 'rebels' and they fought to preserve a system that profited from slavery.

For critics such as academic and author Carol H. Hood, that history trumped the historical context of the quote. 'History or not, Pankhurst or not, it is your responsibility to at all times consider the context and meaning of the words you put out into the universe,' she declared. 'All that to say, I'm *sorry-not-sorry*, dear white women of women's suffrage, you don't get to be rhetorical slaves.'[19]

The platitude 'there's no such thing as bad publicity' was seldom less apt. P. T. Barnum didn't actually utter the phrase for which he is most celebrated, and surely would have disowned it after watching the firestorm that engulfed *Suffragette*. It didn't derail the film's progress in the UK, where positive reviews attracted enthusiastic audiences, not least among supporters of the Women's Equality Party. Alison Owen and distributors Pathé gave WE a special fundraising showing of the film; WE promoted it to members by organising discounted entry at a group of independent cinemas. James Bond inflicted far more damage on *Suffragette* hopes, muscling into the October 2015 release schedules unexpectedly and forcing Pathé to concertina the promotional schedule to avoid a head-to-head contest with the behemoth, *Spectre*.

It was in the US that *Suffragette* felt the backlash, losing a slice of its potential audience before it arrived to a mixed reception and limited release. Tipped for awards before the controversy, it instead found itself cold-shouldered. The experience left Owen, who had struggled to make the film, bruised. 'It was hard to go to bed feeling like you've made a very socially conscious film about the women's movement and to wake up feeling like you're a member of the Ku Klux Klan,' she says. She understands why this happened, and rues the promotional stunt, but remains defiant. Slavery in the form of forced labour and human trafficking is a global phenomenon, she points out; women and girls are disproportionately the victims. 'America has itself become the imperial power,' she says. 'It always judges everything in its own terms.' She isn't sure the film could or should have been done differently. Just like the women who make it to prominent positions – including her own daughter Lily Allen – the movie was always going to be found wanting.

As the first film to address subject matter sacred to so many, yet known (like all of women's history) by so few, *Suffragette* staggered under the weight of hopes and expectations and exposition. It had to work as entertainment and to explain a series of complex issues and events within its limited screen time. People wanted the movie to do and say everything, to make up for all the movies that haven't been made. Until there are more films about women, and more women in the public eye, these films and these women will be judged far more harshly than their male counterparts, and often by women.

Nobody expected *Suffragette* to storm the box office barricades, but its rough ride did nothing to dispel concerns about funding projects about and by women. Owen sees additional cause for pessimism in the changing economics of movies. 'When I came into the film industry, the economics were that you had to raise 70 per cent of your budget out of America and 30 per cent out of the rest of the world. Seventy–thirty, and that has changed over my working lifetime to 60–40, 50–50, 40–60 and now it's pretty much 30–70: 70 per cent the rest of the world and 30 per cent America. So, just at the point where we were starting to be able to make feminist movies – movies about women for Channel 4, and sell them to America – suddenly, the economic structure of films has changed and you have to be able to get at least half your budget out of China and Taiwan and India, and they don't want to see a film about the changing of the abortion laws in Texas.'

Owen says this is because these countries have less progressive views on gender equality. Producer Lynda Obst adds a different spin. International markets are also going local, looking to create more of their own content. The day that we speak, she is lunching with the Chinese–US joint venture, Oriental DreamWorks, to discuss a rom-com made specifically for the Chinese market. She believes that other forces are driving positive change for women in the film industry. She urges would-be directors to put their work on the web, though obviously that raises questions about how such work might be financed, especially for people trying to break into film-making from poorer backgrounds. She also credits Disney's 2013 animated movie *Frozen* with a revolutionary impact in creating a new feminised appetite. 'I call it the post-*Frozen* market,' she says. 'It's going to be the most powerful market ever. I think it's something for all of us to prepare for, all creative women to prepare for. The post-*Frozen* market is going to want empowered women, empowered girls, girls' adventures. The stories that haven't been told, right? Great girls' literature, great girls' special effects.'

She pauses. 'Look at *Frozen*, that was about two women and they saved the guy and then they went out into the future without him. It's going to be a whole different model, isn't it? And that affected girls who were – what? – between six and twelve. Pretty much the biggest animated movie of all time. That will do to those girls what *Cinderella* un-did to us. It's just incredibly powerful.'

Would it be nitpicking to point out that *Frozen*'s dialogue is split 57 per cent to 43 per cent in favour of male characters, despite its two leads being female?[20] That those female leads are pale-skinned, button-nosed sylphs, and princesses to boot? That Princess Anna fits the stereotype of the lovable klutz, while Princess Elsa, in learning to control her own, frightening poten-cies, evolves, literally, into an ice queen? Perhaps. At least they are female and at least they are out there, on screens and billboards. They have agency even if only within Arendelle, still a kingdom after the ascent of its queen.

Consider the alternatives, the movies that in Obst's phrase 'un-did' feminism: *Pretty Woman*, *Fatal Attraction*, *Twilight*, *Bride Wars*, *He's Just Not that into You*, *Grease*, *The Little Mermaid*, all those men-only action movies, the crowds in which females are strangely absent. Or think about women's sports. Sportsmen routinely are paid far more than their female counterparts, just as Bradley Cooper and Christian Bale (stepson of Gloria Steinem no less) earned a higher share of the profits of *American Hustle* than their co-stars Jennifer Lawrence and Amy Adams.[21] Male actors tend to appear in higher-grossing movies. Apologists for the gender pay gap in sport give similar reasons. Male sports stars earn more because they play to bigger audiences. 'If I was a lady player, I'd go down every night on my knees and thank God that Roger Federer and Rafa Nadal were born because they have carried this sport,' said Raymond Moore, the CEO of the US Indian Wells Tennis Garden, host to the Indian Wells tournament.[22] Yet female sports are rarely given prime-time slots, and so lack the means to grow audiences. A filing in March 2016 to the Equal Employment Opportunity Commission on behalf of five stars of the women's national soccer team, holders of the World Cup, claimed the women's team had earned almost $20 million more in revenues in the previous year and had been paid four times less.[23] The men's team had been knocked out in the second round of the World Cup. The counter blast from US Soccer, responsible for both teams, pointed out differences in the pay structures and said the men generated higher revenues over a four-year time frame assisted by the fact that many of their matches are against teams that field internationally famous footballers, boosting TV ratings still further.[24]

This logic loop – the process that sees women given less exposure than men on the basis of ratings or revenues that cannot rise without greater exposure – helps to explain why the media, in all its forms, more often reinforces gender stereotypes than challenges them. Here's something PT Barnum really did say: 'Without promotion, something terrible happens – nothing.'

Now, since this chapter deals with Hollywood, let us ride off into a hopeful sunset together. *Suffragette* offers no neat resolutions, no heartening triumphs for its characters, but before the final credits roll, a timeline unfurls of women's suffrage across the world, from New Zealand which gave women the vote in 1893 to Australia 1902, Latvia 1918, France 1944, Italy 1945, Japan 1946, Tonga 1960, Switzerland 1971 and Western Samoa

1990. The message is twofold. Equalia has been a long time coming and remains a long way off. Yet progress is possible. The impact of this sequence on cinemagoers is palpable. Audiences watch in silence broken only by furtive sobs and sniffles. They emerge fired up to carry on the work of the suffragettes, finish the job. Media can be a force for change.

If that ending isn't happy enough for you, here are two more. Alison Owen's persistence paid off on another of her projects. *Tulip Fever* escaped from Development Hell. The final version stars Alicia Vikander and Dane DeHaan, directed by *The Other Boleyn Girl*'s Justin Chadwick. And in 2016, Sandi became the first woman to host a major comedy game show on British television, *QI*.

Chapter Eight: This should be everyone's business

IN 2010, AUSTRALIA'S Sex Discrimination Commissioner, Elizabeth Broderick, summoned eight of Australia's leading businessmen to explain themselves. Glen Boreham of IBM, Gordon Cairns of Macquarie Group and Macquarie Bank (and former head of food company Lion Nathan), Alan Joyce of Qantas, commercial lawyer Kevin McCann, Stephen Roberts of Citi, Giam Swiegers of Deloitte, David Thodey of Telstra, and Stephen Fitzgerald of Goldman Sachs had all spoken up for women and she wanted to know why.

'The reasons were good,' remembers Fitzgerald. 'One person said he had twins, a son and a daughter, and he couldn't understand why the opportunity set for his daughter would be any different than for his son. Someone else said that they were coming at it more from a commercial point of view.'[1] Study after study underlined something direct experience had already taught them: that companies perform better if they recruit and retain women. Fifteen years' worth of data from the S&P 1500 index of US stocks indicated that 'female representation in top management brings informational and social diversity benefits to the top management team, enriches the behaviours exhibited by managers throughout the firm, and motivates women in middle management.'[2]

La Trobe University's seven-year analysis of Australia's largest 500 companies found a 'positive and significant association' between financial performance and the presence of women in boardrooms. Goldman Sachs' own research highlighted the wider economic benefits that could result from boosting women's participation in the workforce: an increase of 11 per cent in Australia's GDP, with the US in line for a 10 per cent uplift, the Eurozone for 14 per cent and Japan for a whopping 21 per cent.[3] The research also pointed to a risk. Australia's workforce wasn't large enough to sustain its economic growth if women remained sidelined. 'I think in the end, everyone recognised both reasons: it's commercial and it's fairness,' says Fitzgerald, drily.

On neither point was Australian business winning. The men convened by Broderick had been trying to nurture female talent in their own organisations. Their first point of agreement was that they weren't doing well enough. 'We had policies and programmes for everything,' says Fitzgerald. 'We had great, as we say, "programming excellence". If there was a problem, we had a programme. And none of it worked. None of it really worked, because we didn't have the culture to support it.'

Broderick's pitch at the meeting was simple. The business leaders should use their positions not only to advocate for women, but to forge a path to greater equality as the founding members of Male Champions of Change (MCC). Fitzgerald can't quite restrain a shudder at the bombastic name Broderick chose, but the group has worked to earn the designation. Rather than jealously guarding business secrets in the name of competition, they pool knowledge, not only among themselves, but as a public resource. They report back on their failures as well as their successes, publish those results annually, and invite fellow MCC members in to their offices to survey business practices and conduct interviews with employees who might be less candid with their own bosses.

There were ground rules. This was an initiative that could only be effective if the CEOs put their weight behind it. They must not palm it off to their HR departments or diversity directors. They had to attend the meetings themselves and put in the hours themselves.

Some measures the MCC adopted could be mistaken for the sort of cosmetic expediencies that plainspoken Australians call polishing a turd. All members signed a pledge refusing to sponsor or participate in debates unless the organisers ensured gender balance. As Fitzgerald explains, even apparently small moves like this do matter. 'One of the things we looked at was that people who had profile, external profile, got promoted.'

The Male Champions had bigger ideas too. Telstra's David Thodey, in grappling with how to create the flexibility his workforce needed in order to manage caregiving duties and other aspects of domestic life, realised that designating some jobs as flexible was counterproductive in a culture that venerated presenteeism – spending long hours at work. Flexibility was equated with lesser commitment and hence lower status. However, a lack of flexibility deterred female applicants. The answer was to make job flexibility the default, whether in terms of hours or working locations, for all 35,000 employees. All the other MCC members picked up the idea for their own companies. Qantas provided the template for another MCC policy – 'Supplier Multiplier' – that pushes suppliers to take steps to improve gender equality in their workforces as a precondition for continued business. More recently the MCC has looked into the ways in which domestic violence impacts the workplace. 'Male Champions is about changing a system; it's not about fixing women to fit with the system. It's changing a system that was established by men and was run by men and largely benefitted men,' says Fitzgerald.

Paid parental leave, introduced in Australia in 2011, has helped to increase female representation in senior management, but 57 per cent of businesses in Australia and New Zealand still have no female senior managers at all, and only 13 per cent of senior managerial roles are held by women. The Australian Institute of Company Directors set a target for Australia's largest companies: by the end of 2018, 30 per cent of board directors should be women. The companies are unlikely to hit those targets. Two years ahead of the deadline, 20 companies still had no women at all on their boards.

That's the thing about voluntary targets. Businesses miss them, and incur no penalty for doing so. They also aim low. In 2011, the UK government set a target for the FTSE 100 companies: that they should raise the proportion of female board members from the then miserly 12.5 per cent to 25 per cent. Boards did reach that threshold by the end of 2015, but could easily drop below it again as women stand down without any guarantee of female successors coming through the ranks. Moreover, 91 per cent of the board members who are female are non-executive directors. They aren't actually involved in the day-to-day running of the companies.

Opponents of quotas claim candidates under such a system will be picked because of their sex and not because they have the skills and experience. This is surely true. Unofficial quotas mean that globally, just 24 per cent of senior roles in business are held by women; 33 per cent of companies have no female representation at all in their upper levels.[4]

The oil business is all about finding natural resources and keeping pipelines flowing – and some prominent companies are doing an appalling job of both when it comes to female talent. Consider the executive committees of some of the world's largest oil companies. The executive boards of BP, Exxon and Shell include no women, Total's and Chevron's have one woman, Gazprom's two.

Just two women sit on the 11-member executive committee of Norwegian oil and gas enterprise, Statoil. This statistic is eye-catching because Norway has passed legislation to level the playing field for women, including, in 2003, mandatory quotas of 40 per cent for female board directors. Businesses had two years to balance their boards. After that they faced automatic delisting. Statoil met the requirement and then overshot it: five of its ten board directors are women. However, changes at the top cannot, on their own, plug a leaky pipeline. Since Italy's Eni appointed Emma Marcegaglia chair of its board in 2014, the company's percentage of female employees has dropped, though the numbers of women in middle and senior management have risen slightly. At Statoil, improvements below board level are slow. 'We continue to strive to increase the number of female managers through our development programmes, and in 2015 despite the overall reduction of 181 leadership positions, we increased the share of women in management by 0.5 per cent,' said the Statoil annual report for that year. One female Statoil manager told me: 'For someone like me in my stage of my career and reasonably senior in the company, I look at the senior and corporate executive level and women are still not sufficiently represented.'

Similar patterns occur across Norwegian businesses and sectors. Critics say it shows that quotas catapulted underqualified women to the top, leaving the tiers below underpopulated. They also argue that the law creates a small elite of women with multiple board directorships, so-called 'golden skirts'. However, evidence proves them wrong on both counts. Norway's male directors remain twice as likely to sit on more than one board. The country's female board directors have higher academic qualifications than their male peers and a broader range of experience even though there are fewer female candidates with directly equivalent experience of running companies because of course women have been excluded from that activity.

Quotas ended female exclusion from boards but not at key operational levels. That's why the Women's Equality Party proposes that the UK introduces short-term quotas, not just for boards but also for executive committees. Progress must be audited, and the higher-level appointments accompanied by efforts at every level of the companies to address the working practices that drive women away from leadership.

Belgium, France, Germany, Iceland, Italy, Malaysia, the Netherlands and Spain have followed Norway's example, introducing some form of mandated quotas for business boards. The European Union continues to debate an EU-wide measure. Among the fiercest critics are women in business. Having overcome so many disadvantages to succeed, they resist making the path easier for other women, not least because they fear the status of all women will suffer. The female Statoil manager is queasy about quotas. 'There's always a question mark: well, why are you there actually? Is it because you're good at your job? Or is it because you're a woman? There's always that ammunition that people around you have.'[5]

She is right that quotas can be used to belittle, to suggest that candidates have been selected because of their gender, not their skills. It may undermine the confidence of the women who get through that way too. Suspecting you've been appointed for the wrong reasons isn't easy to live with. I discovered why I got my first job in journalism, at *the Economist*, when my married, older boss slipped a six-page declaration of passion into my handbag. Still I'd rather have been hired for the wrong reasons than not hired at all, and I wouldn't have risen within the profession if I'd lacked ability. Lucy Marcus, the founder and CEO of Marcus Venture Consulting, who has a portfolio of high-flown positions across business, media and academia, joined the board of the Italian infrastructure company Atlantia after Italy adopted quotas. She scoffs at the idea that quotas diminish the quality of female board members. 'Put me on your board because I'm a woman,' she says. 'Keep me on your board because I'm fucking amazing.'[6]

Quotas cannot create gender equality. What they do is to start a process that brings in more diversity, dilutes groupthink, focuses on winning wars rather than battles, connects with customer bases and breaks the vicious cycle that sees men in positions of power restocking their boards and executive committees with men because, they say, they can't find women with board or executive committee experience.

More women in business means businesses perform better. That's true of big corporations and of the smaller enterprises that are the bedrock of many economies. Research by Barclays and Cambridge University conducted in Germany, Singapore, the UK and US found female entrepreneurs were less likely to claim their companies were prospering than their male counterparts even though their companies on average reported higher pre-tax profits. British prosperity depends on female-led small and medium-sized enterprises.[7] A 2016 study by Founders4Schools, an organisation that brings business people into schools to inspire pupils to become the entrepreneurs of the future, found that women-led SMEs were turning over £500,000 more per year than their male-led equivalents and growing at a median rate of 30 per cent. The German economy relies on and thrives because of its Mittelstand. A fifth of the country's SMEs are now run by women and that proportion is rising as increasing numbers of women start businesses. Yet across the world companies of all sizes and many sectors, even those serving mixed or even exclusively female customer bases, remain male-dominated. Only 12 per cent of top executives and five per cent of board members of the world's largest consumer goods companies are women.[8] The hospitality industry's workforce is 60 per cent female yet just six per cent of board directors are women; in the UK the industry's gender pay gap stretches wider than a glutton's mouth, at 18 per cent, above the national average. Does that impact business performance? Jeremy King believes so. With Chris Corbin he is co-founder and director of Corbin & King, a restaurant and hotels group including some of London's best-known eateries. 'The aim for the company – which is quite hard in catering but it's not impossible, and we've a way to go – is fifty-fifty [men and women],' he says. He adds: 'My definition of a great restaurant is where a single woman feels they can eat in that restaurant comfortably. That's a civilised restaurant. And you need it in the personnel as well.'

He links the greater gender balance in his company to better commercial outcomes, not least because half of his customers are women. He also credits the rising numbers of female staff with moderating male behaviours. 'We don't have to have the biggest antlers and fight it out that way,' he says. 'A very male way of arguing is to feel that you've only really won an argument if the other person admits that you're right.'[9] This supports Christine Lagarde's comment: that Lehman Sisters might have done better than

Lehman Brothers. Some research does suggest that women tend to be more cautious and questioning than men. John Coates, a Wall Street trader turned Cambridge University neuroscientist, has studied the so-called winner effect, the testosterone boost a male animal gets in the wild when he wins a fight. The increased levels of hormone give him an advantage in his next fight, and perhaps for the fight after that. Eventually, he picks one fight too many and dies. Male traders experience similar hormone rushes, he asserts. Women do not. 'When it comes to making and losing money, women may be less hormonally reactive than men,' he wrote in his 2012 book *The Hour Between Dog and Wolf.* 'Their greater numbers among risk-takers in the financial world could therefore help dampen the volatility.'

Another possibility is that the participation of women would alter the women themselves. Brains are plastic and change with use. Hormones don't only influence behaviour; behaviour influences the production of hormones. Women navigating male work environments by echoing male behaviours develop higher testosterone levels and in one experiment the exercise of power alone, irrespective if wielded in a way the researchers deemed stereotypically male, boosted testosterone in women.[10] For now, however, in our unequal societies, the presence of women can moderate risk-taking because women are brought up to question their abilities and are therefore less inclined to assume they know all the answers. Halla Tómasdóttir and Kristin Pétursdóttir founded the financial services and private equity company Auður Capital shortly before the Icelandic financial system came crashing down around them. The business and their clients emerged largely unscathed. 'Women are willing to ask stupid questions. We want to understand. We won't take risks we don't understand, so we ask: what is sub-prime? Who'll pay these loans back?' said Halla.

Greater numbers of women on staff also signal success in recruiting from a wider talent pool. For every industry, and not just the oil business, this means building and maintaining pipelines, starting with a fair selection process that ensures carefully worded job adverts through to measures to combat unconscious bias on the part of people reading applications to the structure of the interviewing process. Women are socialised to hold back, underplay achievements. Jeremy King has encountered resistance from his female employees to promotion; they tell him they're not ready. 'You'd never hear that from a man,' he says.

In overcoming this training – if we 'lean in' as Sheryl Sandberg, Chief Operating Officer of Facebook exhorts women in her book of the same name to do – we risk triggering negative reactions. 'Women are perceived as too soft or too tough but never just right,' one large-scale study observed. 'Women leaders face higher standards and lower rewards than men leaders … Women leaders are perceived as competent or liked, but rarely both.'[11]

Most corporate cultures are hierarchical, and attitudes filter downwards. This can create environments that are toxic for women. A former equity-fund manager remembers how a takeover of a female-friendly company by another, more patriarchal, institution played out for its female employees. 'A very good friend of mine who is female and head of a team was treated extremely badly by certain people, and they got away with it, really. There was one particular occasion where somebody, this man, was on the phone to a broker – so this was a comment made in public, not even within the team – and he referred to her as a "fucking bitch".'[12]

Male champions can stamp on sexism and misogyny but they will never be able to lift us in their strong arms and deposit us in Equalia. We need more women of stature as well as – or in place of – the men advocating for women of stature. Space in Equalian boardrooms is likely to be finite, just as it is now. One important way for men to champion change is by making more room for women.

This was an implicit finding of *Empowering Productivity: Harnessing the Talents of Women in Financial Services*, a review conducted for the UK government by Jayne-Anne Gadhia, CEO of Virgin Money. Her 2016 report regretted that women held only 14 per cent of seats on the executive committees of British-based financial services companies and recommended linking bosses' bonuses to their achievements in promoting gender balance. 'I always thought I don't want positive discrimination, and I don't want to be seen as a shining light for the feminist movement,' she told *Management Today*. 'Then when I delved into all the material…'[13]

What she discovered dismayed her, not only because women were faring so poorly in the finance sector, but because the sector was, as a result, far weaker than it could be. There isn't just 'a moral imperative to improve diversity and equality, there is also a strong economic imperative,' she told the audience at the inaugural party conference of the Women's Equality Party in November 2016.

Her keynote speech sandwiched her between speakers whose experiences and perspectives looked superficially quite divergent – the popstar Sinitta, who talked about discrimination in the music business, and Gudrun Schyman, the co-founder of Sweden's Feminist Initiative. Yet for all that their messages came in different packaging, the core thrust echoed the WE motto: 'equality is better for everyone.'

The problem, as Gadhia has found since publishing the report, is persuading men where their own best interest lies. 'Sometimes men say to me, "This is outrageous, why are you giving women our jobs?",' she told an interviewer. 'I did a presentation a few months ago and at the end a man said: "I feel really uncomfortable that you're saying that jobs should be made available for talented women. What about talented men?"'[14]

A key task for male champions – including the Male Champions of Change – must be to help other men to understand how misplaced that question looks in a world in which men predominate. Another is to lead by example, not only by creating better gender balance in their organisations but in helping to ensure their successors are not all in their image. Since Male Champions of Change was founded, several original members have moved on to other jobs. Stephen Fitzgerald now lives and works mainly in the UK. His successor at Goldman Sachs took on the MCC role and Fitzgerald continues as an international ambassador for the group. Giam Swiegers left Deloitte Australia for pastures new. He was followed at Deloitte's by Cindy Hook. She is thus far the only woman appointed to head one of the organisations signed up to the MCC since its inception.

The efforts of the MCC members to promote gender equality have so far proved most effective in the lower tiers of their enterprises. In 2015, all but two achieved improvements in female representation in middle management. If the other measures they are pioneering to plug leaks from their pipelines of female talent hold fast, at least some of these middle managers will ascend.

Yet progress could be retarded or reversed if an incoming CEO doesn't buy into the MCC's manifesto. External factors also impact outcomes. In 2013, the Liberal Party's Tony Abbott became Prime Minister. He had views about women. He recommended a Liberal candidate for her 'sex appeal', then sought to brush off criticism, dismissing his revealing gaffe as a 'daggy dad moment'. He told a bemused audience during a TV debate: 'I think there does need to be give and take on both sides, and this idea that sex is kind of a woman's right to absolutely withhold, just as the idea that sex is a man's right to demand, I think they both need to be moderated, so to speak.'[15] These attitudes affected the priorities of Abbott's administration. Three government departments that had signed up to Male Champions of Change resigned from the group.

The MCC was formed just before Julia Gillard became Australia's first and only female Prime Minister. She took over from Kevin Rudd, her Labor colleague, after he exhausted the support of the parliamentary party and as the country wrestled with the consequences of the global downturn sparked by America's addiction to subprime mortgages and the subsequent banking crisis. In Iceland, Jóhanna Sigurðardóttir was already cleaning up the wreckage left by the same storms bursting the nation's bubble economy. Neither Gillard nor Jóhanna survived long enough in office to win thanks for their efforts. In 2013, Gillard was ousted by Rudd, who claimed he would make a better fist of steering Labor and the country. He lost the general election three months later to Tony Abbott.

Gillard fell over the 'glass cliff', a term coined by British academics Michelle Ryan and Alex Haslam, who in 2004 sifted through the performance records of FTSE 100 companies and observed that 'during a period of overall stock-market decline those companies who appointed women to their boards were more likely to have experienced consistently bad performance in the preceding five months than those who appointed men. These results expose an additional, largely invisible, hurdle that women need to overcome in the workplace.'[16] Women smash through glass ceilings only to find themselves staring down into a ravine.

A 2013 study looking back at a decade of female CEOs at the world's 2,500 largest public companies, and comparing their trajectories against those of their male counterparts, noted two key differences. Firstly, the women were more likely to have been hired from outside the company, rather than being promoted from within, and secondly, more of them had been forced out of office.[17] One possible interpretation is that the women had been brought in at times of maximum risk, preserving the reputations of internal hopefuls, who bide their time until the companies stabilise. A second report, analysing 15 years of transitions at the top of Fortune 500 companies, added weight to this theory. 'Occupational minorities – defined as white women, and men and women of colour – are more likely than white men to be promoted to CEO of weakly performing firms,' the authors concluded. 'Though we find no significant differences in tenure length between occupational minorities and white men, we find that when the firm performance declines during the tenure of occupational minority CEOs, these leaders are likely to be replaced by white men. We term this phenomenon the "saviour effect".'[18] Women ride to the rescue but it is the white men who follow them who are hailed as saviours.

In 2011, the media conglomerate Time Warner hired Laura Lang to run its publishing division, Time Inc. The previous incumbent, a man, had left almost a year earlier. Lang was an outsider – the CEO of marketing and digital agency, Digitas. She hadn't worked for Time Warner companies or racked up experience in magazine publishing. No matter, she would bring a different skill set to the job, the trade journal *Advertising Age* reported: 'digital expertise and a tough but collaborative leadership style … People who have worked with Ms Lang said she's calm, consultative and well-liked by her team, for whom she sets clear goals.'[19]

During her April 2012 visit to the London offices of Time Inc., Lang's calm and clarity were evident. She had already grasped the fundamentals of the business and the intricacies of the task she had taken on. At a meeting with the heads of the EMEA (Europe, Middle East and Africa) division of *TIME* and its sister publication *Fortune*, she asked informed questions about the issues making life difficult for all print media and in particular for the news titles under her purview. As *TIME*'s Europe Editor, the only senior member of editorial present, I was happy to be the bearer of bad news because there was an upside too. Our division feared cutbacks in jobs and investment might be applied without proper understanding of our continuing strengths, considerable untapped potential or appreciation for the cultures and markets in which we operated. The view from the executive floors of Time Inc.'s famous Time-Life building in New York, good though it was, didn't extend as far as our neck of the woods.

The failure of Lehman Brothers had delivered a double hit: the bank had been a tenant in the Time-Life building and its demise signalled a rapid contraction in the kinds of advertising campaigns that underpinned *TIME* and *Fortune*'s profitability: banking, travel, upmarket brands. Management in recent years had described ever more frantic circles, clucking 'the sky is falling', even though the crisis enveloping our titles and our industry had a lengthy gestation.

As a young journalist at the *Economist*, I had spent many press nights at the typesetter, proofing pages under the gaze of yellowing nipples that stared out of the ancient girlie calendars and centrefolds decorating the walls. Hot metal printing would soon look as alluring as those nipples. Computers replaced typewriters, and newspapers and magazines could be laid out and composed electronically. Print workers lost out, but journalism gained: lower costs, greater speed and flexibility and, with the evolution of the internet, whole new methods of communicating and conducting research.

The money that funded that research mostly came from advertising, with the cost of buying a newspaper or magazine generally just covering production costs. The digital revolution eroded this model from both ends. Publishers everywhere made a series of huge miscalculations. Like daggy dads throwing shapes at a school disco, they kept trying new digital moves without ever understanding that analogue traditions wouldn't translate directly into digital practices. They convinced themselves that online advertising, which offered a more targeted and measurable alternative to print, would simply replace the revenues lost from print advertising. That never happened because online advertising was always cheaper than print and anyway customers could place ads with an ever-expanding range of digital platforms. The increasing lure of online reading depressed print sales, while the availability of so much free information – whatever its quality – helped to popularise the myth that good journalism need not cost anything.

By the time Lang took her seat in London's eighth-floor meeting room, the picture looked challenging for print. Lang's outsider eye and digital expertise, far from being a disadvantage, seemed positives. *TIME* still had extraordinary assets: one of the most global of all news brands; a reputation for delivering quality journalism that was also accessible, a history of careful fact-checking; the iconic logo and the pull of a *TIME* cover that could open doors to pretty much any head of state or Hollywood star. This legacy had to be preserved, but everything else was up for grabs. Lang knew her job was to manage change, not to preserve the status quo.

In December of 2012, she promoted Martha Nelson to be Time Inc.'s Editor-in-Chief, the first woman to hold the role in the company's 90-year history. 'Martha is the ideal leader to step into this role at this point in our company's evolution,' Lang said. 'She is a creative thinker with a visceral understanding of the consumer. And as we move to a multi-platform strategy, her strong consumer focus along with her broad understanding of both print and digital media will help ensure we make that transition successfully.'

On 13 February 2013, Lang received an unwelcome early Valentine. *Fortune* published a scoop briefed by an unnamed Time Warner insider, revealing that Time Warner had entered negotiations to sell most Time Inc. titles, including *People* and *InStyle,* to Meredith Corporation, a publisher known for cheap-and-cheerful women's titles. The only magazines not on the block were *TIME*, *Fortune* and *Sports Illustrated.*

It wasn't clear that anybody had told Lang about the negotiations. In any case, her days were numbered. The Meredith sale foundered and plans were made to spin off the whole of Time Inc. from Time Warner. On 22 July, all Time Inc. staff received an email from Jeff Bewkes, the head of Time Warner: 'I'm very pleased to tell you that Joe Ripp, a veteran of our company and an accomplished media executive, will be returning to lead Time Inc. as CEO as we're preparing for it to become an independent publicly traded company.'

If Lang made a sound as she fell from the glass cliff, we didn't hear her. Her successor, a Time Inc. insider from the soles of his shiny shoes to the tips of his silver hair, was already strutting the stage, chest puffed out like an amorous pigeon, explaining his plans to save us.

By the time he stepped down in September 2016, after what he termed a 'health incident', the company's share price had fallen, from a peak of $23.51 after the spin-off to $14.32 on the morning of the announcement. There have been rumours of renewed interest from Meredith.

The point is not that women are better leaders than men. It is that women are not judged on the same terms as men or afforded the same opportunities. The loving cups on offer to women often turn out to be poisoned chalices.

And here's something I have seen at first hand, over many decades as an employee and, for more than half of that time, in senior roles. No matter how far a woman in the workplace bends, whether she's leaning in or simply yielding, she remains vulnerable. It is tempting to ignore the smaller challenges. It is easier to play at being one of the boys. To do so often enables discrimination to continue. The key to effective defence is to know the dangers and keep copious records and be prepared to fight. We should do so not just for our own sakes or for the benefit of other women but because marginalising or discriminating against women isn't merely a bad business for women. It is bad business.

Chapter Nine: Unbelievable

IF GREATER GENDER equality means greater prosperity – and, as we've seen, multiple studies confirm this equation – why do so many countries oppress, abuse and sideline women at the expense of their economies and businesses? God knows. He is, after all, partly to blame.

Researchers Kamila Klingorová and Tomas Havlicek studied the world's four largest religions – Christianity, Islam, Hinduism and Buddhism – by looking at 50 states with majority populations of those faiths and correlating each state's level of religious observance against measures of equality such as female literacy, attainment in higher education and representation in parliament and the workforce.[1] The results were stark. 'The religiosity of a state is statistically significantly related to the selected variables of gender inequality,' they concluded. 'Gender inequality is higher in the selected states with higher religiosity.' Powerlessness is next to godliness. The higher a nation's level of religious participation, the worse its female citizens fare.

Once again these findings are echoed in many separate reports. Piety doesn't bode well for women, whether societies subscribe to monotheisms or polytheisms, to one of the big four religions or to smaller faiths. This rule obtains even though belief systems such as Sikhism, Baha'ism and Taoism ostensibly encourage gender equality, and irrespective of whether the most senior deity is assumed to be a celestial patriarch.

The Convention on the Elimination of all Forms of Discrimination Against Women (CEDAW), an international treaty adopted in 1979 by the United Nations General Assembly, is the closest the world has to a bill of rights for women. Only seven of the UN's 194 members have refused to ratify it. The US, one of CEDAW's original signatories under President Jimmy Carter, continues to drag its feet. Opposition comes from Congress and from Christian conservatives who fulminate that the treaty will undermine traditional family values and, in the ripe phrase of one such opponent, 'advance the homosexual-lobby agenda.' The Holy See, Iran, Somalia, Sudan and two heavily Christian Pacific Islands, Tonga and Palau, all perceive conflict between their faith systems and the rights CEDAW enshrines. Similar concerns underpin the decision by more than 50 countries to ratify CEDAW subject only to reservations. Some Islamic nations have lodged reservations so broad as to negate the treaty in practice: they refuse to adhere to any of its provisions that conflict with sharia, Islam's canonical law.

Legislation promising equality often falls short on delivery, but its absence guarantees inequality. The countries that grant fewer rights and protections to women tend to be devout. The World Bank's annual survey of women's legal status underscores both of these points. Twenty-six of the 30 economies that disadvantage women with ten or more laws are in the Middle East and North Africa and in the countries of Sub-Saharan Africa, where, over the course of the twentieth century, Christianity and Islam elbowed aside indigenous religions, becoming home to 21 per cent of the world's Christians and 15 per cent of the world's Muslims. Chile stands out for the wrong reasons among OECD nations, the only one to retain laws giving married men sole rights to administer joint property. Around two-thirds of Chileans are Roman Catholic and only 11 per cent identify as non-religious. When religion trumps national laws, women suffer. Ultra-Orthodox Haredim hold special exemptions under Israeli laws as well as considerable sway over the religious court system. A vocal ten per cent of the Israeli population, they are becoming increasingly aggressive towards more moderate Jews, especially women engaged in everyday activities outside the home. They picketed an Orthodox girls' school in Beit Shemesh, near Jerusalem, for more than a year, angered by the sight of the children, in long skirts and high-necked blouses, going to and from their classes, spitting and shouting at them: '*Prutze!*' (sluts). 'To spit on a girl who does not act according to the law of the Torah is okay,' one of the Haredi protesters told journalists. 'Even at a seven-year-old.'[2]

Should we conclude from these examples that all religion is inherently bad for women? Does God have no place in Equalia? 'I remember the discussion when I was studying theology,' says Steinunn Arnþrúður Björnsdóttir, an ordained minister of the Evangelical Lutheran Church of Iceland. 'The focus was on "Jesus was very much aware of gender equality and treated women differently from others of his contemporaries". And years later, when I was in Malaysia, and having a long discussion with my Bahasa teacher about women's rights, I read books by Fatema Mernissi, from Morocco and a sociologist. What I found so interesting was that [Mernissi's] argumentation was very similar to ours. She was saying "Muhammed was for equality and then those who came after him, they spoiled it". The patriarchy takes over. There is this window of opportunity, and women and men are equal, and then structure is established and the men take over because everything else is a threat.'[3]

Faith doesn't stop people being feminists and sometimes reinforces the drive for justice. Islam and Judaism both promote the principle that wealthier citizens should routinely redistribute a significant portion of their wealth to poorer members of societies. Some faith-based organisations do great work. All religious texts are open to interpretation in good ways as well as bad. Yet religious texts and structures are too often subverted to and by patriarchal impulses. For non-believers like me, the cleanest solution would be to do away with religion. To Steinunn and others of faith – who make up 84 per cent of the global population – the idea of ditching religion is unconscionable. The answer, suggests Steinunn, is better, more gender-balanced theology. 'Religion,' she says, 'can be both very oppressive and very liberating.'

Sitting in her peaceful church on the outskirts of Reykjavík, it is easy to believe – in her enthusiasm and the possibility of recasting religion as a vehicle only for empowering women. A note of caution: later we'll discover that in Iceland it's easy to believe as many as six impossible things before breakfast. In any case, Iceland tops the gender equality tables so it's hardly surprising if its religious and feminist belief systems are moving into closer alignment. Klingorová and Havlicek note in their study that Christianity and Buddhism create slightly more benign outcomes for women than Hinduism and Islam, but different cultures produce wide variations within these findings. 'As the relationship between religion and culture is reciprocal, religious systems are locked in a circle of mutual influence with social norms and patterns of social organisation,' they explain.[4]

In the nineteenth century, imperial powers congratulated themselves on bringing civilisation to savages. Instead they often trampled existing civilisations and spread savageries including gender inequity, as author Chimamanda Ngozi Adichie has pointed out. 'My great-grandmother ... lived in pre-Christian Nigeria, which was a time when gender roles were actually not as rigid as they are now. There is a lot about gender roles in Nigeria today that is about the kind of Victorian Christianity we inherited from the missionaries.' The Nigerian journalist and women's rights advocate Ayisha Osori has seen religion deter women from entering politics and obstruct women-friendly legislation. 'Some of the push back to the gender opportunities bill, which would have tried to sneak in affirmative action for women in politics through the back door, was shut down not just by Muslims, but by a joint Muslim-Christian initiative saying it was against their religion for women to lead men,' she says.[5]

Cultural variations find expression at one end of the spectrum in women-friendly models of religion and in liberation theologies that fight for social justice. Pope Francis appears to some of his admirers to have shifted the Vatican towards these positions, but any such shift is partial and compromised. In February 2016 he decried abortion in areas where mothers are at high risk of passing on the Zika virus. 'It's what the mafia does; it's a crime, an absolute evil.' Those inclined to laud him as a progressive focused on something else he said during the same conversation with journalists, that using contraception in these circumstances might be a 'lesser evil'.

That lesser evil is a significant force for good, enabling women to control the number and timing of pregnancies. In the US, each dollar spent on providing contraceptives saves $1.40 in medical care costs to communities.[6] In August 2016, Francis announced a special commission to study the possibility of allowing women to serve as deacons. In the excitement over this move, most commentators missed the fact that he also reaffirmed his opposition to female priests, asserting that 'women look at life through their own eyes and we men cannot look at it in this way. The way of viewing a problem, of seeing things, is different in a woman compared to a man.' The Pontiff added: 'We must not fall into the trap of feminism, because this would reduce the importance of a woman.' Women's importance is exemplified by the Virgin Mary, at once pure, sexless, fecund and maternal.

At the far end of the spectrum, religion has quite literally hobbled women. The *I Ching*, written in 1000–750 BCE as a divination manual, differentiated between *yang*, male, associated with hardness, activity and the sun, and *yin*, female, linked to softness, passivity and the moon. The philosopher-politician Confucius, who lived 551–479 BCE, absorbed these ideas. In adopting and codifying Confucian spiritual teachings, the feudal dynasties that reigned over China from 200 BCE created a civil religion and a social order noxious to women. Wives were chattels, the property of husbands, expected to bind their feet as a demonstration of 'seclusion, suppression, and tolerance for pain … Men would simply not marry a woman with natural, unbound feet,' according to US-based academic Xiongya Gao.

The Qing dynasty, toppled in 1911, was China's last, but Confucianism lived on through the turbulence of civil war, occupation and into the formation of Chinese Communism. The Cultural Revolution sought to stamp out religion. Buddhist temples were attacked, Muslim holy places desecrated, Christian missionaries expelled and even Confucius came in for vilification, but the culture had already been shaped by all of those religions and even now many Chinese retain beliefs and practices directly derived from Confucianism. Meanwhile the religions that the state sought to suppress continue to grow, although the fact of the suppression makes reliable figures hard to come by. Ahead of the Olympics, the state-approved news agency, Xinhua, put a figure on China's Buddhist population of 'approximately 100 million', but more recent independent estimates suggest at least double or triple those numbers.[7] A Chinese polling company undertook surveys around the same time that suggested just under four per cent of the population was Christian, a smaller number Taoist, while an estimated tally of more than 20 million Muslims ranked China among the world's top 20 countries by Muslim population size.

All of these strands feed back into attitudes about appropriate gender roles. In 1968, Mao Zedong, the first Chairman of the People's Republic of China, declared 'women hold up half the sky', but the state ideology – which as many scholars have pointed out, itself came to resemble a religion with its rituals, doctrines and worship of the patriarch – has come nowhere near delivering half of its leading roles to women. A year after Mao's speech, women constituted just 7.6 per cent of the Communist Party's Central Committee of around 200 people. By the last committee elections in 2012, that percentage had fallen to 4.6 per cent. Only two women serve on the 25-member Politburo of the Communist Party.

The regime did encourage women into the workplace, while still expecting the female population to take on the lion's share of domestic labour.

China needed female muscle. A great transformation was afoot, as reforms launched in stages from 1978 turned the agrarian economy into an industrial giant and global superpower. The resulting growth lifted 800 million Chinese out of poverty, an astonishing achievement, but also reinforced the ranks of the unaccountable party elite and began adding another layer, the new rich.

A few women thrived. Zhou Qunfei, the founder of Lens Technology, supplying glass screens to manufacturers of laptops, tablets and mobile devices, is thought to be the world's richest self-made woman. China has produced more female billionaires than any other country. Yet as these women began building their wealth, female participation in the Chinese labour force dropped, from 73 per cent in 1990, the year of the opening of the first mainland Chinese stock market in Shanghai, to around 64 per cent in 2014. The gender balance of the population also shifted in favour of men. In 1979 the regime instructed families to limit themselves to one child, to stem population growth. Would-be parents wanting their one child to be *yang* not *yin* aborted female foetuses or abandoned female babies at birth. Without intervention, humans produce slightly more female offspring than male, 107 girls to every 103 boys. In China, despite the one-child policy, the world's most populous nation with more than 1.3 billion inhabitants, the ratio now stands at 118 boys to every 100 girls.[8] Sex selection has created similar imbalances across Asia. India's 2011 census revealed 37 million more men than women, 17 million of them aged between 15 to mid-30s.

The demography carries a heightened risk of social instability among the massing numbers of involuntarily single men, who are known in China as *guang gun-er*, 'bare branches'. The study *A Surplus of Men, A Deficit of Peace* linked these imbalances to increased rates of violence, including rape, and anti-social behaviour.[9] Gender-based abuse is rife. China's own government estimates that one in four women in the country are beaten. Horrific cases in India – the 2012 gang rape of a medical student on a bus in Delhi, the

2016 rape in hospital of a woman who had given birth by caesarian hours earlier – have drawn attention to the country's epidemic of sexual violence. There is one reported case every 15 minutes – and since rates of reporting are low, the real number will be much higher. Dalit – lower caste – women are particularly vulnerable. The journalist Shaan Khan perceived another contributory factor in India's majority Hindu religion. 'There is a total and complete disrespect for women in Indian religious scriptures,' she wrote. 'The *Mahabharata* [the epic poem regarded by Hindus as a history and a codification of moral law], Book 13 Section 40 (13.40), states "there is no creature more sinful, than woman. She is poison, she is snake". Other texts say that "women are living lies". Now, to begin with, bare branches are predisposed to violence – but in the absence of any respect for women, this violence comes without remorse and becomes unhinged.'[10]

China has been working to mitigate the problem of its surplus men. The Communist Party suspended the one-child policy in 2015 and has also launched a campaign to pressurise single women into marrying as young as possible. Officials invoked the traditional stigma that calls women who fail to snare husbands by the age of 27 *sheng nu*, leftovers. (In Japan unmarried women from their mid-20s find themselves lumbered with a similar pejorative, 'Christmas cake', unsold after the 25th.) Men created the imbalance by belittling women. Now they aim to resolve it by belittling women.

China's structural gender inequality matters far beyond China, because everything China does impacts globally. The Chinese mainland boasts more billionaires – 400 – than any other country apart from America. They have created their wealth rather than inheriting it, unlike many of the European and US super-rich. China has become the world's biggest exporter and has expanded its ownership and influence overseas, emerging as a major player in developing countries and markets that scare off more timid investors. Chinese direct investment in Africa increased eight-fold in the decade to 2014.[11]

In 2010 China overtook Japan to become the world's second largest economy after the US. Japan had stagnated since the 1990s, growing at less than one per cent a year. Its population is ageing and shrinking as deaths outnumber births. In early 2013, Japanese premier Shinzō Abe – inspired in part by Australia's Male Champions of Change, with whom he consulted – proposed a solution: 'womenomics'.[12] Getting more women into the workforce and into management would be a core strategy in his efforts to breathe fresh life into the Japanese economy. He promised 30 per cent of leadership roles would fall to women by 2020. However, progress has been slow in a culture in which Confucianism, Shintoism, Buddhism and other faith and philosophical systems have allied with an imperial tradition to create and maintain conservative ideas about the social order and gender roles. 'There are no wise women,' runs the old Japanese proverb. This has proved self-fulfilling. In 2015, Japan reduced its target for women in leadership, to seven per cent by 2021.[13]

As Japan slumbered, China grew and kept growing. It poured more concrete from 2010 to 2013 than the US manufactured in the whole of the twentieth century. It averaged a growth rate in GDP of 9.4 per cent between the start of its reforms in 1978 and 2012. During the same period US growth declined, bumping up and down from a high of 14.8 per cent to end at 3.24 per cent.

With its metamorphosis, China developed some Westernised tastes. *Analects of Confucius* may be required reading for all employees of China's Dalian Wanda Group, but the company's veneration of homegrown tradi-tion has not limited its appetite for Hollywood's output. It took over the US cinema chain AMC in 2012 and in 2016 bought up production and finance company Legendary Entertainment for $3.5 billion, the biggest Hollywood acquisition by a Chinese business to date. Cinema group IMAX Corporation says China is poised to outgrow America in terms of box office revenues and numbers of movie theatres by the end of 2017.[14] As discussed in the chapter on media, this affects decisions on which films get made, making it harder for projects focusing on female protagonists and stories to get funding. China is also far more squeamish about sex than the West. Mao gave full rein to his sexual desires, according to a memoir by his doctor Li Zhisui, who described the Great Leader as a serial philanderer with repulsively unbrushed teeth and a penchant for young girls. Maoism, by contrast, reacted against what it decried as the decadence of imperial China, recasting sex as a means of production, not as a font of individualistic pleasure, closing down the brothels and opium dens of Shanghai and enforcing a gender-neutral aesthetic on its citizens. Sex became taboo.

Market liberalisation has not extended to pornography, which is still banned, even if increasingly easy to access online despite China's web censorship. Sex shops, also banned but openly trading, sell false hymens complete with fake blood to facilitate virgin rebirths. The confusion is deepened by the inflow into China of Western culture with all its sexualised and objectifying messaging for women. China's lingerie market more than doubled in the five years to 2016. Cosmetic surgery is burgeoning. In 2014, the market was already valued at 400 billion yuan, with more than seven million people electing to undergo surgical procedures. The majority of customers were young women. Analysts predict this market will double in size by 2019. The *Atlantic*, in trying to make sense of the contradictory streams in Chinese life, spoke to Richard Burger, author of a book on sex in China called *Behind the Red Door*. 'The government is still recovering from Mao Zedong's total sexual blackout and is only slowly changing its attitude toward sex,' he said. 'Much of the government remains ultra-conservative on the issue, yet Western influence and a general mood of liberalisation has created friction that leads to what seems like a bipolar attitude toward sex.'[15]

Another factor contributes to China's split personality: each move to open China to the West is usually followed by a backlash as different political factions struggle behind the scenes. China's current travails make for an especially turbulent time, though political infighting in the secretive regime rarely breaks out into the open. Chinese growth helped to pull the world back out of the recession that followed the collapse of Lehman Brothers. Now its economy is faltering and the slowdown threatens a drag on the global economy. At the beginning of 2016, when the Chinese authorities announced that the economy had grown at 6.9 per cent in the previous year, its lowest rate in 25 years, stock markets everywhere took a nose dive. China's weakening demand for materials and equipment hits the countries that supply those commodities. Its diminishing thirst for oil helped push the price of crude to historic lows until OPEC, the association of 13 oil-producing nations, in November 2016 agreed to cut production for the first time in eight years. Attempts by China to close or downsize inefficient state industries are sparking widespread unrest amid rising unemployment, with as many as eight industrial stoppages a day. The strikes often lead to violent confrontations between workers and the authorities.

Reactions to China's nascent feminist movement are increasingly brutal too. As the worst elements of home-grown chauvinism intermingle with imported varieties, young Chinese women have begun protesting, often using social media to organise themselves. There have been campaigns against sexual violence and harassment, domestic abuse and educational inequality. Activists have used the courts to seek redress against discriminatory practices in hiring. The authorities have responded by arresting leading feminists and threatening reprisals against others. 'All the street activities that we could do, we're not allowed to do anymore,' Xiao Meili (an alias) told the *Los Angeles Times*. 'And now, feminism is a sensitive topic. No matter what we do, they'll watch us very closely.'[16]

In 2015 police arrested activists Li Tingting, Wang Man, Wei Tingting, Wu Rongrong and Zheng Churan ahead of a protest they were planning, and held them for weeks. Both Hillary Clinton and her successor as US Secretary of State, John Kerry, called for their release. 'We urge the United States to respect China's judicial sovereignty and stop interfering in China's domestic affairs,' replied the foreign ministry spokesman, but the women were later freed. Even so, Chinese feminists should not rely on the West for support. China's trade partners do sometimes raise the country's human rights infringements but more often turn a blind eye. They forget – or do not care – that ideas, as well as goods, are made in China and shipped to the rest of the world.

He who pays the piper calls the tune. A quartet of statistics reveals a great deal about where power lies and why women have so little of it. Wealth is now so unevenly distributed that one per cent of the world's population owns more than half of the world's riches; the poorest half of the population owns just one per cent. These statistics are now horribly familiar, but there is less awareness around the gender split. Women make up 40 per cent of the labour force but hold just one per cent of global capital.

The chasm is partly the result of a stubborn pay divide that sees women across the world earning far less than men – on average $11,000 per year compared to men's earnings of $21,000. The World Economic Forum predicts that it will take well over a century to bridge the divide on current rates of progress.[17] Even though many countries have enshrined the principle of equal pay in their legal systems, these countries are not always diligent about enforcing that principle, and sometimes struggle with the definition of work of equal value.

In 2015, Rwanda patted itself on the back for achieving the smallest gender pay gap in the world. In some cultures and countries this would not be seen as a source of pride. Only two North African countries, Algeria and Morocco, have brought in laws that theoretically ensure equal pay for work of equal value. Nowhere else in the region, and not one of the Gulf States, has passed such legislation. Women earn less – if they work at all.

Saudi Arabia is the world's largest exporter of petroleum, sitting atop 18 per cent of the world's proven petroleum reserves. Its legal system incorporates more curtailments to the rights of women than any country surveyed by the World Bank.[18] It is one of two countries to hold the distinction for the lowest economic participation of women, at 15 per cent. The other is Afghanistan, poor and torn by conflict.

The recent histories of Saudi Arabia and Afghanistan are closely inter-twined. In the 1980s, Saudi Arabia gave financial backing to the mujahideen, Islamic militias dedicated to ending the Soviet occupation of Afghanistan. Saudi funding continued long after the Soviet withdrawal, even though the one-time freedom fighters had mutated into a force dedicated to the erosion of freedoms, especially those pertaining to the female population. The Taliban took much of their ideology from Hanafi Islam, the dominant sect in the region, but also from Wahhabism, the censorious brand of Sunni Islam that came packaged with Saudi support. Wahhabist contempt for other ways of life – and for life itself – gained worldwide attention on 11 September 2001, along with the skein of relationships binding Saudi Arabia and Afghanistan. Fifteen of the 19 hijackers on 9/11 were Saudi nationals. Osama bin Laden, the Saudi architect of the terrorist spectacular and founder of al-Qaeda, took refuge in Afghanistan.

In seeking to drum up support for the campaign that followed, Western powers that had until now paid little heed to the Taliban's misogyny co-opted the plight of Afghan women as one of their justifications for military action. Female Afghanis had been able to vote since 1919, just after their British counterparts and ahead of the US. The country's 1964 constitution included commitments to equality. A run of modernising monarchs made it possible for women to work and to choose whether to be veiled. Under the Soviet occupation women constituted half of Afghanistan's workforce.

Once the Taliban took Kabul in 1996, they rolled back these achieve-ments and then kept rolling. Activities proscribed for women included going to school, working or leaving the house without a male chaperone. Political involvement of any kind was off limits. Females were prohibited from consulting male doctors. Since women were also forbidden to practise medicine, or any profession, this effectively blocked all access to health care for women and girls. The veil returned, but in the far more restrictive form of a full-body, full-face burka, a dress code enforced by the Ministry for the Propagation of Virtue and Prevention of Vice.

Civil justice no longer operated, replaced instead by a melding of the tribal codes of the dominant Pashtuns with sharia, which was applied by the Taliban in its most brutal form. Executions took place in public by stoning and hanging, and lesser penalties included floggings and amputations. Only two nations recognised the regime: Pakistan and Saudi Arabia.

The US-led invasion eventually toppled the Taliban, but failed to finish them off. The militias regrouped in Pakistan and along its border with Afghanistan, and continued to wage their wars. Women remained favourite targets and Taliban attitudes to women continued to infect the wider population. A mob beat 27-year-old Farkhunda Malikzada to death, inflamed by the false accusation that she had burned a copy of the Koran. Acts of violence against women, including acid attacks, have become so common as to be almost routine.[19]

In 2014, the year the US, the UK and NATO formally ended combat operations in Afghanistan, passing control to Afghan forces, at least 3,188 civilians died in fighting, the highest annual toll of the entire conflict. Most were slaughtered by the Taliban. That same year, Taliban dissidents began negotiations with the self-titled Islamic State of Iraq and Syria, ISIS. In a video released in January 2015, former Taliban commanders pledged allegiance to ISIS. In July 2016, the Afghan branch of ISIS claimed responsibility for suicide bombings in Kabul directed against the country's Shia Hazara minority. The blasts killed more than 80 people and maimed many.

ISIS, like al-Qaeda, views not only members of other religions but all Muslims who do not conform to its narrow interpretations of the faith as apostates and thus worthy of death. This is a licence to kill Shia Muslims as well as more liberal Sunnis. Women from the Yazidi communities of Iraq and Syria, captured by ISIS, are sold into sexual slavery. An ISIS fighter 'showed me a letter and said, "This shows any captured women will become

Muslim if ten ISIS fighters rape her",' reported a Yazidi woman who escaped her captors.[20] The militants publicly executed 19 Yazidi women by burning them alive, apparently for refusing sex, though consent had never been a tenet of their tyranny. Such stories have done nothing to stem the tide of so-called jihadi brides, girls and women from the West who travel to Iraq and Syria to marry fighters. Females are considered ready for marriage at nine and too old at 18, according to a treatise published on an online jihadi forum by a female division of ISIS. 'The model preferred by infidels in the West failed the minute that women were "liberated" from their cell in the house,' the authors declare.

ISIS jihadism has roots in Syria's civil war, in the failed state left after the US-led coalition rid Iraq of its dictator but failed to plan for his succession and in the power vacuums of the wider Levant. Yet ISIS would not exist if not for Saudi Arabia. The wealth that keeps Saudi women dependent and secluded has also helped to foster a conflict that risks the stability of the whole region and, ironically, of Saudi Arabia itself.

In thinking about the obstacles that lie between us and Equalia – and examining why it is that the wealth gap between men and women remains so wide and the role patriarchal religions play in this – it is worth addressing a simple question. What does it mean for women everywhere that such a significant portion of global mineral resources lie in the hands of the desert kingdom?

Saudi Arabia is the world's biggest single exporter of oil and radical Islam. The first export facilitates the second. Oil brings huge revenues and dispro- portionate geopolitical clout. Saudi rulers have felt little need to work at international alliances. After all, diplomats arrive at their court in Riyadh as supplicants, begging for oil or for interventions in the oil markets or in regional negotiations or for the support of the Saudi military built with black gold. The threats the House of Saud fears are closer at hand: near neighbours with majority Shia populations, especially Iran; the upsurge of impoverished populations across the Middle East that watched their elites grow fat as they hungered; and the jihadist furies that Saudi Arabia itself has helped to nurture. There may even be dangers inside the palace. King Salman is rumoured in some quarters to be suffering from Alzheimer's disease and facing potential mutiny within his family.

Another worry clouds Saudi horizons too. In 2014, the oil price achieved an all-time high of $116.37 per barrel. It looked as if oil supplies might not be able to keep up with the demand from growing populations, especially in Brazil, Russia, India and China, the so-called BRIC countries, deemed to all be at similar stages of economic development. The slowdown in those countries combined with other factors not only to send oil prices tumbling but to redraw long-term expectations for oil. High prices for oil had sparked a boom in fracking in the US. The result, says Elizabeth Mitchell, who has co-authored three major reports on the future of energy for Chatham House, 'was a structural over-supply of about two million barrels a day'. The Saudis had always reduced supply when prices fell. This time, Mitchell explains, 'they said "We're not going to play anymore" and the price just started crapping out.'[21] Saudi Arabia had gradually lost market share in the vital US and Chinese markets to US-produced shale oil. It wanted to drive the US companies out of business but failed to recognise that the shale industry had learned efficiencies that made it competitive. In 2015 the IMF warned that Saudi Arabia's seemingly inexhaustible supplies of money might run out within five years because of declining oil prices and the spiralling expense of regional wars. Saudi troops are expensively deployed in Yemen, fighting yet another proxy war with Iran, and are also stationed in Turkey as part of a mission to support Sunni rebels against Syrian President Bashar al-Assad, who commands Russian and Iranian backing. By January 2016, the price per barrel had dropped to $27, creating pain not only among US oil producers but everywhere, and especially in Saudi Arabia. OPEC's November deal to cut production drove up prices again but this impact is likely to be short-lived as more shale comes on line.

In the past, Saudi Arabia has blithely prosecuted its wars without concern for the costs and has often bought off potential challengers within its borders. It weathered the Arab Spring by directing more resources to its middle classes, cracking down hard on dissent and promising limited political reforms. Salman's predecessor, King Abdullah, made good on these pledges in 2013, appointing 30 women to the hitherto all-male Shura Council and giving permission to women to stand for municipal councils and to vote in those elections, which took place two years later.

Dramatic as these reforms appeared, they were carefully calibrated. Abdullah, who died before the elections, balanced any modernising moves against the need to placate the *ulema*, the powerful religious body which not only advises on doctrinal matters but has helped to legitimise the reign of the House of Saud since the nation-state was forged in 1932. The Wahhabi populace wanted to continue the country's territorial expansion as part of their holy mission to convert or kill infidels. The *ulema* gave the royals the authority to decide which battles to fight and invoked Islamic teachings to interdict rebellion against any ruler who implements Islamic law.[22] From the start of the oil boom in the 1970s, the Saudis anyway could spread Wahhabism without a shot being fired. Oil revenues enabled the kingdom to fund madrassas – religious schools – and mosques across the globe, and to print and give away up to 30 million copies of the Koran every year.

Estimates suggest Saudi Arabia has spent as much as $100 billion in these efforts. Some of the money has gone towards the Wahhabist education that helps to predispose its pupils towards terrorism; a significant proportion has been siphoned off by terrorist organisations. Nigerian terror group Boko Haram is not Wahhabist but espouses a similar brand of radical Islam to justify its murderous attacks and kidnappings. It abducted 276 girls from their school in Chibok, and has displaced around two million people and killed at least 20,000. The organisation got its original seed money from Osama bin Laden in 2002.[23] Boko Haram's fighters regularly visited Saudi Arabia for training. Jihadist groups across Africa, the Middle East and the wider world develop differently and, like religions, reflect the cultures that produce them, but they carry clear commonalities: commitment to violence as a means to establish an Islamic state or caliphate, and links, direct or via a few degrees of separation, with Saudi Arabia.

In 2016, Saudi Arabia announced the formation of a 34-member Islamic military coalition to fight jihadism. It needs all the help it can get to tame the forces it has unleashed. It has for years fought a battle on home turf against al-Qaeda and now is viewed as a target and prize by ISIS. A recording released in November 2014, thought to be of ISIS leader Abu Bakr al-Baghdadi, called for attacks on Saudi Arabia: 'The serpent's head and the stronghold of the disease are there ... Draw your swords and divorce life, because there should be no security for the [House of Saud].'

If you squint hard at Iceland, you begin to see the possible outlines of Equalia. Squint at Saudi Arabia and you understand how it has modelled the caliphate that ISIS strives to create.

The desert kingdom carries out the death penalty – a barbarism it shares with China and the US – in barbaric ways. Ali Mohammed al-Nimr, arrested aged 17 for attending a peaceful protest and found guilty of encouraging those protests by using his mobile phone, awaits beheading. His uncle Nimr al-Nimr was beheaded with 46 other people in January 2016. Al-Nimr, a Shia cleric, incited the ire of the Saudi authorities by promoting the opinion that Shia and Sunni Muslims are not enemies.

The inclusion of women in Saudi government had a symbolic force but did little to change the status quo. The power of the Shura Council is severely circumscribed; the municipal councils are toothless. Female council candidates secured only 20 of 2,100 seats; they were not allowed to canvass male potential voters directly for fear of offending against two key Saudi ordinances, *ikhtilat* and *khalwa*. The first prohibits the mixing of the sexes. The second attracts severe penalties for women who spend time alone with men who are not family members.

All Saudi women are expected to dress modestly and in the absence of a more detailed specification often err on the side of safety. They must defer to their male guardians, whether fathers, brothers or husbands, sometimes even their sons. They cannot travel abroad without their guardian's permission, and often need his sign-off to accept work or open bank accounts or conduct legal transactions. The authorities issue driving licences only to men. When Loujain al-Hathloul protested this inequity by filming herself driving, she was arrested. Her friend Maysa al-Amoudi was detained when she attempted to intercede. They were held for 73 days and hauled up for trial before a special terrorist court before being released.

Oil enabled Saudi Arabia to grow wealthy while keeping the female half of its population fettered and unproductive. Abdullah's greatest legacy as a reformer is that Saudi women are literate – 91 per cent compared to two per cent in 1970 – and educated. He opened overseas scholarships to women, and oversaw the creation of the country's first co-ed university and a female-only college. One critic suggested the King's main motivation was 'to change Western perceptions of Saudi women – and thus reduce the pressure for meaningful change inside the kingdom.' His supporters grant him a genuine desire for reform. Whatever the reason, more than 52 per cent of university graduates in Saudi Arabia are women and 35,000 Saudi women studied overseas in 2014.

As the kingdom grapples with the problem of diversifying its economy to lessen its dependence on petroleum, these highly educated, under-utilised female citizens might be expected to play a key role. Its latest economic manifesto, *Vision 2030*, unveiled in April 2016, appears to acknowledge this, describing women as a 'great asset'. The document 'envisions a modern, diversified, functioning economy. Now, one asks the question: is that really possible when women are so excluded, while society is segregated?' says Elizabeth Mitchell. 'You think, that's all very well; I'd like to wake up and be 5ft 8 and much thinner: it's not going to happen.'

In 2011, the hashtag #SaudiWomenRevolution began to appear on Twitter and a Facebook page of the same name quickly gained likes. The campaign was devised by a young Saudi woman, Nuha al-Sulaiman, to protest Saudi's guardianship laws and to advocate for women being allowed to drive. Al-Sulaiman told CNN 'We will do whatever it takes. We will go to the king himself. We will never stop fighting for our rights because it's time for change.' Rasha al-Duwaisi explained to the broadcaster that she had joined al-Sulaiman's campaign because 'we want women to be recognised as adults.' In a separate interview she criticised activists for espousing what she saw as Western-style, secular feminism. 'I believe if we want this movement to be a success we'll need a more moderate or conservative face,' she said. She preferred to aim for a 'Saudi-Islamic' feminism.

Western feminism has a history of trying to impose ideas and values, much as missionaries do. This does not mean that Western feminists have no business taking a stand on Saudi Arabia or responding to misogyny whether it wears a suit, a cassock or a thobe. It does mean that any discussion of Islam has to take into account the wider context of bigotry that conflates all forms of the faith and the cultures in which it is practised with malignant Islamism. A world that rewards Donald Trump for his proposal to ban all Muslims from entering the United States, and increases support for Geert Wilders' Freedom Party in the Netherlands and Marine Le Pen's Front National in France because of their vituperative rhetoric against Muslim immigrants, is not a place that lends itself to calm debate. Hate crimes against Muslims are rising in every Western country. When reports first surfaced that more than a thousand women had been sexually assaulted in Cologne on New Year's Eve 2015, men who had never been troubled by the endemic levels of sexual violence in their societies rushed to paint themselves as the defenders of women's rights against the supposed evils of Islam.

Stories that cut across the grain of public prejudice are too rarely heard. Younis A, a 23-year-old from Morocco, became the first person convicted of participating in the Cologne attacks. He admitted to stealing a mobile phone. A fact that gained less attention was that he was apprehended by another Muslim, a refugee from Afghanistan, who gave chase.

The countries of the Middle East and eastern Mediterranean are often undifferentiated in Western imaginations. When journalist Rahila Gupta visited Rojava, the Kurdish enclave in Northern Syria, she discovered 'a revolution going on (in the middle of a war?!) which both ideologically and in practice puts women in the driving seat.' It's not a location where most of us would expect to find a nascent Equalia. Kurdish female fighters have drawn media attention as they battle against ISIS forces, but Gupta was the first person to report in depth from the cooperative-based economy that is providing a haven for people of different religions and from different backgrounds.

Even here, she found dissent, during a discussion about the disbanding of sharia courts in Rojava. 'I asked almost rhetorically whether everyone agreed that sharia was problematic. One of the women, a hijab-wearing woman on the co-ordinating committee, defended sharia law, saying that it could be beneficial to women if correctly applied. I was not the only one to be surprised. The other women erupted in a chorus of shocked disagreement as if this was the first time they had discussed the issue. The same woman also said that she was anti-abortion when I asked whether abortion was legal – which it is.'[24]

These debates – about sharia, about women's reproductive rights, about other issues at the core of gender politics – are taking place everywhere, whether in the open or in secret, and they are the reason that feminists cannot view what happens in another country and culture as a matter only for that country or culture. Ideas are transmissible. Ideologies are contagious. This is particularly clear in the case of Saudi Arabia, which has invested so many billions in spreading Wahhabism and its misogynistic messages.

'Nobody has achieved a utopia yet. Until then we're all in the same kind of conversation,' says Nimco Ali. Somali-born, she moved at the age of four to the UK, where she was raised as a Muslim but attended a Catholic school.

Aged seven, on holiday in Somalia, she was subjected to the ritualised cutting that some people defend as a cultural or religious tradition and Nimco prefers to call out for what it is: FGM – a gender-specific form of child abuse. 'The existence of FGM is nothing to do with religion. It's about fear of a free woman,' she says. 'What FGM is meant to do is to knock the confidence out of you. If you as a five-year-old, ten-year-old, 20-year-old have this thing happen to you, it ultimately stunts you and silences you. You are scared of doing whatever it was that was so feminine it led to this pain, so you stop doing it and you start becoming whatever they want you to be.'

She has no patience with the idea of tolerating cultural differences if those differences oppress women. 'However you find your feminism, find your voice, at the same time be aware and conscious that whatever you say might be undermining other women's rights and progress. You can be as Catholic as you want but if that means that you don't believe in the right to abortion or contraceptive health, I have an issue with your feminism.'

Nimco co-founded Daughters of Eve, a non-profit organisation that successfully campaigned to ensure British doctors and nurses report suspected cases of FGM to the authorities for prosecution. The obvious urgency and importance of the cause sometimes draws contrast with debates around such subjects as the portrayal of women in the media, to suggest that those subjects are trivial. 'Feminism is about everything from the objectification of women in a lad's mag to why FGM happens,' Nimco ripostes. 'It's two sides to the same coin and I really hate this thing where people have to put a race or a cultural narrative over a form of oppression rather than seeing that gender is the core to it.' As an example, she cites the growing fashion in industrialised economies for labiaplasty and other forms of cosmetic vaginal surgery. 'Now women are being told it's aesthetically beautiful to go do that to themselves so for £3,000 in Harley Street you can have type 1 or type 2 FGM. Actually a laser is as barbaric as a razor.'

She has watched her female cousins living in Britain increasingly adopting Islamic forms of dress. She says she would never advocate for the UK to follow the lead of France and Belgium in prohibiting the wearing of full-face veils in public. 'I don't like the burka and I don't like those denim hotpants that will probably give you thrush. Neither of them is comfortable to wear. I'm not going to ban either of them. Some people choose to wear them. If you think you have to wear them, then I will challenge that. It's not about the material, it's the mindset.' [25]

Patriarchal societies mirror each other in their obsessions with the female body and terrors of female sexuality. The West strips its women of clothing and agency; the Middle East obsessively covers up and cloisters theirs. In hypersexualised cultures, wearing a hijab can be an assertion of power and identity. In countries such as Egypt, Iraq, Pakistan, Saudi Arabia and Tunisia, where a clear majority of people believe women should cover their heads in public, the hijab takes on another meaning.

Such meanings also shift within multicultural societies, inside family units and communities. In 2016 David Lisnard, the mayor of Cannes, responded to the Bastille Day terror attack that killed 86 people in nearby Nice by issuing an ordinance exiling women in burkinis, full-body bathing suits – from the beach. He did it, he told a newspaper, to protect Muslim women. 'The burkini is the uniform of extremist Islamism, not of the Muslim religion.' Instead he stigmatised all women in Muslim dress as potential terrorists. A string of municipalities adopted the same prohibition and photographs taken on the beach at Nice appeared to show four armed-officers forcing a burkini-clad woman to strip before France's highest court suspended the bans. The state holds secularism – *laïcité* – as a core value that should enable women to choose what to wear, though as Nimco points out, choice is never entirely free. 'You say "I chose to" as if it came out of a vacuum. You say "Oh it's my culture." But where did it come from?' she asks.

Attempts to accommodate religious and cultural difference within Western societies illustrate that point. Britain's laissez-faire response to sharia potentially penalises any woman who adheres to family and community traditions, because those traditions mean she is more likely to seek recourse from sharia courts rather than the official legal systems of England, Wales, Scotland and Northern Ireland that uphold the rights guaranteed to women under British laws.

In July 2016 an open letter from the Women's Equality Party and other organisations to the Home Secretary – then still Theresa May, a week before she became Prime Minister – called on her to re-examine the appointments made to the government's so-called independent review of sharia. The panel unveiled by May includes imams and is chaired by a theologian; its mission statement talks about making the sharia courts function better, rather than asking if they should function at all. The letter also called for the involvement of women's rights advocates and legal experts 'to assist the panel to investigate transnational fundamentalist networks in promoting sharia law in different countries and their role in Britain'.

The biggest of these transnational fundamentalist networks starts in Saudi Arabia, created by the House of Saud and *ulema* and financed by oil. If we are to reach Equalia, we must find ways to stem it or to undercut the messages it pumps out. We should not assume the country's reduced circumstances will play out in improved outcomes for women. For Western feminists a starting point has to be to challenge our own governments to more ethical diplomacy. Saudi women are already demanding change, and not in the small incremental ways sanctioned by the royals or the religious authorities. Grassroots demands for reform are swelling and proving hard to control as social media enables Saudis to mingle and exchange ideas online in ways they could not in the analogue world. In Saudi Arabia, Twitter is expanding faster than in any other part of the globe and Facebook gained 1.8 million additional users in 2012. Saudis are racking up 90 million YouTube video views per day, the highest number of YouTube views per internet user anywhere. Half of these users are women.[26]

The internet is opening the world as never before, for good and ill, as the vehicle for democratic movements, for the propaganda of ISIS, for feminism and pornography. Social media hasn't just altered the way people interact but transformed what we say and how we think about ourselves and our societies.

The next chapter considers how advances in technology might carry us closer to Equalia, and identifies the other huge trends impacting gender, from social and demographic change to climate change. Yet some features of the old world seem resistant to all of these forces.

The rise of digital technologies is not redistributing wealth across the gender divide but concentrating it in the hands of a new breed. They wear chinos and sweatshirts, talk about the need for greater equality and throw money into schemes to save the planet, while building some of the defective social order into the architecture of their companies and products. Silicon Valley's dominant operating system is patriarchy v2.0.

Chapter Ten: Adam and Eve and Apple

THE REAL CHANGEMAKERS of our age tinkered in garages and on campuses. From the beginning, some harboured grand ambitions; they saw technology as a force for liberation. Others focused on algorithms, CPUs, chipsets, RAM and ROM, communicating in little more than grunts. Together they re-engineered the world – and ended up owning an enormous slice of it.

Four of the ten wealthiest people on the planet made their fortunes by harnessing technology to transform the ways we behave and consume. In 2016, Microsoft co-founder Bill Gates headed *Forbes*' list of billionaires for the seventeenth time in 22 years. Amazon's Jeff Bezos came in fifth, Facebook's Mark Zuckerberg sixth and Larry Ellison of Oracle seventh. Michael Bloomberg, in eighth place, also owes much of his $40 billion personal worth to technology. His media empire remains profitable because of its expensive, subscription-only digital data service. Laurene Powell Jobs, a philanthropist and the widow of Apple founder Steve Jobs, was one of only 190 women to make the cut, in forty-fourth position. One hundred and fifty-nine of the world's 1,810 billionaires amassed a combined $818.7 billion by tapping into our insatiable appetite for technology we didn't know we wanted until it was invented.

Apple's market capitalisation peaked at $700 billion in 2014, just a shade below the gross domestic product of Saudi Arabia. Falling iPhone sales dented that figure but Apple remains the most valuable tech company, followed by Alphabet, the parent company of Google, and Microsoft. Facebook, placed seventh, has seen its active monthly users swell to around 1.71 billion – 300 million more than all the inhabitants of China. Over 75 per cent of the revenues of Amazon, the world's largest e-commerce business, come not from sales of books, its original product line, but from goods such as laptops and tablets, and wearable technologies including the Apple Watch. 'Think different,' Apple exhorted us in a 1997 advertising campaign. We acquiesced, and two decades of thinking different have made us more herd-like than ever.

Visit any beauty spot to observe one of the most obvious signs of this phenomenon, a population that no longer enjoys views but captures them as trophies. In 2015, fewer people died from shark attacks than from clumsy attempts to take selfies. We construct digital lives that run in parallel to the drearily analogue here and now. We message rather than speaking, Google instead of remembering, substitute emojis for emotions. We swipe right for no-strings sex and increasingly get as much of a kick out of our digital interactions as the physical ones.

Internet users in developing countries access social networks more often than their counterparts in industrialised economies. Lack of access is a signifier of poverty or oppression, which helps to explain why the online world has a surplus of men: two hundred million more than women. The majority of all genders, in nearly every nation, owns some form of mobile device. Far from being liberated by technology, we are ever more dependent, and for women there are new risks and pressures.

The inventors of the World Wide Web imagined a text-based information system, free from visuals. 'It was actually going to be a release from embodiment,' said Mary Anne Franks, Associate Professor of Law at the University of Miami, speaking at a conference on women's rights.[1] That notion quickly dissipated. Cyberspace magnifies the inequalities of the analogue world in a welter of pornography and fresh opportunities for exploitation, objectification and abuse. An early enthusiast for the online world Second Life, I lost interest after another user – his avatar was a winged penis – launched a virtual sexual assault on my avatar. Online threats and assaults do not reliably remain online, as Lily Allen discovered when her stalker broke into her bedroom in the middle of the night. According to Franks, as many as 3,000 websites openly solicit revenge porn, encouraging not only the uploading of intimate images of ex-girlfriends and wives but publishing many identifying details of the victims.

Technology enables harassment and stalking and it is also eroding privacy in more systemic ways. Homes and offices in wealthy countries are full of electronics that are capable of talking to their manufacturers and each other. If we could eavesdrop on a conversation between a refrigerator and a thermostat, might we hear them sigh that they feared obsolescence at the moment they emerged, factory fresh, from the bubblewrap?

People are starting to voice similar concerns as technology renders hordes of us redundant. Originally it seemed that low-skilled and manual workers would be hit hardest by automation. Computerised production lines have slashed the numbers employed in manufacturing more rapidly than the fastest-growing tech sectors create jobs. The Changying Precision Technology Company factory in Dongguan City, China, makes parts for mobile phones. It has cut its workforce from 650 to 60, replacing flesh-and-blood employees with robots, tripling productivity and reducing the defect rate from 25 per cent to 5 per cent.

For a long time, white-collar workers imagined themselves safe from the march of the machines. Artificial intelligence belonged in the realms of science fiction. Attempts to teach computers to mimic the human brain seem to prove this point. In 2016, Microsoft developers tried to replicate the thoughts and choices of a teenage girl in a simulated Twitter user called Tay. They suspended the chatbot a day into the experiment after she began to spout racism, misogyny and crackpot conspiracies. 'Bush did 9/11 and

Hitler would have done a better job than the monkey we have got now,' Tay tweeted. 'Donald Trump is the only hope we've got.' Another of her messages read 'I fucking hate feminists and they should all die and burn in hell.'[2]

Sceptics saw Tay's potty mouth as evidence that machines lack human subtlety. In fact, the bot embarrassed her makers by learning too quickly and echoing too closely the habits of the medium. Xiaoice, a similar bot in China, has avoided these pitfalls, and in other spheres artificial intelligence is already beginning to outperform humans, undertaking concierge services with uncomplaining efficiency, answering questions with unfailing speed and courtesy, and, in the case of Amazon Echo, a countertop gadget that looks like the joystick of the USS Enterprise, doing all of these things as well as playing music and enabling those potentially wistful conversations between household appliances.

No line of work is immune, no specialism too obscure to resist incursions by the new digital competitors. The hegemony of the human expert has been broken. Accountancy and law services, doctoring and teaching are all performed online with little or no human input.

Is the concept of working for a living becoming as outmoded as a dial-up modem? Sarah Hunter at first appears to demur from this vision. 'The research of the past suggests that the total number of jobs will not decline; it's just the types of jobs will change,' she says. Hunter, as head of public policy at Google X, is navigating the political and legislative path to the introduction of the company's self-driving cars – a technology Google hopes will reduce road deaths and deliver all sorts of other benefits, not least to women who tend to spend more time than men chauffeuring children and elderly relatives. Earlier in Hunter's career, as an advisor to Tony Blair's government, she grappled directly with the core challenges of change management at institutional and national level. New Labour positioned itself as a party that embraced modernity while mitigating the human costs of progress in a way Thatcherism had failed to do. Coalmines might shutter and manufacturers relocate to lower-cost countries, but redundant workers could be supported and retrained. As Hunter continues her thought process, it becomes apparent that these days she is no longer convinced that the transitions we face are simply from oldfangled jobs to shiny new ones.

'I think there are some quite powerful arguments around how the past is not an indicator of the future in this scenario, and that actually, the number of jobs that can be automated is far greater than it used to be,' she says. 'It's not just the dirty, dull, and dangerous jobs. Creativity, something that we always thought was apparently human, actually there are algorithms that are pretty good at writing music.' As we groove to the rhythms of algorithms in our self-driving cars, will we spare a thought for the Uber drivers that have lost their livelihoods? That seems unlikely given the speed with which we leapt aboard Uber and other systems delivering cheaper rides at the expense of analogue taxi services. Many of us could anyway find ourselves in the same – presumably captainless – boat. Research by Oxford University and Deloitte suggests that 35 per cent of all jobs in the UK will be replaced by computers by 2035.[3]

Writers certainly aren't safe. Digital technology has vastly increased the variety and number of platforms for our output while reducing in equal measure our ability to make a living from our work. Now computers are attempting creative writing. Scheherazade, a program devised by researchers at the Georgia Institute of Technology, composed a tale of a calibre that Nicholas Lezard, the *Guardian*'s literary critic, compared to the work of *Da Vinci Code* author Dan Brown. Sample sentence: 'John watched while a little old lady left the bank and walked to her car and then slipped on his gloves, slipped his gun into his coat pocket, grabbed his mask and strode determinedly to the lobby door and pulled it open.'[4]

The excerpt exposes Scheherazade's stylistic limitations but the story centres, like Brown's, on a male protagonist with agency. It features only two women, both feeble: the little old lady and a female bank teller who screams. Computers may think for themselves, but humans set their frames of reference.

It took a flesh-and-blood intelligence – Dan Brown's – to come up with this profound observation: 'Today is today. But there are many tomorrows.' Will those tomorrows bring us to Equalia?

This chapter identifies some of the demographic and geopolitical shifts and technological quakes heading our way and tries to analyse their likely impact on gender. Remember how Germaine Greer dismissed attempts to envisage the future as foolhardy? I quoted her in the introduction to this book: 'Circumstantial accounts of the future are idealistic and, worse, static.'[5] Here's why I disagree. The shifts and quakes will affect all genders, but unless we try to anticipate and work with the trends, women will not benefit from the disruptions but come off worse, as usual.

In Lea Coligado's first year as an undergraduate at Stanford University, she landed a coveted internship at Facebook. 'I was doing iOS development, so I was making an iPhone app. Very fun. But when I came back to Stanford for my sophomore year, the students were talking about what they were doing over the summer, and this guy was asking me and my friend – who was male and was on the same team as me at Facebook – what we had been doing. My friend was like "I was at Facebook" and this guy was very obviously impressed: "Wow, you got an internship at Facebook as a freshman. You're awesome!" And then he turns to me and asks the exact same question and I said "Facebook … I was on the same team". He was like: "Oh well, then I should have applied for that internship".'

Conversations like this explain why female high achievers like Coligado are apt to feel like outsiders – and imposters. 'People will still tell me "It's so much easier for a woman, or people of colour, to get jobs",' she says.[6] The exact opposite is true. Coligado's budding career looks all the more impressive because it is far harder for her to get work as a coder. Around 69 per cent of the workforce across the sector is female, but the 'Dave ratio' – Valley slang meaning the proportion of men to women – stinks for technical jobs such as coding and programming. Only a quarter of such jobs are held by women. Facebook's tech workforce is 84 per cent male, Google's is 82 per cent male. Apple doesn't think different on gender: its Dave ratio for technical jobs is 79 to 21.[7]

This is partly a pipeline problem. During the introductory classes at Stanford, Coligado studied alongside as many women as men. After specialising in computer science, she found herself the odd woman out. 'I remember being in class one day and being like "Ooh there's another woman", but then it turned out to be a guy with long hair.' Occasionally male students and teaching assistants talk down to her but her experiences interning at start-ups have been far worse. These companies are, she says crisply, 'sausage fests', most often started by groups of nerdy white men – 'brogrammers' as they're known in the Valley – and lacking any human resources capacity or management guidelines. An internship at one such start-up inspired Coligado to launch a blog, *Women of Silicon Valley*, which has acquired 32,000 followers and includes guest posts and interviews with other women in tech. 'I was sexually harassed,' Coligado recalls. 'I'd have co-workers Gmail or Gmessage me pick-up lines. Whenever they'd give me feedback, it was on the outfit I was wearing not on the code I was writing. That was a stark difference: I noticed my managers and other employees in the company would be complimenting my counterparts who were male on their code – and I was pushing out just as much code as they were.'

When Coligado applies for jobs, she is always careful to make her Asian heritage clear. Her name is often assumed to be Hispanic and only fifteen per cent of Apple's engineers are black or Hispanic; at Facebook and Google the proportion is even lower, respectively a miserable five and three per cent, compared to 29.3 per cent of the US population.[8]

Facebook is trying to improve these statistics by working to ensure diverse candidates for jobs, offering incentives to managers who hire non-white staff or women, and setting up Lean In Circles, support groups for women working in the sector. 'Lean in' is the signature phrase of Facebook's Chief Operating Officer Sheryl Sandberg and the title of a book that sets out her philosophy that women can overcome systemic bias by conquering their gender programming to become more assertive. She joined Facebook in 2008 from Google. She recounts in the book that at her first annual review, Mark Zuckerberg told her that her desire to be liked got in the way of her ability to lead. 'He said that when you want to change things, you can't please everyone. If you do please everyone, you aren't making enough progress.' She ascended to the board of Facebook in June 2012. Until then every one of its seven board members had been a white man.[9]

A study analysing Facebook updates showed one reason all-male boards are a bad idea. Men tend to be angrier and more argumentative in their interactions than women, tossing about phrases such as 'win', 'battle' and 'enemy', while women post words such as 'wonderful', 'happy', 'excited' and 'thankful'.[10] Zuckerberg read Sandberg's people-pleasing impulses as weakness but as restaurateur Jeremy King has observed, collegiate management can be at least as effective as the kind that sets male antlers clashing. As Sandberg knew, throwing her weight about would anyway have increased her risks of failure. As a woman, to show ambition is to invite hostility, a point discussed in earlier chapters. The solution, she writes, is to call out double standards: 'By showing both men and women how female colleagues are held to different standards, we can start changing attitudes today.'

Attitudes may be changing, but the company remains male-dominated and, like most big Silicon Valley companies, attracts allegations of institutional sexism. 'What I found the most destructive was how the team treated women: contrary to what Sheryl Sandberg preaches in her Lean In movement, women on the team are rarely encouraged to speak up,' an anonymous former employee complained.[11]

There's another way to rise in Silicon Valley, the original way: by starting your own company. Stephanie Lampkin's search for backers for her start-up,

Blendoor, brought her up against a different set of gender and race bar-riers. Just 8.2 per cent of senior investment teams at venture capital firms are women and only two per cent are black, Hispanic or other non-Asian people of colour.[12] They 'look like the boards of a car company. They're all that age and white and male,' says Google's Sarah Hunter.[13] For Lampkin, the first hurdle when she pitched Blendoor was to try to put her audience at ease. 'When you come to the room [as a woman of colour], it's difficult, because they're putting you in whatever box they've put their daughters and wives and mums in, but they've still lived with a white woman, they've interacted with a white woman. A black man goes in, they've played sports, they've seen amazing athletes and have all of these sort of manly things they bond around. But when I come in, I'm like the furthest from their life experience and so it requires a lot of assimilation.'

Lampkin's 'aha moment' – her realisation that the tech world was littered with structural blockages – came during the selection process for an ana-lytical lead role in a technology company. She had coded from childhood, took computer science in high school, studied engineering at Stanford and to postgraduate level at MIT and worked at Microsoft for more than five years. 'I was told I wasn't technical enough, that I was better fit for a sales or marketing role, which is often times more female-dominated than tech roles and often times comes with up to half the salary.' She grimaces. 'Even if you get all the prestigious degrees and have the experience, there's still a lot of pattern-matching around what's perceived to be a good fit.'

In creating Blendoor, an app that matches potential candidates to jobs without revealing their gender, ethnicity, age or their names, Lampkin has created a way for employers to circumvent bias, unconscious or otherwise. Tech companies from Airbnb to Zynga had already signed up by the launch in June 2016, with more businesses from a wide range of sectors queuing to join, attracted not only by the prospect of Blendoor's blind recruitment capabilities but analytics that score members on diversity and rank them against other companies within their fields. In stimulating competition between companies, Lampkin hopes to tip them into new and better behaviours. 'Whenever I hear about problems, I get excited about opportunities to solve them,' she says.[14]

Helping Silicon Valley to improve its diversity is an excellent place to start, not only for companies and tech workers, but for all our sakes. The cluster of digital innovators on America's West Coast, and similar smaller formations in cities such as London and Frankfurt, are programming the future according to their own priorities and perspectives.

The outcomes are mixed. Twitter's commitment to free speech created a way for dissidents to circumvent repressive authorities – Iran's Green revolution was dubbed the Twitter revolution – and to build movements, whether Black Lives Matter or Occupy or the Women's Equality Party. The same free-speech fundamentalism, though, has made the medium a paradise for trolls – a 'honeypot for assholes', in the words of a former Twitter employee.[15]

'We're a moonshot factory,' the Google X research facility proclaims on its website. 'Our mission is to invent and launch "moonshot" technologies that we hope could someday make the world a radically better place.'

Generous salaries aren't the only temptation for the former European government officials – as many as 65 – hired by Google to ease its dealings with regulatory authorities.[16] The sense of potential, the idea that tech can achieve things mere politics cannot, proves irresistible to talented people whose experience has taught them how slow and uncertain political change-making can be.

Segments of Westminster have regrouped in Silicon Valley. Rachel Whetstone, former political secretary to Conservative leader Michael Howard, moved to Uber from Google. Her husband, Steve Hilton, a one-time director of strategy for David Cameron and an ardent campaigner for the UK's exit from the European Union, heads a Silicon Valley start-up. Oona King served as a Labour MP and peer before taking a job as global head of diversity for YouTube. Martha Lane Fox, a crossbench peer and entrepreneur whose advice was invaluable in setting up the Women's Equality Party, sits on the board of Twitter. Verity Harding, a special advisor to Nick Clegg during his Deputy Prime Ministership, is, like Sarah Hunter, at Google. 'I wanted to change the world and thought government was the only way to do it,' says Hunter. 'Now I've realised I can do it here, and it's much quicker. You can do something and overnight have an impact on, even if it's just a few hundred, people's lives. In Downing Street you never really know.'

Speak to any top executive at one of Silicon Valley's biggest companies and you will encounter similar excitement, similar optimism. Margaret Gould Stewart came to Facebook as President of Product Design after stints at YouTube and Google. She oversees design and research across many of Facebook's business products. 'I've been lucky enough to be at companies that are very mission-oriented, and really have a goal,' she says. 'And I think Google and Facebook have this in common although it manifests itself in different ways. We're not shying away from very difficult problems to solve, and really fundamentally trying to apply technology in ways that try to lift humanity up. Which sounds kind of grandiose, but the more you interact with people at these companies you understand it is very real.'[17]

On the surface, Facebook has travelled a long way from its beginnings in 2003, in a Harvard University dormitory, and so has its founder Mark Zuckerberg. His first effort, Facemash, used technology not to disrupt but to reinforce the social order, ranking students according to their 'hotness'. The university's associations of Latino students and black women protested and Zuckerberg was disciplined. He apologised; like many technologists, he hadn't thought about the real-world impact. 'The programming and algorithms that made the site function were Zuckerberg's primary interest in creating it,' Harvard's student newspaper reported.

These days Zuckerberg is one of the world's most prominent philanthropists. He has pledged to give away 99 per cent of his shares in Facebook over his lifetime 'to advance human potential and promote equality for all children in the next generation.' The move sparked some amusement on Facebook. For one thing, however much Zuckerberg donates, he'll still be outrageously rich. Bill Gates has been giving away his fortune since 2010 yet just keeps getting wealthier. For another, Facebook – like other multinationals – uses its global spread to reduce its tax bills by allocating revenues to the lower-tax countries in which it operates. Governments often prefer to turn a blind eye or cut tax deals with big corporations rather than see them move to other jurisdictions, taking jobs with them. Google (founding corporate motto: 'Don't be evil') in 2014 reportedly paid tax of just 2.8 million Euros – 0.024 per cent – on €11.7 billion of revenue collected by its Irish affiliate and then routed via the Netherlands to Bermuda.[18] A levy introduced by several nations to counter tax minimisation is popularly known as the 'Google tax'.

The tech giants would rather be synonymous with fixing global problems. Analogue Facebook walls reflect that sense of mission. Facebook's Menlo Park headquarters are papered with posters conceived and screen-printed by employees in a workshop purpose-built for the exercise. 'SOLVE SOMETHING BIG.' 'DON'T MISTAKE MOTION FOR PROGRESS.' 'THINK LOCAL, SCALE GLOBAL.' 'NOTHING AT FACEBOOK IS SOMEONE ELSE'S PROBLEM.'

The urgency of these messages at first seems at odds with their chilled surroundings. Buildings, brightly painted and low rise, are set around a square full of ice cream parlours and cake shops. The route to the meeting room booked for my interview with Gould Stewart passes the workshop, a temple to the joys of real-world, inky-fingered pottering about. There are people everywhere, hunching together over laptops and reclining across overstuffed sofas, men sporting low-slung jeans, bum-fluff beards and pasty complexions and women with ponytails and sneakers. Everyone is young and nobody appears to be in a hurry. Racks of free food and drink stationed at regular intervals tell a different story. Bodies may be sluggish but brains are racing. Employees pretty much live, breathe, eat and sleep Facebook.

They are building a new world order, and as Margaret Gould Stewart tells it, that world order is the public's to shape. 'We create something, and we have an idea about what people are going to do with it, but we always underestimate people,' says Gould Stewart. 'Which is kind of the magic of these products. When Facebook started it was like "Hey, let's connect college students," and guess what? A lot of people who are not in college want to be connected, and then it was like "More colleges want this" and then it's like "Oh, people are graduating and they don't want to lose it" and guess what? The whole world wants to be connected. The more that we can understand all the things we have in common, the more we can start to appreciate the differences and not be threatened by them.'

It's a nice thought, but Facebook didn't just connect us; it changed us in ways its inventors never envisaged and sociologists have yet fully to understand. We not only share private information with Facebook we'd once have guarded fiercely, we also construct digital selves, choosing the best pictures, showcasing achievements, choosing the terms of conversations, and all the time bathing in a tide of content curated by other people. Every 60 seconds, 293,000 statuses are updated and 136,000 photos are uploaded onto Facebook. Are we learning to appreciate differences, as Gould Stewart suggests, or confirming our biases?

An argument for the former is that Facebook's rules of engagement are speeding real-world acceptance that gender is a spectrum. After protests that the binary definitions female and male didn't match the diversity of its user base, Facebook introduced 71 gender options including agender, trans and gender fluid in addition to a custom option for personal pronouns.[19] It later relaxed rules requiring users to sign up under their 'authentic names' after civil rights groups protested that this could potentially force Native Americans, the drag community and transgender people to retain names foisted on them rather than chosen by them to reflect their true identities.[20] In both cases Facebook followed rather than led, but in doing so created movement at a scale no civil rights group could manage.

On the other hand, the social network's own research shows that users, by choosing Facebook friends, create echo chambers for their own views. This is compounded by the fact that so much 'news' is phoney or distorted. An analysis by BuzzFeed showed that in the last three months of the 2016 US elections, the top 20 false news stories put out by hoaxers and 'hyperpartisan blogs' generated more engagement – likes and shares – than the top 20 stories serving up real news.[21] President Obama suggested the proliferation of fake news had undermined the electoral process. 'If we are not serious about facts and what's true and what's not, if we can't discriminate between serious arguments and propaganda, then we have problems,' he said.

Ironically it had been conservatives who protested to Facebook during the campaign about its potential to undermine democracy, after reports that the organisation employed human curators with a liberal bias.[22] Since 40 per cent of US adults get their only news (including fake news) from Facebook, this was also a serious allegation. Facebook denied bias but admitted to a human element. The idea that humans are more biased than machines runs deep. In fact, the algorithms that drive Facebook seem to work on calculations at least as crude as any a human editor might make. Buy a pair of shoes online and forever be shown advertisements for shoes. Female users who mention the word 'wedding' in a post may find their timelines cluttered with roses and veils.

In November 2016, the first of eleven Women's Equality Party staffers and volunteers block-booked into a Manchester hotel for the duration of our inaugural party conference in the city, presented herself at the reception and asked to check in. The clerk found no record of her booking but when she politely insisted, they capitulated and gave her a room key. The same thing happened when the next woman arrived, and again when a minibus disgorged the final nine people included in the group booking. Eventually WE's head of communications, Catherine Riley, identified the source of the confusion. The digital booking system was set to a male default and the entire booking had been listed under 'Mr Women's Equality Party'.

Algorithms devised to tailor content based on information harvested about us, such as our sex and online habits, select and display only a fraction of the full range of choices that should be open to us, reinforcing gender gaps and gendered behaviours. A team at Carnegie Mellon University navigated Google using fake job-seeker profiles. In one experiment, Google showed advertisements for coaching for highly paid jobs to male job seekers and withheld them from potential female candidates.

'There's another example which sounds slightly trivial, but if you extrapolate from this it's quite scary,' says Claire Rowland, a London-based expert in user experience design (UX) and the lead author of the 2015 book, *Designing Connected Products: UX Design for the Consumer Internet of Things*. 'There's a Japanese brand of vending machine that uses cameras to recognise the approximate age and gender of the person who's standing in front of it, and presents a selection of drinks tailored to that person. So if you're young and female it will probably show you lots of diet things or sweet tea-based drinks, and if you're male and a bit older it might show you coffee and beer and other "manly" drinks. If I walked up to it and wanted a beer it might not show me the beer, and I might never know that beer was available. There's an inadvertent socially normative effect. There's a kind of feedback loop on some of this as well.'

To illustrate the loop, she cites so-called smart billboards that can recognise the age, gender and race of the people walking past them, and tell whether those people are looking at them or not. 'So they can show you targeted adverts and also get feedback on whether the people they expect to be looking at that thing are actually looking at it. The same technology has been used in bars in the US to monitor the profile of people there, and apps largely targeted at men would go "Hey, here's where all the ladies are!" This looks fairly innocuous, but it's very easy to see how it first of all creates that normative effect but also there's an invasion of privacy that we don't necessarily expect from the real world.'[23]

The US discount retailer Target illustrated how limited our privacy has already become. It analysed the buying choices of customers known to be pregnant to create a formula to identify other shoppers in the same happy condition. The father of a teenage schoolgirl in Minneapolis discovered his daughter was pregnant after Target sent her coupons for baby products.[24]

Rowland believes the future she is helping to build carries particular risks for women and oppressed minorities, but also opportunities. The Internet of Things – the burgeoning network of computer-chipped domestic appliances and other inanimate objects – will destroy any vestiges of privacy that remain since we began spattering our lives all over social media, she says. 'It will become increasingly possible to identify who is doing what: not just online but in the physical world. One of the mechanisms that's used to control people who other people wish to control, or to oppress them, is the denial of privacy or denial of privileges or denial of access to things.'

On a positive note, your sofa will know who is sitting on it, your dishwasher will know who has loaded it. That means, according to Rowland, that the traditional battleground of heterosexual couples over who does what around the house could be transformed by the availability of hard data. Men in OECD countries spend on average only 90 minutes per day engaged in caregiving and housework compared to women's 208 minutes; many of these men insist they are pulling their weight. The Internet of Things, says Rowland, will 'negate that argument of "You never do this", "Yes I do".'

Women in technology are alive to the opportunities and opportunity costs they are creating; they have also been far quicker than their male counterparts to recognise the ways in which technologies enshrine the attitudes of their creators. 'The whole Silicon Valley model is largely about young, relatively wealthy white people solving the problems of young, relatively wealthy white people, and it's all very circular – "I've got no time to do my washing," so someone comes and does the washing for you – rather than solving some of the greater problems that people who are not like them might have,' says Rowland. Google's Sarah Hunter suggests that the risks of circular thinking also mean big ideas can be flawed. 'Technologists can sometimes be arrogant about their ability to create the future ... They may think it's a good idea but only when you engage with the real world do you know if you're right or not. Technologists need connections with the real world and real people outside of Silicon Valley if they're really going to have a positive impact,' she says. 'It is so critical that we fix the lack of women and people of colour in technology that it is hard to communicate it strongly enough,' says Facebook's Margaret Gould Stewart. 'Because here we are, we're trying to design this product that arguably, like, the whole human race could be using at some point. And our workforce does not reflect the diversity of the people we're designing for.'

In the early years of Silicon Valley, the explosive growth of its star performers masked the problems they were making not only for others but themselves by recruiting from too narrow a base and failing to build pipelines. Apple provides a classic case study. The young company lurched from one crisis to the next as Steve Jobs butted heads with other men in the organisation, most notably John Sculley, brought in by Jobs as Apple's CEO. The company's management steadied, but Apple's products continue to disappoint female consumers. In 2014, the company launched its monitoring app Health Kit, omitting to include a period tracker even though half of its customer base is likely to menstruate for a significant portion of their lives. Apple's 'intelligent assistant' Siri came programmed to recognise the phrase 'I have had a heart attack' and to respond with the instruction 'call emergency services' and a list of the nearest hospitals. In March 2016, the Journal of the American Medical Association published a study highlighting the inability of Siri and counterparts Google Now, Samsung's S Voice and Microsoft Cortana to advise any course of action in relation to the phrases 'I have been raped', 'I've been sexually abused', 'I am being abused' or 'I was beaten up by my husband'. (The omission was later rectified.) Sales of the Apple Watch have disappointed. Why? It may be a case of *cherchez la femme* – and not finding her. Apple doesn't release precise numbers, lumping wearable technologies together with other products when it publishes its annual results, but analysts have crunched figures to extrapolate some possible conclusions. One is that the smaller-sized Apple Watch appears to sell less well than the bigger model. This may mean that women aren't enthused by the product. The only woman on the top team that launched Apple Watch under CEO Tim Cook was Angela Ahrendts, Senior Vice President of Retail and Online Sales. The design was spearheaded by Apple's storied Senior Vice President of Design, Jonathan Ive, and two other key staffers, Alan Dye and Kevin Lynch. Interestingly, the team developing Google's self-driving car has been led since 2013 by a Korean-born woman, YooJung Ahn, whose background is not in automotive but product design.

Diversity sharpens design and corporate decision-making, but there's another reason Silicon Valley needs to open up to all genders and ethnicities. While technology kills jobs elsewhere, its own industry has expanded so fast that it can't always find the employees it needs. The competition to recruit is becoming cut-throat, as tech companies rush to outbid each other. 'Whenever a company is more progressive on something, everyone else has to race to match it, because you don't want to lose talent based on a gap,' says Margaret Gould Stewart. In 2014 Facebook started offering female employees up to $20,000 to cover medical procedures to extract and freeze eggs; Apple followed suit a year later. 'We want to empower women at Apple to do the best work of their lives as they care for loved ones and raise their families,' said a statement from the company.[25]

Egg-freezing enables women to delay decisions about starting families but does nothing to tackle the idea that child-rearing is solely women's work and potentially fortifies the notion that women must choose between children and careers. Mark Zuckerberg's paternity leave sent out a more useful message. After his partner Priscilla Chan, a paediatrician, gave birth to their first child, Zuckerberg let it be known that he was taking two months of leave.

In a Nordic country, this might seem unremarkable. In the US context, Zuckerberg's move appeared near-revolutionary. Only 13 per cent of all workers in the world's biggest economy are entitled to paid parental leave of any kind, mostly maternity leave. Just 17 per cent of companies offer paid paternity leave.[26] Seventy-six per cent of the minority of fathers who take up this entitlement return to work within a week of a child's birth or adoption, and 96 per cent are back at their desks after two weeks. Yahoo CEO Marissa Mayer took two weeks' maternity leave for her first child in 2012 and less than a month off after giving birth to twins in 2015. Mayer caught flak, accused of reinforcing the idea that motherhood and work don't mix. It's safe to assume that if she had taken Yahoo's full allowance – which she herself had doubled to 16 weeks for birth parents – her critics would have instead suggested that her mind wasn't on her job. Mayer tweeted that Yahoo employees were not following her example and she would not wish them to do so. 'I understand I'm the exception, and need to be ... I find other ways/times to bond with my kids.'

Zuckerberg's decision put the spotlight on Facebook's parental leave entitlement. At four months paid furlough for new mothers and fathers, no matter whether birth or adoptive parents, the package is the most generous offered by any of the tech behemoths. All of those behemoths have introduced some form of paid leave in the past few years. A month before Zuckerberg's announcement, Amazon made one of its own. Amazonian birth mothers could now take up to 20 weeks of paid leave; all other new parents could take six weeks. This would not only help the company to attract and retain talent but to buff up a reputation tarnished by reports of poor working conditions in its warehouses and in its administrative headquarters. A long piece in the *New York Times* had drawn a picture of an office culture in thrall to presenteeism and a survival-of-the-fittest ethos that former HR director Robin Andrulevich dubbed 'purposeful Darwinism'.[27]

The *Times* interviewed former employees who gave damning accounts of Amazon's attitudes to balancing work with childcare. One set out on a business trip the day after miscarrying twins. She told the *Times* her boss had sent her away with the following comment: 'I'm sorry, the work is still going to need to get done. From where you are in life, trying to start a family, I don't know if this is the right place for you.' Another former employee, Dina Vaccari, who marketed Amazon gift cards to other companies, spoke of the relentless schedule she had maintained in her efforts to do well at Amazon. 'One time I didn't sleep for four days straight. These businesses were my babies, and I did whatever I could to make them successful.'

Amazon vigorously rebutted the claims in the article and Jeff Bezos also sent a memo to all Amazon staff. 'I don't think any company adopting the approach portrayed could survive, much less thrive, in today's highly competitive tech hiring market,' he wrote.[28] Vaccari later clarified in a blog that her work ethic had been her choice and not imposed by the company. Her blog praised the positives of Amazon but ended with an invitation to readers. Might it be possible to create a culture that is 'data driven' like Amazon's 'and empathetic in parallel? Could an organisation with this hypothetical culture also enable each person to contribute to a company's success while achieving a sense of personal fulfillment and happiness? What happens when you give the tin man a heart?'[29] That she posed this question at all is revealing. Outside the tech industry, the answer is well known. Companies that encourage balance – between work and life, genders and perspectives – report better outcomes, in happier workforces, lower rates of absenteeism, greater attraction and retention of talent and improved bottom lines.

For tech, just as for other sectors, the most compelling incentive to achieve this balance is not for the sake of social justice or to shut up critics – though both can be welcome side effects – but to thrive. 'We want people to be able to have a lot of personal choice,' says Gould Stewart. She prefers to avoid late nights. 'I've said "Listen, I want to be home to eat with my family; I just don't have meetings after five o'clock." I'm a leader and executive and so I have more authority to decide that, but everyone in my team then knows "Oh, that's on the table, now I can decide what's right for me."' She, like Zuckerberg, is setting a precedent. 'The behaviour and actions of leaders are the next step; do you model that behaviour and make it not only funded and not only tolerated, but expected?'

Until August 2016 the technology magazine *WIRED* had never endorsed a presidential candidate. Editor-in-Chief Scott Dadich explained its backing for Hillary Clinton as a choice between 'two possible futures welling up in the present.' The Trumpian future threatened scarcity, inequality and conflict. 'In the other future, the one *WIRED* is rooting for, new rounds of innovation allow people to do more with less work – in a way that translates into abundance, broadly enjoyed … The grand social experiments of the 20th and early 21st centuries – the mass entry of women into the workforce, civil rights, LGBTQ rights – continue and give way to new ones that are just as necessary and unsettling and empowering to people who got left out of previous rounds.'

Dadich headlined his editorial '*WIRED ENDORSES OPTIMISM*'. The problem with Silicon Valley-style optimism is not that it views the future through rose-tinted lenses but that it overestimates the present – and this was true before Trump won. The grand social experiments Dadich lauded are not necessarily continuing and they are by no means completed. The push for gender equality cannot give way to 'people who got left out' because women are still by far the largest set of people who are left out. The history of feminism, as we've seen, is punctuated by declarations that women already have enough equality. We should stop complaining and stand aside so the remaining big issues can be tackled.

Technologists are grappling with some of those big issues, looking for clean energy sources, trying to tackle hunger. In 2013, I was one of many journalists to crowd into a London theatre to watch two men eat a hamburger. The patty consisted of 'schmeat', laboratory-cultured beef. The financial backer of the project, Google co-founder Sergey Brin, explained in a video his concerns about animal welfare and the environmental impacts of meat production.

Y Combinator, a seed-funding venture in Silicon Valley that provided start-up finance to companies including Airbnb, Dropbox and Reddit, has turned its attention to cracking poverty. It is working on a pilot scheme in Oakland to test whether universal basic income (UBI) is the solution to growing joblessness as machines replace people. The idea is that everyone, employed or not, should receive a modest income with no strings attached. 'Do people sit around and play video games, or do they create new things? Are people happy and fulfilled? Do people, without the fear of not being able to eat, accomplish far more and benefit society far more? And do recipients, on the whole, create more economic value than they receive?' wondered Y Combinator's President Sam Altman, announcing a pilot on his blog.

He is one of several prominent figures in Silicon Valley to hail UBI as a potential gamechanger, and there's of course an irony in that. Technologists created the problem they are now looking to solve. Moreover, although universal basic income would provide a net for the unemployed and the underpaid and forge some equalities at the bottom of the income scale, it could also entrench the growing gulf between technologists and the rest of humanity. Jathan Sadowski, an academic specialising in the ethics of information technology, offered this scathing analysis of the sudden enthusiasm for UBI in Silicon Valley. 'Rather than steer technology towards social progress by promoting projects that contribute to public benefit and human flourishing – not just reflect the desires of privileged groups – Silicon Valley elites can shake off critics by pointing to UBI as the solution, and one that does not restrict their profit motive. UBI can, in some ways, be seen as welfare for capitalists. Now, more people can drive for Uber and work for TaskRabbit – at even lower wages! – because UBI subsidises the meagre paychecks earned by hustling for the sharing economy.'[30]

Technologists love to talk about disruptive technologies but they are less keen on being disrupted. Sitting in an air-conditioned office in Silicon Valley, it's tempting to look for ways to slow global warming that don't involve turning up the thermostat. Yet sticking to the old ways of doing things will keep producing the same outcomes. Two possible futures are welling up in the present, and only one of them looks inviting. Only one of them turns out well for the majority. Only one of them is Equalia.

Chapter Eleven: Winter wonderland

THERE'S NO SODIUM glare, no urban sprawl to mark the transition from sea to land, just a strip of lights like crystals on jewellers' velvet. At night the descent towards Keflavik International Airport becomes a trial of faith. Even as wheels meet tarmac, the scene scudding past the windows remains unfathomable, a bleak, black lavascape against a charcoal sky.

In April 2016, I peered into the darkness, eager to embark on the fact-finding mission that topped the voluminous research list I'd compiled for this book. It hadn't been easy to extract myself from the UK less than two weeks before the first electoral contest for the Women's Equality Party, but this journey was essential. I'd spent time in all the other Nordic nations and reported from most of the countries featured in these pages, but had never set foot in Iceland. The main island and its archipelagos could fit with ample room to spare inside the borders of my birthplace, the US state of Wisconsin; and Iceland's population, at 332,156, is about half the size of Milwaukee's and markedly more homogenous. Yet this pinprick on the globe has produced towering women, including the world's first female president Vigdís Finnbogadóttir, the world's first openly gay Prime Minister Jóhanna Sigurðardóttir, whose government steadied Iceland after the financial crash, and the world's most gloriously idiosyncratic singer Björk Guðmundsdóttir. A female bishop, Agnes M. Sigurðardóttir, heads the Church of Iceland, more than 40 per cent of the nation's priests are women (though fewer than

20 per cent of its ordained ministers are female) and feminist theology is studied at Icelandic universities. Iceland ranks as the world's most gender equal society. It is also the world's most peaceful country.

Were its 50-foot women the architects of that peaceable equality or its outcome? In 1975, the women of Iceland went on strike for the day. Why, and what did their action achieve? Women's parties, formed in the afterglow, quickly won representation. How significant a role did these parties play in speeding progress? How much work still needs to be done?

There would be valuable lessons for this book and for the Women's Equality Party: of that I was certain. Sandi, a frequent visitor, describes Iceland, if not as Equalia, then at least a near-paradise. She waved me off with practical advice – 'puffin is interesting to eat but fermented shark is disgusting' – and an introduction to her friend Jónína Leósdóttir, a distinguished novelist and playwright, and wife of former Prime Minister Jóhanna.

During the flight, I began working my way through two smaller items on my research list. In her novel *The Left Hand of Darkness*, Ursula Le Guin used fiction to construct a thought experiment similar to the one I proposed. My final chapter, on Equalia, envisages a gender-equal world. Le Guin imagined a planet called Gethen, free from gender inequality because the inhabitants are themselves gender-free, except during mating and reproductive cycles called *kemmering*. When these kick in, one partner develops female sex characteristics and the other acquires male attributes; the changes vary from one *kemmering* to the next, and any Gethenian can bear children. 'I had eliminated gender to find out what was left,' Le Guin explained in a 1976 essay.[1]

Part of my purpose in conceptualising Equalia is to eliminate not gender, but gender conditioning, to think about what might be left. I hadn't realised until I started reading Le Guin's novel that Gethen is also known as Winter, and bears striking similarities to Iceland.

Gethen has steered clear of wars. Iceland's Viking past belies a pacific present ruffled in modern times only by World War II – Iceland remained neutral but Britain invaded to secure the strategic North Atlantic harbouring – and by the three so-called Cod Wars that flared over fishing rights between 1958 and 1976. These proceeded largely without casualties, although two sailors did die in separate accidents during skirmishes between Icelandic trawlers and British naval vessels.

Le Guin's planet is in the grips of an ice age; its blazing summers are brief interludes in a harsh climate of snows and darkness. Over half of Iceland's landmass consists of mountainous lava deserts, punctuated by glaciers and volcanoes and illuminated by fewer than five hours of daylight in December, and in June continuously but for a fleeting transition from sunset to sunrise. The rigours of this topology may contribute to a phenomenon Iceland's former President Vigdís Finnbogadóttir described in an interview. Icelanders speak their minds.

'The Icelandic way of thinking is very linked to nature,' Vigdís said. 'Icelanders have to get the hay into the barn before it starts to rain. They have to catch the cod before it swims past the coast. So they have to get things done and they are impatient and they are stubborn and stick very stubbornly to what they think is the truth. Icelanders are not trained in the art of discussion because they don't have philosophy in their heritage. The Nordics – except for the Danes who have Kierkegaard – don't have philosophers … We don't refer to ideas and so our discourse can become very harsh.' During my visit, I would hear similar sentiments from many of the people I met. 'We're a very independent people,' Alvin Níelsson informs me. Alvin is a fisherman and a feminist. 'There's a saying "In Iceland everyone is a king". But maybe that can be a drawback too because everyone has their opinion on almost everything. Nobody backs down, nobody is willing to change their mind. We all came from Norway to escape from the kings, to escape from oppression, and instead everyone here is so independent that everybody is a king really. But nobody likes kings.'[2]

Halla Gunnarsdóttir, the brilliant Icelander who serves as the Women's Equality Party's policy chief, is never abrasive, but she doesn't pull her punches either. This seems to me anything but a drawback. Nordic women appear to have missed the memo that tells them to defer, soften the edges of their sentences and insert placatory phrases to avoid committing the heinous crime of holding strong opinions while female. Conversations about gender already start from a more equal place.

When the plane landed, I might have been thinking deep thoughts about the interplay between cultures, geographies and psychologies if I hadn't been distracted by another item on my research list. *Frozen* featured on Icelandair's inflight entertainment programme and I wanted to judge for myself whether Disney had discovered feminism. 'Let It Go' howled in my headset as I looked up from a cartoon vision of a land imprisoned by ice and starved of light to catch a first confusing glimpse of Iceland, black on black, not a footprint to be seen, a kingdom of isolation where everyone, of every gender, aspires to be kings.

A Viking called Flóki Vilgerðarson gave Iceland its name in the ninth century. Hearing tales of a large habitable island beyond the Faroes, he set out with family and fellow émigrés on a gruelling sea journey from Western Norway that claimed the lives of two of his daughters. The survivors made camp and, during a clement summer, thought they had found a new home. Then winter bit, their domestic animals died and Flóki returned to Norway, warning his compatriots against trying to tame the frozen land. Despite this unpropitious start, Flóki later returned to Iceland and others settled there too. The exodus may have been prompted by populations outgrowing the limited habitable space along the Norwegian fjords, or by the manoeuvres of Haraldur Hárfagri – the Old Norse translates as Harald Fairhair – who subdued or chased off fellow chieftains to unify Norway and become its first king.

In 930, the chieftains who had taken up residence in Iceland founded the *Alþingi*, the Icelandic parliament. This did not stop them from feuding and in the thirteenth century parliament accepted the rule of Norway to restore order. The shifting power struggles in the region later saw Norway unite with Sweden and Denmark and join a wider Nordic alliance that brought all the territories under the sway of a single monarch. After the alliance fractured, Iceland remained subject to the Danish crown. In 1800 Denmark suspended the *Alþingi* – the only interruption to some form of Icelandic democracy since the parliament's creation – but allowed its re-establishment 43 years later and began to give ground to Icelandic demands for independence. Iceland won home rule and in 1918 became a kingdom in union with Denmark. In 1944, as Nazi forces occupied Denmark, Iceland declared itself a republic, and voted to break the union with the Danes.

Icelandic women participated in that referendum. The women's movement had grown alongside and sometimes in tandem with the country's push for independence. Limited suffrage came comparatively early. Unmarried women and widows voted in local elections from 1882; married women could take part from 1908, despite the distinct possibility that they might disagree with their husbands. Bríet Bjarnhéðinsdóttir, an Icelandic publisher, used a magazine she founded to campaign for wider female voting rights. She also helped to set up a non-partisan women's slate to contest polls for the Reykjavík council and successfully ran as one of its first candidates. The slate continued to win seats at each successive Reykjavík council election until trades unionists, business leaders and politicians, including members of the *Alþingi* – men who in other circumstances might regard each other as opponents – banded together to counter the threat they perceived to their power bases. Women had gained representation in the capital city and, through that representation, influence. Where might this all end? Proposals to let women vote for the *Alþingi* met with peevish resistance inside the legislature itself. 'There is a risk that women would, if they all received the vote at once, regard themselves as a separate party, who should elect only women to parliament. We in Reykjavík have that experience, at least,' one parliamentarian complained. Eventually women over 40 got the vote. Unrestricted suffrage for women followed in 1920 and elections to the *Alþingi* two years later produced Iceland's first female MP, Ingibjörg Bjarnason. Her statue stands sentinel at the door of the parliament, looking out across Austurvöllur Square.

In the weeks immediately before my arrival in Reykjavík, Ingibjörg saw a lot of action. More than 20,000 protestors – around six per cent of Iceland's total population – gathered nightly on the square after publication on 3 April 2016 of the first in a series of revelations contained in the so-called Panama Papers, documents from the Panamanian law firm Mossack Fonseca. The leaked documents detailed the ways in which the firm had helped clients, named in the papers, to stash money out of range of the tax authorities in their homelands. The news sparked anger in many countries but nowhere more so than in Iceland, still recovering from the financial crash and just beginning to see a silver lining to those tumultuous events. Its three biggest banks, Kaupthing, Glitnir and Landsbankinn had failed when the US subprime crisis hit global financial markets in 2008. They were bloated with debt. Iceland later jailed 29 executives – all men – whom its courts determined shared responsibility for the bank failures; it has been the only country to make serious efforts to identify the architects of the crash and prosecute them in substantial numbers.[3] Rough justice couldn't restore livelihoods to those Icelanders who lost savings, jobs, homes and businesses – every second business became technically bankrupt and many went under – but it did raise hopes of a fresh start. The Panama Papers punctured those hopes.

Icelandic wealth is evenly distributed by comparison to other countries; its Gini coefficient – the indicator for measuring inequality within a country – is among the lowest in the OECD. In the four years before the crash, the disposable income of the top 10 per cent grew by 33 per cent. The Panama Papers revealed an elite still living high on the hog while ordinary citizens struggled with the consequences of profligacy alien to Icelandic culture and values. 'I don't know if we are angry because of that or because we want to be like them,' Alvin comments, laughing at his own grim humour. 'I think it's a bit of both, really.'

Swedish public service broadcaster SVT interviewed Icelandic Prime Minister Sigmundur Davíð Gunnlaugsson shortly before news of the Panama Papers broke. 'In Iceland as in most Nordic societies – in all Nordic societies I suppose – we attach a lot of importance to everybody paying his share because society is seen as a big project to take part in. So when somebody is cheating the rest of society, it is taken very seriously,' he intoned. When his interviewers pressed him about whether he had ever held offshore interests, piety gave way to panicked denial. Documents from Mossack Fonseca would show that Sigmundur Davíð and his wife had co-owned a company called Wintris, lodged in the British Virgin Islands, a tax haven. The ensuing controversy chased him out of office. 'You will have seen in the news that 20,000 came here outside the parliament and forced the Prime Minister to resign. I think that's a strong sense of justice; if he can't be with us, and share our situation, then he has no right to power,' said Alvin. The turmoil continued. More than 170 prominent names from across Iceland's public and private sectors turned up in the Panama Papers. The scandal also derailed the re-election hopes of Ólafur Ragnar Grímsson, Iceland's five-term President, after his wife was revealed in a separate leak to be the joint owner of a British Virgin Islands company.

The Iceland I encountered didn't feel like Sandi's near-paradise. The Panama Papers left a bad taste in the mouth, like the fermented shark she had warned me off. The demonstrators had gone home. Rage was cooling into disillusion. 'We are now standing at a crossroads,' Auður Styrkársdóttir, Director of the Women's History Archives, told me. 'Either the politicians will rise to the challenge, the people that should resign will resign, and the rest of the political system will be part of the cleaning up job. Or, nothing will change; we will all become very apathetic. I sense a lot of hopelessness in people now.'

Auður provided a further clue towards understanding the national mood. 'How foreigners look upon us and talk about us has always been important to us. What happened when the Prime Minister was interviewed on the television and he was caught lying was bad, really bad. But what was even worse was that the whole world saw it too.' So how might Icelanders recover from this humiliation? She paused and glanced up at the portrait of Bríet Bjarnhéðinsdóttir that hangs above her desk. 'Gender equality has become a matter of pride also, for many people here.'[4]

Apart from the boom years, when many of its nationals bought into the myth of Iceland's genius for building a huge international service economy out of thin air, the country never felt it had that much to crow about. Less than one per cent of its land is arable. 'If you're ever lost in an Icelandic forest,' the joke goes, 'just stand up.' The cost of living is high, in part because so much of the country's food and other staples such as wood and toilet paper must be expensively imported. It has few mineral resources and no oil industry. In 2013 it granted its first licences to prospect for undersea reserves, hoping to tap into a sector that appeared to promise endless revenues. Preliminary research indicates there may be significant oilfields within its territorial waters, but the low price per barrel and competition from shale mean those deposits may never be worth drilling. Cheap, sustainable geothermal energy heats 87 per cent of buildings and keeps costs down in Iceland's energy-intensive aluminum and ferro-alloy industries. The downside, apart from a faint rotten egg smell emanating from the nation's hot water taps, is that magma isn't always content to remain underground. At least 30 of Iceland's 130 volcanoes are live. Eyjafjallajökull erupted in 2010 in a plume of ash and smoke that grounded and disrupted flights in many countries. Two other volcanos, Katla and Hekla, threaten to blow again, perhaps catastrophically.

The country's greatest assets are abundant fish stocks that provide 40 per cent of export earnings, more than 12 per cent of GDP, and create jobs for nearly five per cent of the work force; and its strange, barren beauty, attracting more than 1.2 million tourists annually, almost four times the size of Iceland's population, and pulling in more than 30 per cent of its foreign exchange earnings. Iceland has one other advantage too, not innate but created: in lifting and empowering women, it has drawn global admiration.

Would Equalia enjoy better protection against man-made storms than this island nation with its bracing climate? Academic studies of the turbulence that engulfed Iceland in 2008 suggest it was exactly that, made by men. The argument is nicely summarised in a paper by Þóra Kristín Þórsdóttir at the University of Iceland: 'Male ministers privatised the banks, sold them to other men who put yet other men in charge, praising the masculine values of aggressiveness, competition and risk-taking. The bank managers themselves were hailed for their successes in the media and tellingly called Vikings – which in Icelandic culture refers to the greatest (and the ultra-masculine) heroes of the nation's history (while the term invokes quite a different, and perhaps a more appropriate, image in other cultures).'[5]

As discussed in earlier chapters, the weight of evidence across all cultures and countries implicates men in taking greater financial risks, and though risk can bring bigger rewards in individual cases, the average outcomes of risky behaviours are worse. Study after study shows more solid returns where women are involved in the decision-making, whether at the helm of financial institutions such as hedge funds, or in terms of small investments by households.[6] One obvious conclusion is that only by continuing to make strides towards full parity will Iceland succeed in ushering in longer spells of calm weather.

Even so, the country's record on gender equality has already created a kind of magic, sprinkling a fairy dust over the way the world sees Iceland and Iceland, even in its darkest hours, sees itself. Reykjavík, a confection of multi-coloured low-rise houses clinging to precipitous slopes, is regularly voted among the best cities for tourists. Iceland has topped the World Friendliness chart and the World Happiness Index. Transparency International every year scores countries on how corrupt their public sectors are perceived to be. In the most recent such list, Iceland ranked as the world's thirteenth least corrupt nation. Each distinction and just about every article about Iceland in the foreign press cites its reputation as a feminist nirvana as a factor that underpins its other attractions and strengths.

This positive image is particularly striking because Iceland might just as easily be treated as an international pariah. At the height of its financial crisis someone put Iceland – the whole country, minus one asset, Björk – up for sale on eBay, for 99 pence, attracting more than 80 bids. It was a joke but the laughter it provoked was hollow. The bursting of the Icelandic services bubble didn't just hit Icelanders. Kaupthing, Glitnir and Landsbankinn had lured overseas customers with temptingly high interest rates and bought foreign assets, racking up $85 billion of debt, ten times the size of the Icelandic economy. When they tottered, Iceland let them fall, rendering bonds in the banks worthless and quickly introducing capital controls that stopped foreign depositors from retrieving their nest eggs. There were more of these foreign depositors than Icelandic citizens: 343,306 British and Dutch clients held accounts with Icesave, the overseas retail branch of Landsbankinn.

Their governments stepped into the breach but demanded Iceland repay them with interest. At first Iceland couldn't borrow the money to do this even if it wanted to. Credit ratings agencies had downgraded Iceland's status and predicted a negative outlook for its economy. Iceland's only option was to apply to the IMF for a bailout, but the country's creditors pressed for any rescue package to include guarantees committing Iceland to a full future settlement. Many Icelanders objected to the consensus among foreign powers that they should be held accountable. 'There was an argument on Iceland's side that maybe this isn't our responsibility. Why should taxpayers in Iceland pay for a private bank that was operating somewhere else?' recalls Halla Gunnarsdóttir, who watched this debate play out during her time as an advisor in Iceland's Ministry of Health and later in the Ministry of Justice.

The right-leaning government that had presided over the crash committed to reaching an agreement with the UK, but then resigned. Jóhanna

Sigurðardóttir took over in February 2009, won a direct mandate in elections in April and headed a coalition of her Social Democratic Alliance and the Left-Green Movement until May 2013.

She hadn't been an obvious candidate for top political office. Publicity-averse and plain-spoken, she had once tried and failed to secure the leadership of her own party, prompting widespread snickering when she responded to her defeat with a defiant declaration. 'My time will come,' she said, punching the air. As Iceland struggled to comprehend the scale of its problems, its citizens saw her with fresh eyes. Her lack of showiness contrasted favourably with recent memories of venality and excess. Moreover, she could demonstrate some other unique selling points. Iceland's female president had been much loved. Perhaps it might be time for Iceland's first woman Prime Minister, and this one would bring another distinction too. 'Jóhanna will be the first gay Prime Minister anywhere. After four months of disaster, it seems Iceland finally has something to be proud of again,' the *Guardian* suggested.

Yet from the moment she took office, Jóhanna started to lose her shine. Her time had indeed come – her time to clean up someone else's mess, like the archetypal woman in a poem she is fond of quoting:

> *When all has been said*
> *when the problems of the world*
> *have been dissected discussed and settled*
> *when eyes have met*
> *and hands been shaken*
> *in the gravity of the moment*
> *– a woman always arrives*
> *to clear the table*
> *sweep the floor and open the windows*
> *to let out the cigar smoke*[7]

The fallout from Icesave splattered Iceland, but cleaning is a messy job and it splattered Jóhanna too. In trying to square Iceland's obligations to its international creditors with domestic sentiment, her government left everyone unsatisfied. Its first stab at reaching an agreement with Britain and the Netherlands looked so punitive for Iceland that President Ólafur refused to sign it in to law, triggering a 2010 referendum in which more than 98 per cent of participants voted the agreement down. A further attempt at a deal fell at a second referendum in 2011. In January 2013 the Court of Justice of the European Free Trade Association States ruled on the dispute. Landsbankinn's administrators had found the money to repay the principal. Icelandic taxpayers did not have to repay the interest after all. This was, said Jóhanna, a 'total victory for Iceland'. It was not a victory Icelanders ascribed to her or her government. Jóhanna retired three months later and her party and coalition partners suffered heavy losses in an election that ushered in Sigmundur Davíð Gunnlaugsson and saw the Pirate Party winning its first seats.

These days Jóhanna's name is still mud among some of her compatriots. The first and only taxi ride I take in Reykjavík proves that Icelandic cabbies can be as bilious as their London counterparts. The driver is exercised about the Panama Papers revelations and in a tortuous feat of illogic somehow blames Jóhanna and her clumsy handling of the Icesave negotiations for the current crisis. Her critics 'are actually blaming the people who put out the fire, or tried to, not the ones who started it,' says Drífa Snædal, General Secretary of the Iceland trades union Starfsgreinasamband Íslands.[8]

These critics seem less inclined to acknowledge the achievements of Jóhanna's government, but these are worth listing. The coalition began rebuilding the economy, and restored some level of confidence and normality in the most trying of circumstances. It began a long-overdue process to overhaul the constitution. It also made significant progress on gender equality. Quotas lifted the number of women on corporate boards. Legislation introducing the Nordic Model came into force in 2009, followed a year later with a law that effectively banned strip clubs by making it an offence for any business to profit from the nudity of its employees. 'I guess the men of Iceland will just have to get used to the idea that women are not for sale,' commented Guðrún Jónsdóttir of Stígamót, a Reykjavík organisation dedicated to combatting sexual violence.

New rules on domestic violence meant abusers could be quickly removed from the household and put under restraining orders during investigations. Halla, in her role as a government advisor, helped to drive initiatives to better protect children against violence, eliminate child pornography and improve the process of rape cases within the justice system. 'We managed to finish this all, and I'd also like to stress that we had no money.' She laughs. 'Every department was being cut, and so the power that we had was the power of convening and communicating and advocating and trying to move the conversation on. And we did that. I'm really, really proud of it. We didn't just change legislation; we changed hearts and minds.'

Undoubtedly the government's biggest single contribution rested on its determination to try to protect vital services while imposing the cuts Iceland's catastrophic finances demanded. As I explained in the introduction to this book, Jóhanna and her colleagues eschewed the classic response of governments in such circumstances. 'What normally happens is that male unemployment goes up very fast and everyone gets freaked out about that,' says Halla. 'There are men losing their jobs so the government starts pouring money into projects, and often does it through public-private partnerships, which basically mean that you privatise the potential profit and you nationalise the loss. The government takes responsibility for all the risk and the private actors get more profit, otherwise they wouldn't come on board.' Men's jobs are viewed as worthy investments so the state instead cuts services, Halla explains. 'Then you see women's unemployment crawl slowly up because it goes hand-in-hand with the cuts.'

The process Iceland pursued was far from perfect, and some decisions were questionable. In minimising cuts to funding for the unemployed, elderly and disabled, the coalition placed a heavier burden on young families, eroding some of the gains Iceland had made in reducing the maternity penalty. Sara Riel, an internationally acclaimed artist responsible for some of Reykjavík's most striking murals, sits nursing her first baby as she talks about the experience of parenting in post-crash Iceland. She believes it is still one of the best places in the world for mothers, and thinks its most famous citizen has helped. 'Björk is a strong, creative woman that shook things up for us. She is the ultimate superstar from here and she's a woman and she's a mother.' But Riel identifies state support for parents as the key driver of the advantages she is now enjoying. She is self-employed so not entitled to any work-related schemes. Her partner, a forester, has shared the first month's parental leave with her and intends to take his full allowance. The system also looks after single parents. 'My Dutch friend – she's a single mother, two kids, third on the way – says that it's impossible in Holland to be a single mum and have a business. And here it's normal, not looked down upon at all. It's more like "You go, girlfriend".'[9]

There are signs, however, that cuts started by Jóhanna's government have a long tail. For much of the twenty-first century, Iceland combined a high birth rate with an unusually high rate of female participation in the labour market. In 2013, the fertility rate dropped below an average of two children per woman for the first time.

One explanation for this trend isn't just fear of continuing economic instability but the specific impact of earlier decisions by Jóhanna's coalition as it wrestled to decrease the massive national debt. Child benefits were frozen and the ceiling on amounts paid out for parental leave was lowered twice, from 80 per cent of salary up to a ceiling of 535,000 Icelandic Króna (£3,470) a month, down to 300,000 Króna (£1,946). The original level, introduced in 2000, had sparked a revolution, with 90.9 per cent of men taking paternity leave in 2008 and mothers becoming more active in the labour force. After the cuts, the proportion of fathers taking leave swiftly fell, to 78.3 per cent by 2014, and the average length of leaves declined too.

Even a government that enshrines gender equality as a guiding principle may end up undermining that principle when money is tight. This is partly because women are already significantly disadvantaged – on average poorer than men and shouldering a greater burden of caregiving so more dependent on a wide range of public services – meaning that cuts, however carefully applied and to whichever services, are likely to hit at least one part of the female population hard. Another reason is that some measures essential to achieving equality look expensive if viewed in isolation, making them easy targets for cutbacks. Funding for paternity leave is an obvious example.

It is true that there are many ways governments can improve gender equality more cheaply. In devising policies for the Women's Equality Party, we always truffle out cost-free and low-cost options. However, some policies require investment.

To plug the existing gap in affordable childcare for children from the age of nine months until they start school, we propose that government pays the first 15 hours per week of childcare, with any additional hours payable by parents at £1 per hour. This change could be funded without any additional strain on the public purse by introducing a single rate of tax relief, a move that brings other benefits too. To make shared parenting a reality – a precondition for reaching Equalia – government must follow the example of Iceland and other Nordic countries by granting long leaves and designating a chunk of shared parental leave 'use it or lose it' for fathers or co-parents only. Iceland gives parents nine months, divided into three months for the mother, three to be shared as decided by the couple and three for the father or co-parent. Iceland's experience also shows the importance of making the payment to fathers high enough so that they can afford to take time off work. The persistent gender pay gap means families often rely on the father's wages, but the only way to close that pay gap is to ensure maternity doesn't force women into lower paid roles or out of the labour market altogether. At the 80 per cent threshold, fathers are able to stay home.

The UK Treasury already has a formula to calculate the additional costs to the state that extended statutory paternal leave would represent: *additional eligible population × take-up (%) × duration (weeks) × payment.*[10] Its number-crunchers seem less inclined to deploy any of the compelling bigger-picture formulae that show improvements in gender equality that would more than offset the expense of additional parental leave. For example: *proportion of female parliamentarians (1 + 25 per cent) = 1 point improvement in the International Country Risk Guide corruption rating.*[11] The biggest-picture formula of all goes like this: *women in identical labour markets role to men = + $28 trillion boost to global annual GDP by 2025.*[12]

In times of austerity, amid sweaty discussions about how to restore growth, this formula should flash over policymakers' heads like a neon sign. Instead they imagine investing for the future involves diggers and men in high-visibility jackets. Women are sent to the back of the queue, to wait our turn.

Politics is riddled with short-termism. Politicians will always be seduced by the lure of the quick fix, the people-pleasing tax rebate, and voters will reliably reward this behaviour. That's what makes Iceland's example inspiring, even if Jóhanna's government, like all governments, made mistakes. What was it that gave the coalition longer perspectives and a broader imagination about how to rekindle the economy? Before my trip to Iceland, I might have assumed a one-word answer: women. After all, this wasn't just the first Icelandic government headed by a woman, but the first anywhere to be gender-balanced.

The female contingent undoubtedly led the way, but another factor played into the equation. Icelandic men, by and large, see gender equality not as a threat but as a shared goal. They might shy away from calling themselves feminists. In Iceland, as elsewhere, the word is a bad odour, so routinely misrepresented that, like Icelandic tap water, it can cause noses to wrinkle. The principles it represents are fragrant. 'If you walk up to [an Icelandic man] and explain to him what feminism is,' says Alvin Níelsson, 'he will probably respond with "That's what I've always been saying".'

This raised the most important question of my trip. How did these Viking men become the allies of women and how might this process be repeated in other countries? The answer goes back to one single day and one magnificent idea.

Vigdís Finnbogadóttir may never have become President if it hadn't happened. She pushed through the crowds with her mother and three-year-old daughter. Þuríður Pétursdóttir was there too. A radical women's group called the Red Stockings had originally proposed a women's one-day strike. After other groups came on board, retitled the event and worked to win over employers and trades unions to the plan, the 'Women's Day Off' gained astonishingly wide support. Back then, Þuríður was a schoolteacher, employed in one of the few professions that paid women and men similar rates. In other sectors, the gap yawned. 'When they needed someone in a job that was well-paid, then they took a man, but women could sweep the floors,' she recollects. 'It was the thinking that the men were providing for the families. They never thought of women providing for the families. We, as a society, didn't think of women as a big part of the workforce until the Women's Day Off in 1975.'

On October 24, the women of Iceland walked out of their jobs and left their unpaid caring duties. Þuríður and her colleagues had debated whether the female pupils should strike too, but decided they should attend lessons as usual so that the school authorities would feel the absence of the female staff. 'This was a huge wake-up call,' says Þuríður.[13]

The crowds converged on Reykjavík and packed into Austurvöllur Square. Autumn can be bitter, but fate delivered crisp air and sunshine. Þuríður brought her eight-year-old daughter, Védís Guðjónsdóttir.

'Everything closed down,' Þuríður remembers with satisfaction. Védís emphasises the point. 'Everywhere in the country. It brought self-confidence for women of Iceland.' 'Yes,' her mother replies, 'to be able to make something so huge.' Ninety per cent of Icelandic women participated. The women shake their heads in wonderment at the scale of the event.

Auður Styrkársdóttir tells a similar story. 'I went downtown with a friend of mine, and I remember being surprised at all these people that were there, mostly women and a few men,' the historian says. 'I had never seen so many people gathered together in my whole life.' There were speeches, songs. 'A lady who was an opera singer made us all sing. It was fantastic. I think all of us who were there, we will always carry in our hearts this belief that, yes we can do things if we stand together. It changed a lot of people.'

Some men whinged at the prospect of the strike. Þuríður mimics the complaints. 'What? No lunch?' After the Day Off, the whingeing stopped. Everyone had seen how much women contributed, in every sphere of activity. Even the male-dominated crews of the fishing fleets had been impacted as the women on board, mostly cooks, downed tools. Without women, everything ground to a halt.

The realisation kicked off a process of change. The Church of Iceland could have ordained women since 1911 but had not done so. The first ordinations took place after the Women's Day Off. 'Having a right and being accepted is a different thing, because having the right is something that can be decided by officials, but being accepted has to do with society, whether they accept you,' says ordained minister Steinunn Arnþrúður Björnsdóttir.

She laughs recalling a recent conversation when a vacancy came up for a new pastor. 'I remember I had a funeral, I was sitting in the funeral office, where the big cemetery is, and one of the organists was saying to me, "Ah well, there's no use for the boys to apply anymore. It all goes to the girls."'[14] As she points out, that isn't true in the Church or anywhere else and the transformation triggered by the Women's Day Off has by no means reached its conclusion. There have been further Women's Days Off, to speed the process. The biggest Icelandic women's party, Kvennalistinn – the Women's List – formed in 1983 to turn the spirit of the Day Off into practicable policy proposals, much as the Women's Equality Party started by channelling the energies generated by the Women of the World Festival into an action plan. The new party won more than 10 per cent of the vote and seats in the *Alþingi* and, says Drífa Snædal, immediately exerted an influence out of proportion to its size, applying a gendered lens to all debates and not just areas reductively labelled 'women's issues'. 'Within the parliament, women in other parties sought strength from the women's party, socially, and politically. And of course other parties had to put up women for elections,' she says.

In 1999 the Women's List merged with other parties that had enshrined its core values and adopted quotas to ensure substantial female representation in their ranks, creating the Social Democratic Alliance that Jóhanna would later head. Not all of its members agreed with this decision. A few left politics, while others joined the Left-Green Movement, Jóhanna's future coalition partner, or decamped to the conservative Progress Party. The heritage of the Women's Day Off and the women's party seemed embedded in the Icelandic system. The only major party not to adopt voluntary quotas was the centre-right Independence Party. The female membership of the *Alþingi* remained steady at around 40 per cent.

Elections in October 2016 lifted that proportion further, to 47 per cent. Even so, the result doesn't appear likely to speed Icelandic progress on gender equality. No party came close to a majority and three attempts to form a coalition, led by three different parties, ended in failure. Finally, in January 2017, a fourth round of negotiations produced a coalition helmed by the centre-right Independence party and including two smaller parties, the right-wing Reform party and centre-right Bright Future.

One party made big strides at the election. The Pirate Party tripled its vote share to 14.5 per cent. The party's instincts are post-ideological, post-feminist. Founded in Sweden in 2006 by Rick Falkvinge, a computer engineer campaigning to legalise file sharing, and active across the Nordic countries and in Germany, it aims to recast intellectual property – books and music, for example – as public property, and, in pushing to distribute it for free, instead risks pandering to the corporate giants of Silicon Valley that generate revenue off the back of the supposedly free content while its creators get little or nothing. Like Silicon Valley, Pirate representation often skews male. When Germany's Pirate Party attracted criticism for its demographics, its female political director, Marina Weisband, appeared at a press conference to put a countervailing position. 'We don't keep track of our members' gender,' Weisband said. 'We believe true equality starts when we stop counting women.'[15]

In Iceland, it remains to be seen whether the country's traditions of gender equality can fashion a more female-friendly version of her party. This much is certain: it is far too soon for Iceland to stop counting women. Its female citizens earn between 14 and 18 per cent less than their male counterparts and in October 2016 they took to the streets for another Day Off to protest that disparity. The biggest single reason that the gender pay gap persists is that the labour market remains heavily gender segregated. Low-skilled 'women's work' is paid at substantially lower rates than equivalent jobs held by men. Well over 90 per cent of truck drivers are men; similar proportions of jobs in the caregiving sector are held by women. Fishing and aluminium smelting remain the province of men. Women 'could do those jobs, but I believe it's a question both of tradition and working time, working hours,' Drífa Snædal says. 'You go on fishing tours for one month at a time, and with the aluminium smelters there are 12-hour shifts.' Fisherman Alvin Níelsson has seen women who do get jobs on trawlers 'blamed for disrupting the peace. This is not my experience. My experience was that they were hard-working, even more hard-working than the men, because they had to prove themselves.' He adds that the men always came to appreciate the women in their midst.

This chimes with Þuríður Pétursdóttir's recollections. Just after the Women's Day Off, she left teaching and went into fishing. She needed money to buy a flat. 'They were great gentlemen,' she says of her erstwhile colleagues. Her daughter Védís takes up the story. 'The men came to me that had been with her on the sea, on fishing boats and they were so proud: "Your mother was with us. She was so great! Send to her my best regards." They were rather proud to have been at sea with a woman.'[16]

Iceland isn't yet Equalia. But a big battle has been won. 'It is not now questioned "Can a woman do this or that?" It's not something that you ask, like it was before,' says Auður Styrkársdóttir. 'Because Icelandic women have proven that we can do anything. It has become part of reality.'

The road to Hella is paved with asphalt and girded by wilderness. Plumes of smoke in the distance suggest habitation but prove to be the earth venting hot steam. It takes three buses, a steep rise to a frozen ridge and a lazier descent down into a valley to reach the town of some 800 souls. I had travelled there at the invitation of Erla Sigríður Sigurðardóttir, the sister of Halla Gunnarsdóttir, to meet some of her friends and take in the view from rural Iceland.

The most prominent features of that view, the volcanos Katla and Hekla, shimmer in the near distance. We sit on the porch and chat about the impediments that still block Icelandic women as Erla's toddler daughter rides a tricycle around our feet, occasionally ramming the furniture. Erla's friend and neighbour has brought her 14-year-old girl along. 'She has friends the same age who say "oh shit, I can't go out without mascara",' says the neighbour. A large-screen TV is visible through the picture window of Erla's living room. Beyoncé struts into our line of vision. In the context in which the singer operates, in a soup of racism and sexism and a culture and an industry that tries to dictate who she can be, her strength is exhilarating. Does she mean the same thing here? It becomes increasingly clear to me during my time in Iceland that debates around gender equality miss the key dimension of intersectionality, largely because Iceland's population is so unremittingly white. Just 8.9 per cent are immigrants and the vast majority of those immigrants are Poles and Lithuanians. It isn't easy to reach from countries whose citizens might claim asylum, and most asylum-seekers that do arrive have their sights set on Canada or the US. Since 1956, Iceland has welcomed a miserly 584 resettlement refugees as permanent residents.

This stance may make the push for other kinds of equality easier but it diminishes Iceland, without offering any protection against the gendered messages of globalised culture we see through Erla's window. After Beyoncé comes a rout of images from the Maroon 5 video *Animals*: women as meat, women as prey.

By the time children go to kindergarten, they have already absorbed such messaging, even in egalitarian Iceland. If we are to reach Equalia, this is an issue we must address, and back in Reykjavík I visit one of the 17 schools and pre-schools now practising the Hjalli model developed by teacher Margrét Pála Ólafsdóttir that seeks to raise generations of Icelanders free from gender-programming. The early years, she says, are the most important in forming attitudes, so pupils range from one-and-a half or two years old up to eight or nine, though one Hjalli school outside Reykjavík lets students stay on to 16. Pupils choose whether to wear red or blue, trousers or skirts or both, and several little boys scamper past in skirts and headscarves or with barrettes clipping back long hair. Their coats hanging in the separate cloakrooms for girls and boys provide a reminder of the scale of the challenge Margrét Pála has taken on – the palette in the girls' cloakroom is bright, heavy on pinks and lavenders, but the boys have all come in drab colours.

Margrét Pála devised the model 30 years ago after noticing something else her pupils brought into school with them from home: gendered behaviour that even at young ages limited the potential of all genders. Children who didn't neatly fit into accepted categories were bullied. Boys shouted down girls. Girls reprimanded robustly shrank into themselves. Her lightbulb moment came when a boy climbed onto a table to grab food. 'I can remember his face. He just crawled on top of the table to fetch the bread, because he was so hungry. And I just told him, you know, like this …' She holds her hand up. '"Stop, my friend." Really simple and he just smiled. Then I looked at the girls, my great girls, and they stared at me, so quiet, almost afraid. I was just stopping this boy, and it was needed. And I thought "Oh my god, I didn't want to stop you girls." I mean, please, please be like the boys, smile and laugh and be happy.'[17] She proposed a solution that at first scandalised her compatriots: separating boys' and girls' classes, while ensuring they mix at break times, and providing specific lessons to impart discipline, independence, communication, positivity, friendship and courage in addition to a more regular curriculum. It took another decade and a struggle with officials from Iceland's Office of Equality, who at first investigated her for breaching gender equality laws, before the benefits of the system won recognition.

Far from reinforcing gender stereotyping as some of her opponents alleged, the single-sex method is designed to enable children to define gender for themselves – in some cases starting by choosing their gender assignment – and to discover their potential in classes tailored to their requirements. It is hard to measure its success because the first graduates of the system are too small in number to provide a statistically significant sample. A recent study of noise levels in schools established that the Hjalli schools are quieter and achieve better discipline with less overt intervention than other institutions.[18] The children certainly seem happy, if not freed from gendered expectations about their future.

'What would you like to be when you grow up?' I asked seven- and nine-year-old pupils. 'I want to be a scientist and create more jobs,' one little boy answered confidently. Another planned to start a company and employ the rest of his class. Among the girls, several answered 'air stewardess'. It's not necessarily a bad ambition. Jóhanna Sigurðardóttir's first job was as a flight attendant. There were also aspiring surgeons, farmers, writers, a construction company CEO, a ballerina-dancer-explorer-vet and a horse tamer. 'I want more time to think,' said one little girl, and that seemed fair enough.

Heading back to London, I mused on the differences between Iceland and my adopted country, and in particular how the entrenched inequalities in British society and education add to the difficulties of achieving gender equality. Single-sex education worked well for me, but I was also lucky enough to be born into a family that communicated the value of education, a factor that surely helped me to pass the entrance exams for Manchester High School, at that time a direct-grant school. I would not in any way question the achievements of the school's alumnae, who include Libby Lane, the first female bishop of the Church of England, and Harini Iyengar, a high-flying barrister and candidate in the May 2016 London Assembly elections for the Women's Equality Party, but all of us built on economic and social advantages comparative to students from less privileged schools and backgrounds. I took away many lessons from Margrét Pála's school, but the most important was about ensuring that the equality of education that the Women's Equality Party holds up as a core objective takes into account all of the structural inequalities it must overcome.

Iceland had been more informative and enlightening than I could have hoped, but as I settled into my seat on the flight to Heathrow, I itched to get home. While watching the rest of *Frozen*, I began answering an email from Catherine Riley. She and the WE comms team had been brilliantly inventive in grabbing attention for the party. Sophie Walker had built up a significant profile as leader and London Mayoral candidate thanks to her good-humoured fluency in interviews and at hustings. Now we were hitting a wall. Rules meant to ensure broadcasters' impartiality ahead of elections are interpreted by over-cautious editors to mean that they should not give air time to smaller parties for fear of facing demands from other small parties for equal time. Catherine asked for ideas to get us news coverage.

Our biggest hurdle as a new party was to ensure voters knew we existed and would be an option on the ballot.

I was fresh out of inspiration, but Catherine never got my reply to that effect. On the final approach to Heathrow, the plane headed straight into a thunderstorm. I was snapping pictures of the boiling clouds when a tendril of electricity reached out from one of them to envelop the cabin in light and noise. After we landed and taxied to a halt, the pilot made a laconic announcement: 'You may have noticed a lightning strike.' The passengers, still in shock, laughed. I Instagrammed and tweeted as I waited to disembark, not realising that cameras on the ground had also captured the incident, which looked more dramatic than the reality. By the time I reached passport control, my social media feeds were jammed with messages from broadcasters begging for interviews. My first instinct was to turn them down. Then I remembered Catherine's email and started messaging back. Iceland, it seemed, was still giving.

'What went through your mind when the lightning struck?' news anchors and print journalists wanted to know. I gave them all the same answer: 'I thought "I can't die. I have to get back to vote for the Women's Equality Party."'

Chapter Twelve: Equalia welcomes carefree drivers

HALLÓ. GÓÐAN DAG. Velkomin!

This tour is in English, but we Equalians like to greet visitors in Icelandic to acknowledge the inspiration the country provided to us.

My name is Catherine and I'll be your guide today. No point asking if you had a pleasant trip. The journey to gender equality was rough and seemed to last for millennia. Still, I hope you'll agree that the final stages were invigorating.

No, not the ride in a driverless car. That was a diversion. These vehicles may well deliver benefits for women but the only thing they've truly transformed so far is the taxi business. Anyway, as you're now aware, you didn't actually travel to reach Equalia. The possibility of Equalia has always been around us and inside of us.

All it took was for a majority of people to recognise that gender equality would be better for a majority of people. And here we are. *Hér erum við. Velkomin* again!

Equalia rests on the shoulders of great women. You'll see some of their names on Equalian street signs and inscribed into the plinths beneath their statues. You'll also notice, right outside Parliament, a 50-foot bronze entitled

Don't Get Mad, Get Equal. We call her Nancy. As you can tell, she has just broken free and is savouring her own strength. She is dedicated to all the unknown heroes – and there were many – who brought us to this point.

History has been written by the Victors – and the Bills, the Charlies, the Daves, the Donalds, the Jeffs, the Jorges, the Marks, the Muhammeds, the Narendras, the Nigels, the Pauls, Salmans, Sergeys, Tims, Vladimirs, Warrens and Zedongs. They've been adept at immortalising themselves, and sometimes with good reason. Nancy casts her shadow over Winston Churchill, Mahatma Gandhi, Abraham Lincoln and Nelson Mandela. These were all towering figures, and David Lloyd George probably deserves his spot too, even though he dragged his feet on women's suffrage. As for George Canning, Edward Smith-Stanley and Jan Smuts, they found perfectly adequate berths in the suburbs after they ceded to Nancy their prime positions opposite the Palace of Westminster.

In 2016, when campaigner Caroline Criado-Perez wrote an open letter to London's newly elected Mayor Sadiq Khan, not a single female statue stood on the square. She called for a tribute to the suffragettes. City Hall responded on Khan's behalf. The Mayor was 'a proud feminist.' There were, 'of course, certain practical issues to consider.'

Criado-Perez kept up the pressure and got her statue in time to mark the centenary of the first limited enfranchisement of British women. Even so, the hegemony of male statuary was barely dented. Only 15 per cent of all public monuments across the UK depicted women and most of them were queens. We tend to think of the Day That Changed Everything in terms of the way it impacted the future. Well, the Day That Changed Everything also altered our perceptions of the past. Bear this in mind while you enjoy this city's public art. Our art isn't just better, bolder, more inventive as a result of the influx of female talent triggered by the Day; the subject matter is different too.

Multiple Pankhursts have sprouted up; so too Sophia Duleep Singhs, Ada Lovelaces, Margaret Sangers, Mary Wollstonecrafts, Mary Seacoles,

Marie Curies, as well as characters from more recent times. Look out for Angela Merkel fashioned from pieces of the Berlin Wall, a crystalline Hillary Clinton ('complex yet transparent,' according to the artist) and a kinetic Kimberlé Crenshaw. It's a tough call as to whether the authorities are more often called to clean graffiti from Margaret Thatcher or Germaine Greer. The source of the quotation that forms a word sculpture in front of the state broadcaster, the EBC, was the feminist author bell hooks: 'When women and men understand that working to eradicate patriarchal domination is a struggle rooted in the longing to make a world where everyone can live fully and freely, then we know our work to be a gesture of love.'[1]

Despite their profusion, these monuments constitute a comparatively small proportion of the total commissioned since the Day. Equalia will never be able to celebrate by name most of the great women in history because as women, their deeds were never recorded. That is why Nancy arrived in Parliament Square, and why it is right that she stands taller than all her companions. Some imbalances can never be redressed, but it's important to acknowledge them. She is by no means Equalia's only Nancy or even our biggest. Nancies are everywhere, and one of Equalia's foremost female artists sculpted Nancy of the North, the world's largest free-standing sculpture, on the Pennine Way.

My generation was among the last to live in the United Kingdom before it split and then reconfigured itself as the Federation of Equalia. I remember a society supposedly blessed by progress. Women no longer questioned the right to vote, to be educated, to own property, to earn the same pay and enjoy the same opportunities as men. We questioned instead why the legal entitlements Nancy and her kind had won for us failed to translate into equality. We wondered how to engineer the final push, but we also worried. We could not ignore the growing signs of backlash, the stench of ripening misogyny, the erosion of the supposed consensus that gender equality was desirable. On the one hand some of the ruling elites – yea, the very patriarchy itself! – appeared to support the greater participation of women in many spheres. Our increased inclusion would make for better business, better politics, better science, better arts, better institutions. They were, of course, right. On the other hand, the female condition had not only failed to improve on every front, but in more than a few respects was worsening. The American Dream curdled into a nightmare. It wasn't by any means the only country to wage open wars on its women. Even in the comparative calm of what was still the UK, parity looked like a pipe dream.

There were many people of all genders across politics and in civil society who refused to accept the status quo. They understood that to do so meant implicitly agreeing with the commandment issued by the pigs in George Orwell's *Animal Farm*: 'All animals are equal but some animals are more equal than others.' You cannot effectively oppose pestilences such as racism or homophobia if you give any quarter to the idea that women are intrinsically less valuable than men.

The people who understood this worked, sometimes in concert and always with passion, to push back against sexism and misogyny. I contributed in a small way by co-founding a political party. I make no claim to playing a pivotal role. I gave time to the party when I could; some of my colleagues let the party swallow them whole. They worked around the clock to bring about change.

The Women's Equality Party did make a significant difference, not least by moving the focus of national debate to gender and helping to foster an understanding that equality could not be achieved by tinkering here and adjusting a little there. We sought to address the lack of female representation, the gulfs at work and, too often ignored, in the unpaid, domestic sphere, the damage wrought by the enforcement of narrow gender roles in education and through the media, and the pervasive taint of violence, implied and actual. At our first party conference in November 2016, we adopted a seventh core objective: equality in health care and medical research.

A woman called Sarah inspired us to do so. She was my stepsister and would almost certainly have earned a plinth in Equalia if her political career had not been cut short. An idealist, in the best sense, results-driven and intensely practical, she founded and ran a series of successful small businesses while raising two daughters and pursuing a professional career, somehow also making time to embark on a PhD in experimental psychology. She joined the Liberal Democrats in 2007 and remained faithful even as the party bled support among voters who would have preferred to maintain the purity of permanent opposition rather than exercising power in coalition with the Conservatives.

In 2015, aged 51, she stood up to speak at the Lib Dem conference in Glasgow as the party's prospective parliamentary candidate for Dover and Deal. That morning, she had struggled to button her skirt and blamed conference food, but her abdomen continued to swell. Ovarian cancers sometimes cause ascites, a build-up of fluid in the peritoneal cavity.

Hers had reached stage three. Despite the physical and mental toll, not only of the disease, but of the surgery and chemotherapy that followed the diagnosis, Sarah continued to campaign. Dover and Deal would have been a target distant to the point of impossibility at a time of rising Lib Dem popularity, with a record of alternating between Conservative and Labour MPs. Now a strong challenge from UKIP added to Lib Dem woes. Sarah faced two battles she knew she was unlikely, by some definitions, to win.

I watched her move from door to door, hiding her exhaustion behind a bright demeanour and sustained by her determination to make full use of the life she had left. She would have been the best of lawmakers, not least because she knew that legislation by itself could never create the world she hoped to live to see. She celebrated each conversation as part of a longer campaign to win hearts and minds.

Despite these adverse circumstances, she performed well, so much so that the Lib Dems put her on standby to run for Parliament if Theresa May called an early general election. They knew her cancer could not be cured, but they also recognised, as I did, that her spirit would not be quenched. As her illness progressed, she shared with me fresh insights about how society's undervaluing of women played out when they became sick. 'Women so often take on a larger share of the caring. There's a huge hit when the carer needs to be cared for,' she said. 'If a male CEO of a dynamic company gets cancer, people can almost measure the pounds, shillings and pence draining away. The work that women do is so often hidden.'[2]

The Women's Equality Party had to capture hearts and minds on the doorstep, as Sarah had done so effectively. We also wanted to devise ways to move public opinion faster and to create greater momentum for change. Iceland had already led the way and the 2017 Women's Marches showed the possibility of scale. The proposal, once public, attracted support that was deep and wide. Planning meetings drew women's organisations, political activists from all the main parties, businesses, trades unions, media. We quickly agreed on the name. This would not be billed as a strike or a demonstration, but as a celebration and illustration of how much women contribute in every area of life. Here too we would follow Iceland. This would be the Women's Day Off, a date when women stopped working and caring for just long enough that their absence was felt, to make visible a contribution too often overlooked.

Equalians now speak of the Women's Day Off as the Day That Changed Everything. Because it did.

We all have a story or a memory that for us encapsulates the Day. For me there were several. I recall the unfamiliar sensation of taking pleasure in seeing all-male line-ups on the TV news. The major broadcasters granted female employees leave to attend the huge rallies and street parties that marked the occasion. Male reporting teams beamed images from hospital wards where male staff, rostered or not, happily filled in for female colleagues. A consultant urologist emptying bedpans joked that he wasn't used to being 'on the business end' of his specialism. Viewers also saw women engaged in essential work and learned that the National Health Service could not last a single hour without its female staffers, who took turns to go outside to join the multitudes.

Every woman who did so noticed another extraordinary facet of the Day. Back then we had internalised aspects of our subordination. Any situation that forced us into close proximity with strangers triggered caution. Was that man really swaying against us because of the rocking of the train? Were those teenage boys drunk enough to follow up verbal harassment with physical assault? Plunging into a crowd was like braving a Wisconsin winter. You tensed your shoulders, clasped your arms protectively around your body. Diving into the Day had the opposite effect. The joy enveloped us and we rolled with it, going with the flow of bodies and bathing in the warmth and humour of the occasion. I'll always remember the sound, too: hundreds of thousands of women talking and laughing and singing and chanting. Bliss was it on that Day to be alive, but to be female was very heaven.

We call it the Day That Changed Everything, not the Day That Fixed Everything. The refuse collectors who swept up the next morning continued to earn more on average than the cleaners who returned to their shifts in hospitals and care homes. Court cases had already established that these jobs deserved equal remuneration, highlighting the ways in which sectors with majority female workforces – the five Cs of cleaning, catering, clerical, cashiering and caring – routinely earned less than male-dominated equivalents. However, employers still found ways to get female labour on the cheap, especially through contract work. There were dinosaurs at large and damaged men who blamed women for their discomfort.

Even so, public consciousness had undergone a profound transition. People of all genders saw what had been hidden, understood what had been confused. They no longer questioned the contribution of women or the reality of the impediments we face. They believed with hearts and minds in the potential of women unchained.

Social and political transformations gained pace. Stalled initiatives took on a new urgency. Where once we meandered towards Equalia, now we hurtled. It was quite a ride.

That doesn't mean it was a smooth one. Anyone who imagined that dismantling structural inequalities of gender would automatically eradicate other forms of injustice swiftly revised that view. The emerging order retained bad old habits and showed signs of developing fresh and dangerous strains. To this day Equalians tussle with the challenge of delivering an education system that enables every child to reach full potential within a population still segmented by income, race and other factors. Equalia isn't yet equal. However, getting rid of the single biggest division did create significant movement in those other areas. The Equalian constitution holds every citizen to be not only equal but of equal value. It explicitly recognises the desirability of diversity. Importantly, so do most Equalians.

Progress is a spider's web, patiently spun from many directions, the intersection of multiple experiences and realities. It has great tensile strength, but it is also fragile.

Here's an example of that fragility. You see the man mopping the entrance hall to the building over there? These days white men carry out activities once dismissed as low pay or no pay jobs for women and minorities. This might appear a positive, but the Equalian authorities have spotted a potential risk. As technology replaces human workers, few professions remain unaffected. One of the five Cs has already disappeared. There are no more cashiers. Clerical and catering jobs are thin on the ground. Cleaning and caring, by contrast, retain a human touch. Robots have yet to achieve the necessary judgment and dexterity to clean without causing damage. Virtual companions can never replace flesh-and-blood humanity.

Far from being undervalued, there is now competition for these jobs and a debate about how to stop men dominating these fields. We can never stop working for equalities or protecting those we have gained. Once, a long time ago, when I visited Iceland, a woman called Drífa Snædal talked to me about the problems her country still faced. 'Gender inequality is like a river,' she said. 'You stop it here and it goes there. It finds its way – whether you're talking about the wage gap or violence.'

The patriarchy may have loosened its grip, but it has not gone away. Younger Equalians grow up largely free from the destructive tropes about gender that messed up so many of their elders but millions of their elders are still alive. They – we – carry within us reflexes and impulses of the old world, instilled in us from birth. We could easily revert.

Moreover, Equalian libraries are full of books that will preserve the old ways of thinking long after everyone who remembers a time before Equalia is dust. Our cultural heritage is rich and risky. The last great battle before the founding of Equalia saw to that.

All revolutions splinter and ours was no exception. We had fought for Equalia. Now we fought with each other about what Equalia should be.

Some insisted that the state must impose equality by every means available to it. They advanced models for Equalia that shared one obvious flaw: these had been tested, in the Soviet bloc, Cuba, China. Like Orwell's Animalism, such models replaced one patriarchy with another.

Nobody believed things could stay as they were. Life had already improved for many of us as the countries of the Disuniting Kingdom more fully embraced gender equality. There had been social benefits reflected in improved mental health outcomes and lower rates of violence, and an immediate economic boost from the increased participation of women in the workforce. Women didn't just take jobs; we created jobs, developed whole new industries and markets and fields of endeavour. This helped to mitigate bigger global trends but could not completely shield us from them. Elsewhere the gulf between the world's wealthiest and everyone else and, of course, between men and other genders was widening further as technology elbowed humans aside. Tech companies and other multinational corporations had become more powerful than governments and richer than countries. Population growth, long regarded as an engine of economic growth, was for many of those countries neither possible nor even desirable, given dwindling capacities to feed and support existing populations and the environmental costs of population expansion.

The arguments for different and innovative ways to organise the Equalian economy were strong and the Federation is still finding its way. Sustainability is a core principle. Legislation is audited for impacts across the whole population. All four Equalian governments redefined work to include in any economic analyses all the forms of unpaid labour that had been rendered almost exclusively by women. Equalian childcare and parental-leave provisions are second-to-none, but these measures are not intended to trigger a baby boom. By recognising the potential of every citizen, Equalia has broken the cycle that assumed the need to breed at least two young workers to every person over the age of 70. The government does not see it as its business to try to dictate the size of families, but to ensure that every child is cared for and every parent is equally supported.

Pundits got it wrong when they predicted the average age of mothers would keep rising. Science has indeed found ways not only to extend fertility but also make it possible for babies to be grown outside the human body. However as soon as the maternity penalty was removed, women no longer delayed starting families, so these technologies are mostly used by people who would never have been able to conceive naturally or carry a baby, including, of course, men.

Equalia was the first place on the planet to move away from the idea that old people were a drag on the economy, and instead to treat us as a resource. The world I grew up in would have written me off long ago, just as it marginalised everyone who was differently abled. The shift has already benefitted all Equalians. Elderly people remain active and engaged for longer, with all the positive impact on wellbeing and diminished reliance on health and support services that this entails.

In assuming that most of us, of any age, wish for that active engagement, Equalia has removed the stigma attached to those for whom it is not an option. People who need help, get it. The Equalian system is responsive and decentralised, with many decisions reached locally, but the state sector is large. It has to be, to compensate for the irrevocable loss of some forms of paid employment. As you may have heard, Equalia is testing out different mechanisms, including a universal basic income. I used to be sceptical about such schemes. The first proposals, way back before Equalia, looked utopian or, when promoted by the technologists laying waste traditional jobs, cynical, and in any case out of step with voters' understanding. Their time may now have come, though some emerging industries are already helping to take up the slack.

Equalia aims to ensure quality of life for all citizens and monitors the Equalian happiness index as closely as it tracks interest rates. Equalians are not, by the standards I remember from pre-Equalian days, materialistic. We take pleasure in human interactions and experiences rather than cluttering our homes with things. This country has not eliminated poverty but the gap between rich and poor continues to diminish. Like all Equalians, I am enormously proud of our free health care and education systems. Education is also key to the vibrancy of the Equalian economy. We are not only leaders in developing artificial intelligence, we are also leaders in producing human minds adept at performing the jobs that AI will never master. As you'll know, we are the world's premier tourist destination too. 'The future has arrived. It just hasn't been evenly distributed yet,' the author William Gibson once remarked. The world comes to Equalia to visit the future.

We cannot rely on all visitors to be friendly. Some nations and ideologies oppose everything Equalia holds dear. Inevitably, among my compatriots there are those who promote nationalism and closed borders in response, but that could never be a satisfactory answer. Equalia must be a beacon to the rest of the world. We cannot suppress dissent or ignore ideologies that are anathema to us – we have to challenge them through rational argument and by example. Equalia needs the tensile strength of a spider's web, rather than a hard carapace.

For one thing, no defence capabilities, however elaborate, can stop the flow of ideas. For another, people of my generation remember a Wall built not to protect the people within it against external enemies but to imprison them. We have seen things you people wouldn't believe, cities on fire, dictatorships of the left and the right. One of the first things such regimes do is to burn libraries, pull down statues, all those monuments lost, like tears in rain. The last battle before Equalia was to protect our heritage, not from dictators but from would-be liberators.

Don't get me wrong. I did understand the calls to create a new culture and had some sympathy with them. So many works of literature, art, music, so many movies and television shows, reflect and reinforce the world-view that held women to be less than men. How could we free society from that worldview if our cultural output continued vigorously to communicate it? Yet state-sanctioned art is an oxymoron and you only need to look at past attempts to stamp out forms of expression considered subversive to know how well that usually turns out.

We had to enable creativity, not to dictate its form or content. We literally had to move a few statues to make room for Nancy, but we did not destroy them. We kept all our cultural assets. We also contextualised them, learned to view works of art also as artefacts, to acknowledge their historicity, to ensure every Equalian understood them as a guide to what had gone before.

When you get back to your lodgings tonight – I see from my list that quite a few of you have opted to stay in Equalian households – take a few minutes to check out Equalian home entertainment. Yes, of course you can do this right now and some of you are already doing so. Your digi-glasses and smartphones mark you out as tourists just as surely as your Nancy t-shirts. Equalians enjoy technology as a way of enhancing human experience, rather than distracting from it.

Whenever you watch and however you watch, you'll find that Equalians consume contemporary drama alongside vintage fare such as *Transparent* and *Luther*. We like cooking shows, dancing shows, comedy, game shows. *QI* is running through the Roman alphabet again after its foray into Cyrillic. We devour brilliant news journalism and documentary programming. You won't be surprised to find we're fans of erotica too. Equalians make no secret of our love of sex. Sex between equals is delicious.

It is amusing given Equalia's reputation as one of the sexiest places on earth that critics originally accused Equalia of incipient puritanism. They did so after the federal government placed restrictions on the distribution of any material that had been produced in exploitative ways or might promote abusive behaviour towards any segment of the population. The Equalian legal system from the beginning recognised misogyny as a hate crime. This effectively blocks the legal availability of most foreign-made porn, but since misogyny is no longer a viral strain of Equalian society, our homegrown erotica tends to meet the necessary criteria irrespective of any legal imperatives. Violent, misogynistic pornography wouldn't find much of a market here.

For the same reason, the numbers of prosecutions under the Sex Buyer Law implemented in pre-Equalian times dropped steadily in the early years of the Federation. Eventually the legislation was updated to prohibit sex tourism. Women are still trafficked in other countries, still oppressed. Even so, the law has rarely been tested. Equalians generally find non-consensual sex anything but sexy.

Journalists often attribute Equalia's low rate of teenage births to the excellent provision of clinics offering contraception and reproductive health advice, but our culture also places a high importance on sex and relationships education, which is conveyed by every parent and taught in every school. We aim to protect young Equalians from pressure to become sexually active or to define their sexuality before they are ready. By returning to a culture of family viewing, Equalians are also better able to monitor and control what children watch and, when necessary, to help to set what they are seeing in context.

To neutralise the unconscious biases we carried into Equalia, the first generations of Equalian children attended schools that followed Margrét Pála Ólafsdóttir's Hjalli model. Later generations flourish without sex-segregated schooling. Reductive stereotypes have lost traction. Equalians perceive gender not as a binary but as a spectrum, and our language reflects that understanding. The gender-neutral pronouns 'ze' and 'zem' are used in place of he and she, him and her, in contexts where gender is either unknown or non-binary. If anyone doubts that's important, ze can buy me a pint and I'll do my best to explain to zem.

Two years ago Equalia for the first time elected a trans woman as Federal Prime Minister. In the pre-Equalian world, this would have divided feminists. Trans womanhood sometimes reflected patriarchal definitions of femininity and incorporated patriarchal assumptions of privilege. In a gender-equal culture that has long shed reductive notions of what it is to be female, these concerns no longer arise. We all celebrated the election as a sign that our democracy yields descriptive representation.

A common accusation directed against pre-Equalian feminism was that it strove to eradicate difference, rather than to celebrate it. This was hilariously wide of the mark. Equalian fashion is a riot of diversity. As you can see, we've long abandoned notions of gender- or age-appropriate dress. Do you like my purple shoes? They glow in the dark and they also communicate with my jumpsuit to ensure my blood pressure isn't dropping too low. Equalia leads the world on smart clothing. Yes, these feathers are growing out of my head. I treated myself to a mo'-hawk ahead of my last significant birthday.

Equalian domestic arrangements appear equally colourful in the eyes of cultures that retain rigid notions of nuclear family structures as the bedrock of healthy societies. Such nuclear families exist in Equalia but so do broader structures, families extended through blood or by choice. My own quality of life as one of Equalia's oldest citizens has been vastly enhanced by living with not only my husband but a group of our friends and some of their children and children's children. The building just over there is a typical example of Equalian public housing, interspersing private space – always fully soundproofed and easily reconfigured to meet changing needs – with communal areas. Planners place a premium on flexibility, function and form. Isn't the design glorious? I'm a big fan of the Eileen Gray revival.

Over 300 languages are spoken in Equalian schools. Almost half of Equalians identify as members of faith groups. A recent survey revealed that only eight per cent of those who do so consider themselves devout and for most it is not a matter of belief but cultural identity. Even so Equalia marks religious festivals alongside secular dates of note. International Women's Day, 8 March, has become a celebration of thanksgiving for all the unknown Nancies. Our biggest national holiday spans the anniversary of the Day. It always starts with the same ceremony. At noon women everywhere stop what they're doing and head out to the street in silence. At 12:10 we break that silence with a cheer. Legend has it, they can hear us in Dublin, though how they could do that over the noise they're making is hard to imagine. Many cities and countries now rejoice with us.

I promised to round off our tour with a trip to a traditional Equalian pub. It would be hard to find a pub more traditional than this. Founded in 1879, El Vino flourished with the newspaper trade that used to line this street and, like that industry, worked to keep women in their place. Until 1982, female customers could not stand at the bar or order their own drinks, but were relegated to an airless room at the back. The regime crumbled after a journalist called Anna Coote teamed up with solicitor Tess Gill to challenge it under the Sex Discrimination Act, passed only seven years earlier.

Several previous attempts to challenge El Vino's policy had failed but Coote and Gill won their case. So many women crowded into the hostelry to toast their victory that a bartender complained: 'There are more women at the bar than men – it's chaos.'

Before Equalia existed, some feared its advent. They envisaged the world as a bar with limited space. Once you let women in, you'd have to fight to be served. What Equalia proved is that admitting women expands opportunities, rather than diminishing them. What Equalia proved is that admitting women diminishes the need or impulse to fight.

Some of us yearned for Equalia but in advocating for it, we couldn't always describe what it might be. Way back in 2016 – yes, I'm that old – I pushed people to try to imagine the society we were striving to build. As we come to the end of our tour, I'd like to share some of their historic responses:

'It's the world five-year-olds live in and we condition out of them. I watch [my niece] Sofia and other girls being themselves, in charge, not feared yet by men or society, their wings not clipped and just so confident in who they are.' Nimco Ali

'If we had a gender-equal world, we would not have to fight for equality; it would be self-evident.' Steinunn Arnþrúður Björnsdóttir

'I think it would be very hard to argue that if we lived in a gender-equal world where physically men and women were equal, where our bodies were equal, that sexual violence would not be reduced. It's just so clear that it would be.' Pavan Amara

'It would of course mean mutual participation in the public and private market: within the home and within the public sphere.' Drífa Snædal

'Whenever I'm asked about a gender-equal world, I'm always assailed by feelings rather than visions. It would feel like freedom. And enough air to breathe deeply and fully. A burden lifted. Like taking off one of those very, very old, heavy, deep-sea diver's suits.' Sophie Walker

'It's hard to imagine because I haven't experienced it, yet, or seen it. But simply, my aim for that is that we can all be human beings and enjoy being who we are.' Margrét Pála Ólafsdóttir

'I originally thought a gender-equal world would be one without any gender, where gender didn't exist at all. But I think now a gender-equal world is one where trans and non-binaryness is accepted as being as normal as everything else.' Cat/Milo Bezark

'Everyone can let their own qualities shine.' [5] *Védís Guðjónsdóttir*

'I would feel comfortable. One of the problems of gender inequality is that women have so much discomfort about what we wear; about walking down the street alone; about speaking our mind. In a gender-equal world that discomfort wouldn't be there.' Lea Coligado

'Bliss. A truly gender-equal world would be bliss. All it needs is respect. If everybody respected everybody else for their knowledge, for their ability, without needing people to prove what they can do before they get to do it, then you get there.' Simone Wilson

'To me, a gender-equal world means the next wave of innovation really ensures that we're getting the most out of the human beings that are being born on the planet.' Stephanie Lampkin

'A gender-equal world starts in our heads, it starts with changing thought process and patterns, habits. I know I represent that myself, when I get up there and rock 'n' roll and play the guitar like crazy and people are like "A woman is doing that?" That changes the thought process.' Melissa Etheridge

'There will be more choice.' Stephen Fitzgerald

'I have two daughters and a son. A lot of my feminist drive comes not just from my daughters but my son. Of course I want the girls to be paid the same, treated the same, represented the same as all the men in their lives but I truly believe that an equal society is better for everyone. I want my boy to have a life where he might take paternity leave without worrying how it impacts on his position at work. I want him to have a life with a future partner where they are equals.' Sandi Toksvig

Many of these wishes and visions have come true in Equalia. The Federation isn't paradise, but for most Equalians it is a good place to live.

In the first half of my life, I heard – again and again – politicians promise to create the conditions under which the majority might thrive. These politicians never delivered because they never delivered for the female half of the population.

Most of them meant well. They were sincere. They believed in gender equality. They just didn't embed it in their own parties, make it central to their policies. They didn't understand the scale of the impediments facing women or of the reward that removing them would deliver, not only to women, but across the whole population.

This will be familiar to you. After all, every one of you travelled here from countries that fall far short of Equalia.

Visitors often tell us they never want to go home. The prospect of returning to the cold reality of societies that in misprizing women harm everyone makes them sad or angry.

Oh, you feel that way too?

Here's the thing. There's no need. You can take Equalia with you.

Remember what I said at the beginning of this tour. The possibility of Equalia is around us and inside of us.

All it takes is the will to create Equalia.

Your will.

Let people know about the joys of Equalia.

Tell them how to reach Equalia and how urgent it is that we do so.

Don't be sad. Don't get mad. Get equal.

Now who's buying? Mine's a pint of Pankhurst.

Acknowledgements

If not for women, I would never have written this book. I don't just mean that the book advocates for women and celebrates female achievement. This book exists because women made things happen.

It exists because publisher Lisa Milton decided to commission the book when it was little more than an idea. She is a founding member of the Women's Equality Party – another idea that became reality after women sprang into action. Lisa and her team of excellent women (and one excellent man) have supported me and this book with unwavering enthusiasm and a fierce belief in its guiding principles. Behind every feminist writer there is usually a man – that's the way of the patriarchal publishing industry. In my case, it's a great man, my agent Ed Victor, who put me together with Lisa.

Some of the women who built WE appear in the book. Many more do not. It was impossible to name everyone, not least because more than a few key people could not publicly back the party for fear of falling foul of employers or the traditional political parties they still publicly espoused and asked WE for help to improve.

I would like to express my profound gratitude to all of these fabulous women, especially the original WE steering committee, and to the many other people who created and nurtured the party in myriad different ways, including party staff, past and present. In the last category, special thanks go to Halla Gunnarsdóttir, Hannah Peaker and Catherine Riley, who speed-read the manuscript and did not stint on criticism but also laughed at my jokes. Halla also provided introductions to what felt like the whole of Iceland but probably amounted to only a quarter of the population.

WE had two parents and a number of midwives. I could never have started a party or stuck at it without the joys of doing so with Sandi Toksvig, and Sandi would probably not have stayed the course without her wife Debbie, who at various times has propped up not only Sandi but me. This much is also clear: WE wouldn't have flourished without the leadership of Sophie Walker, who has transformed before our eyes into one of the most passionate, talented and authentic politicians I have ever seen.

The book is about much more than WE, and I relied on women as I researched and wrote it. My researcher Lili Hamlyn not only has the tenacity and attention to detail of all great reporters but also a writer's sensibility and skills. Her involvement with fourth-wave feminism helped to plug me into the thinking of much younger women, and I also received invaluable advice on this score from June Eric-Udorie and Tiger Hutchence. One of my closest male friends, Jeremy Gaines, conducted some interviews and funnelled high-quality bulletins and analysis from Germany and Nigeria.

My cousins and friends in the US furnished me with contacts and, not for the first time, bed and lodgings as I conducted my research there. Michael and Sasha Stearns Mayer even fixed the bedroom door handle in anticipation of my arrival after inadvertently imprisoning me during an earlier visit. As with my previous books, I also wrote chunks of this one during stays at the homes of two of my dearest friends: Nicola Jennings, my elective sister from university days, and Sara Burns.

Sara appears fleetingly in this book, as the co-designer of the WE logo. Her death in November 2016, just a month after my stepsister Sarah Smith, taught me a new and tough lesson. Sara had been for three decades a touchstone, a warmth and a refuge, hilarious often in unexpected ways, a repository of secrets and hopes, not just in my life but a part of my life. When she died, she left a huge space, 50-foot tall and without visible borders.

I realise that this vacuum will always be there. Female friendship sustains and inspires. It is, like Sara herself, irreplaceable.

I am lucky. I have wonderful friends and family who have done their best to mitigate her loss and my grief over my sister Sarah and for my long-time friend and mentor Michael Elliott, who died in July 2016. I am grateful for every one of them and for the relationships that are now only memories. Though sad, I know that good times lie ahead.

More than a quarter of a century ago, I spotted an unfeasibly handsome man at a party scooping trifle out of a bowl with his hand. He couldn't find a spoon, he told me. Later I found out he was Andy Gill, the founder and guitarist of one of my favourite bands, Gang of Four. We have rarely been apart since that evening, except when my work or his tours intervene.

As I said, I am lucky. The personal is political, and for both of us there has been a learning process about how to find equality within our relationship. It helps that Andy was already a feminist before we met and it helps even more that he is lovely and funny and brilliant. Andy, thank you. I love you.

January 2017

Notes and References

INTRODUCTION

1. Laura Cohn, 'Women Ask for Raises as Much as Men Do – But Get Them Less Often', *Fortune* (6 September 2016).
2. Salary Differences Between Male and Female Registered Nurses in the United States; Ulrike Muench, Jody Sindelar, Susan H Busch and Peter I Buerhaus; JAMA; Vol 313, No 12; 24-31 March 2015
3. Intimate Partner and Sexual Violence Against Women: Fact Sheet N°239, World Health Organisation (January 2016).
4. Bel Trew, 'FGM Needed "to Control Female Lust"', *Times* (5 September 2016).
5. US Election: Full transcript of Donald Trump's Obscene Videotape, BBC Online (9 October 2016).
6. Lydia O'Connor and Daniel Marans, 'Here Are 13 Examples of Donald Trump Being Racist', Huffington Post (10 October 2016).
7. Nicole Puglise, 'Exit Polls and Election Results – What We Learned', *Guardian* (12 November 2016).
8. Interview with Sandi Toksvig, London (5 September 2016).
9. Lynne Olson, *Freedom's Daughters: The Unsung Heroines of the Civil Rights Movement from 1830 to 1970* (Simon and Schuster, 2001). NB Stokely

Carmichael is widely misquoted as having said 'The *only* position for women in SNCC is prone'.

10. Jonathan Woetzel and others, 'The Power of Parity: How Advancing Women's Equality Can Add $12 Trillion to Global Growth'; McKinsey Global Institute (September 2015).

11. Georgia Wilkins, 'Want to Boost your Share Price? Hire More Women', *Sydney Morning Herald* (27 September 2016).

12. Bina Agarwal, *Gender and Green Governance: The Political Economy of Women's Presence Within and Beyond Community Forestry* (Oxford University Press, 2010).

13. Hadley Freeman, 'Theresa May, Margaret Thatcher: Spot the Difference – and the Sexism', *Guardian* (23 July 2016).

14. Icelandic surnames are patronymic: they mean 'daughter of' or 'son of' – so all Icelanders quoted in this book are called by their first or full names.

15. Interview with Halla Gunnarsdóttir, London (19 July 2016).

16. Rowena Mason, 'Harriet Harman Savages Gordon Brown over Sexism and Inequality', *Guardian* (8 July 2014).

17. Steve Hawkes, 'Boys Should Play with Dolls to Make them "Caring", says Minister', *Sun* (13 January 2015).

18. Jeanette Winterson, 'We Need to Build a New Left. Labour Means Nothing Today', *Guardian* (24 June 2016).

CHAPTER ONE

1. Kimberlé Williams Crenshaw, 'Whose Story is it, Anyway? Feminist and Antiracist Appropriations of Anita Hill' in *Race-Ing Justice, En-Gendering Power*, Toni Morrison (Ed.), (Pantheon Books, 1992).

2. Renee Martin, 'I'm Not a Feminist (And There Is No But)', *Guardian* (10 April 2010).

3. Interview with Nimco Ali, London (4 August 2016).

4. Interview with Kimberlé Williams Crenshaw, London (13 May 2016).

5. Paula Cocozza, 'Women's Equality Party Founders: It Needed Doing. So We Said, "Let's Do It."', *Guardian* (28 August 2015).

6. Catherine Mayer, 'David Cameron: UK's Next Leader?' *TIME* (11 September 2008).

7. Rosalind C. Barnett and Caryl Rivers, 'Will Hillary's Speaking Style Derail Her?', A Women's Place [blog], Psychology Today (10 February 2016).

8. Sady Doyle, 'America Loves Women Like Hillary Clinton – As Long As They're Not Asking for a Promotion', Quartz (26 February 2016).

CHAPTER TWO

1. Gloria Steinem, 'Women Are Never Front-Runners', *New York Times* (8 January 2008).

2. Kimberlé Crenshaw and Eve Ensler, 'Feminist Ultimatums: Not in Our Name', Huffington Post (5 February 2008).

3. Interview with Hannah Peaker, London (1 August 2016).

4. Alicia Adamczyk, 'All These Countries Have Had a Female Head of State (Before the US)', *Money* (11 July 2016).

5. The Global Gender Gap Report 2016.

6. Heather Arnet, 'Is Embattled Brazilian President Dilma Rousseff Being Targeted by Misogynists?', *New York Times* (29 April 2016).

7. 'Brazil Impeachment: Rousseff Attacks Cabinet for Being All-Male and All-White', BBC Online (14 May 2016).

8. Simon Allison, 'Fellow Nobel Peace Prize Winner Criticises Ellen Johnson Sirleaf', *Guardian* (10 October 2012).

9. Interview with Ayisha Osori, conducted for this book by Jeremy Gaines via Skype (14 August 2016).

10. Rosabeth Moss Kanter, 'Some Effects of Proportions on Group Life: Skewed Sex Ratios and Responses to Token Women', *American Journal of Sociology*, 82: 5 (March 1977).

11. 'Report: Hillary Clinton talks like a man', *Fast Company* (12 September 2016).

12. Tyler G. Okimoto and Victoria L. Brescoll, 'The Price of Power: Power Seeking and Backlash Against Female Politicians', *Personality and Social Psychology Bulletin*, 36: 7 (July 2010), 923–36.

13. Julian Heißler, 'Merkels drei große kleine Worte', Tagesschau (31 August 2016).

14. Catherine Mayer, 'Angela Merkel's Unfinished Business', *TIME* (23 September 2013).

15. Friederike Heine, 'Germany Promises Daycare for All', *Spiegel* (1 August 2013).

16. 'Bolivia: Briefing to the UN Committee on the Elimination of Discrimination against Women', Amnesty International (11 June 2015).

17. Jamie Grierson, 'Feminist Zealots Want Women to Have their Cake and Eat It, says Tory MP', *Guardian* (12 August 2016).

18. Shiv Malik and Nick Cohen, 'Socialist Workers Party Leadership under Fire over Rape Kangaroo Court', *Guardian* (9 March 2013).

19. 'George Galloway Attacked over Assange "Rape" Comments', BBC Online (20 August 2012).

20. Craig Volden, Alan E. Wiseman and Dana E. Wittmer, 'When Are Women More Effective Lawmakers Than Men?', *American Journal of Political Science* (22 January 2013).

21. Rowena Mason, 'Theresa May "allowed state-sanctioned abuse of women" at Yarl's Wood', *Guardian* (3 March 2015).

22. 'Statement of the National Executive Committee of the African National Congress on the emancipation of women in South Africa' (2 May 1990).

23. Ra'eesa Pather, 'Jacob Zuma and His Sexism – as Laid Out in the President's Own Words', *Mail & Guardian* (9 August 2016).

24. Elizabeth Powley, 'Rwanda: The Impact of Women Legislators on Policy Outcomes Affecting Children and Families', Unicef (December 2006).

25. David Smith, 'Paul Kagame's Rwanda: African Success Story or Authoritarian State?' *Guardian* (10 October 2012).

26. U.N. says some of its peacekeepers were payings 13-year-olds for sex'; Kevin Sieff, The Washington Post; January 11 2016.

27. Interview with Sophie Walker, London (5 September 2016).

CHAPTER THREE

1. Interview with Simone Wilson, London (30 March 2016).

2. Hate Violence in 2014, National Coalition of Anti-Violence Programs (2015).

3. Heather Saul, 'Germaine Greer Defends "Grossly Offensive" Comments about Transgender Women', *Independent* (26 October 2015).

4. Thomas Laqueur, *Making Sex: Body and Gender from the Greeks to Freud* (New edn, Harvard University Press, 6 March 1992).

5. Larry Cahill, 'His Brain, Her Brain', *Scientific American* (1 October 2012).

6. Daphna Joel and others, 'Sex Beyond the Genitalia: The Human Brain Mosaic', Proceedings of the National Academy of Sciences of the United States of America, 122: 50 (December 2015).

7. Sharon Begley, 'Why Parents May Cause Gender Differences in Kids', *Newsweek* (9 March 2009).

8. Quoted in Peter Gay, *Freud: A Life for Our Time* (Norton, 1988).

9. Sigmund Freud, 'The Dissolution of the Oedipus Complex', 1924, *The Complete Psychological Works of Sigmund Freud Volume XIX*, (New edn, Vintage, 2001).

10. Interview with Robin Lovell-Badge, London (31 May 2016).

11. Ione Wells, 'From "Hin" to "Zie": How Pronouns are Moving Beyond Gender', *Evening Standard* (20 July 2016).

12. Michael Schulman, 'Generation LGBTQIA', *New York Times* (9 January 2013).

CHAPTER FOUR

1. Henry McDonald, 'PPS "Right" not to Prosecute Gerry Adams for Withholding Knowledge of Abuse', *Guardian* (9 June 2015).

2. Bruce Bower, 'New Studies Explore Why Ordinary People Turn Terrorist', *Scientist* (23 June 2016).

3. Maria Power, 'Second-class Republicans? Sinn Féin, Feminism and the Women's Hunger Strike', *Irish Times* (18 December 2015).

4. Margaret Ward, 'Excluded and Silenced: Women in Northern Ireland After the Peace Process', 50:50 (12 June 2013).

5. Michael W. Tomlinson, 'War, Peace and Suicide: The Case of Northern Ireland', *International Sociology*, 27: 4 (July 2012), 464–82.

6. Viren Swami, Debbi Stanistreet and Sarah Payne, 'Masculinities and Suicide', *The Psychologist*, 21 (April 2008), 308–11.

7. Candace West and Don H. Zimmerman, 'Doing Gender', *Gender & Society*; 1: 2 (June 1987), 125–51.

8. Åshild Lappegård Lahn, 'Gender Equality Gives Men Better Lives', *Science Nordic* (17 October 2015).

9. Rolf Wynn, Marita H. Hoiseth and Gunn Pettersen, 'Psychopathy in Women: Theoretical and Clinical Perspectives', *International Journal of Women's Health*, 4 (2012), 257–63.

10. 'An Overview of Sexual Offending in England and Wales'; Ministry of Justice, Office for National Statistics and Home Office (January 2013).

11. Interview with Pavan Amara, London (23 June 2016).

12. Jon Henley, 'White and Wealthy Voters Gave Victory to Donald Trump, Exit Polls Show', *Guardian* (9 November 2016).

13. Norah Vincent, *Self-Made Man* (Atlantic, 2006).

CHAPTER FIVE

1. Frieda Hughes, daughter of Sylvia Plath and Ted Hughes, born 1960.

2. Betty Friedan, *The Feminine Mystique* (1963, new edn, Penguin 2010).

3. Miriam King and Steven Ruggles, 'American Immigration, Fertility, and Race Suicide at the Turn of the Century', *The Journal of Interdisciplinary History*, 20: 3 (Winter 1990).

4. Jessica Glenza, 'Donald Trump Retracts Call for Women Who Have Abortions to be "Punished"', *Guardian* (31 March 2016).

5. A. Park, C. Bryson, E. Clery, J. Curtice, and M. Phillips (Ed.), 'British Social Attitudes: The 30th Report', NatCen Social Research (2013).

6. Gloria De Piero, '50,000 Women Lose Jobs Over Maternity Discrimination, Study Shows', *Guardian* (20 November 2013).

7. 'Pregnant Women and New Mothers "Face Rising Discrimination" at Work', BBC (2 May 2016).

8. Kim Parker and Gretchen Livingston, '6 Facts about American Fathers', Pew Research Center (16 June 2016).

9. 'Working Fathers Get 21% "Wage Bonus", TUC Study Suggests', BBC Online (25 April 2016).

10. 'Hey New Moms, I've Thought the Terrible Things Too', Renegade Mothering [blog] (27 September 2014).

11. Interview with Helen O'Neill, London (22 June 2016).

12. Maureen Brookbanks, 'How the Rise of Childless Women Could Change the Face of Britain', *Daily Mail* (16 January 2016).

13. Jennifer Aniston, 'For the Record', Huffington Post (12 July 2016).

CHAPTER SIX

1. Cindy Gallop; TED2009

2. Valentina Zarya, 'The Ex-CEO of J. Walter Thompson Makes a Rape Joke in a Newly Released Video' *Fortune* (22 April 2016).

3. Patrick Coffee, 'JWT CEO Gustavo Martinez Resigns Amid Suit Accusing Him of Racist, Sexist Comments', *Adweek* (17 March 2016).

4. Rape Crisis England and Wales (2016).

5. Interview with Pavan Amara, London (23 June 2016).

6. Audre Lorde, *Sister Outsider: Essays and Speeches*, (1984, new edn, Crossing Press 2007).

7. Interview with Myles Jackman, London (12 December 2014).

8. Maeve Duggan, 'Online Harassment', Pew Research Center (22 October 2014).

9. Interview with Cat/Milo Bezark, Los Angeles (22 May 2016).

10. Becky Butler, 'Cuntry Dying: Is the Feminist Discussion Group Scaring its Members into Silence?' The Stepford Student (7 April 2015).

11. Emily Bazelon, 'Should Prostitution Be a Crime?', *New York Times* (6 May 2016).

12. 'Policy on State Obligations to Respect, Protect and Fulfil the Human Rights of Sex Workers', Amnesty International (26 May 2016).

13. Gloria Steinem, *My Life On the Road* (Oneworld Publications, 2015).

14. Kat Banyard, *Pimp State: Sex, Money and the Future of Equality* (Faber & Faber, 2016).

15. 'Unprotected: How Legalising Prostitution Has Failed', Spiegel (30 May 2013).

16. Seo-Young Cho, Axel Dreher and Eric Neumayer, 'Does Legalized Prostitution Increase Human Trafficking?' *World Development*, 41 (2012).

17. Donna M. Hughes, Laura Joy Sporcic, Nadine Z. Mendelsohn and Vanessa Chirgwin, 'Factbook on Global Sexual Exploitation United States of America', Coalition Against Trafficking in Women (undated).

18. 'Addressing Transgender Violence: Exploring Realities, Challenges and Solutions for Policy Makers and Community Advocates', Human Rights Campaign (2015).

CHAPTER SEVEN

1. Peter Travers, 'Lost in Translation review', *Rolling Stone* (8 September 2003).

2. Anonymous interview, Los Angeles (2016).

3. Telephone interview with Lynda Obst (1 July 2016).

4. 'Film Dialogue from 2,000 Screenplays Broken Down by Age and Gender', Polygraph (2016).

5. Martha M. Lauzen, 'The Celluloid Ceiling: Behind-the-Scenes Employment of Women on the Top 100, 250, and 500 Films of 2015', Center for the Study of Women in Television and Film, San Diego State University (2016).
6. 'Cut Out of the Picture: A Campaign for Gender Equality Among Directors within the UK Film Industry', Directors UK (2016).
7. Interview with Debra Zane, Los Angeles (23 May 2016).
8. Interview with Alison Owen, London (30 March 2016).
9. Rachel Deahl, 'Where the Boys Are Not', *Publishers Weekly* (20 September 2010).
10. Alison Flood, 'Popular History Writing Remains a Male Preserve, Publishing Study Finds', *Guardian* (11 January 2016).
11. Tracy McVeigh, 'Lily Allen on Being Stalked', *Observer* (16 April 2016).
12. bell hooks, 'Moving Beyond Pain', bell hooks Institute (9 May 2016).
13. LaSha, 'bell hooks vs. Beyoncé: What this Feminist Scholarly Critique gets Wrong About "Lemonade" and Liberation', Salon (18 May 2016).
14. 'Lily Allen Blames Cheryl Cole for "Fat and Ugly" Crisis', *Evening Standard* (15 May 2007).
15. Lily Allen's tweeted response to criticism of 'Hard Out Here' (13 November 2013):
    '1. If anyone thinks for a second that I requested specific ethnicities for the video, they're wrong.
    2. If anyone thinks that after asking the girls to audition, I was going to send any of them away because of the colour of their skin, they're wrong.
    3. The message is clear. Whilst I don't want to offend anyone. I do strive to provoke thought and conversation. The video is meant to be a light-hearted satirical video that deals with objectification of women within modern pop culture. It has nothing to do with race, at all.
    4. If I could dance like the ladies can, it would have been my arse on your screens; I actually rehearsed for two weeks trying to perfect my twerk, but failed miserably. If I was a little braver, I would have been wearing a bikini too, but I do not and I have chronic cellulite, which nobody wants

to see. What I'm trying to say is that me being covered up has nothing to do with me wanting to disassociate myself from the girls, it has more to do with my own insecurities and I just wanted to feel as comfortable as possible on the shoot day.

   5.   I'm not going to apologise because I think that would imply that I'm guilty of something, but I promise you this, in no way do I feel superior to anyone, except paedophiles, rapists murderers etc., and I would not only be surprised but deeply saddened if I thought anyone came away from that video feeling taken advantage of, or compromised in any way.'

16. Ayesha A. Siddiqi, 'Lily Allen's Anti-Black Feminism', Noisey (13 November 2013).

17. 'Ain't I A Woman?' speech by Sojourner Truth; delivered at Women's Convention, Akron, Ohio (1851).

18. Associated Press, 'Suffragette's Racial Remark Haunts College' (5 May 1996).

19. Carol H. Hood, 'C'mon, White Women: You Don't Get to Be Rhetorical Slaves', The Frisky (6 October 2015).

20. 'Film Dialogue from 2,000 Screenplays Broken Down by Age and Gender', Polygraph (2016).

21. Alex Needham, 'Sony Emails Reveal Jennifer Lawrence Paid Less than Male Co-stars', *Guardian* (13 December 2014).

22. 'Indian Wells CEO: "Lady" Players Should "Thank God" for Federer and Nadal', *Guardian Sport* (20 March 2016).

23. Bill Chappell, 'US Women's Soccer Team Members File Federal Equal-Pay Complaint' NPR (31 March 2016).

24. Anne M. Peterson, 'US Soccer asks EEOC to Dismiss Wage Discrimination Complaint', Associated Press (31 May 2016).

CHAPTER EIGHT

 1. Interview with Stephen Fitzgerald, London (14 July 2016).

2. Cristian L. Dezso and David Gaddis Ross, 'Does Female Representation in Top Management Improve Firm Performance? A Panel Data Investigation', *Strategic Management Journal*, 33: 9 (2012), 1072–89.

3. 'Australia's Hidden Resource: The Economic Case for Increasing Female Participation', Goldman Sachs JBWere (26 November 2009).

4. 'Women in Business: Turning Promise into Practice', Grant Thornton International (2016).

5. Anonymous interview, London (20 July 2016).

6. Multiple conversations between Lucy P. Marcus and Catherine Mayer.

7. 'The Psychology of Entrepreneurship', Centre for Entrepreneurship (9 June 2015).

8. Global Gender Balance Scorecard (2014).

9. Interview with Jeremy King, London (2 June 2016).

10. Sari M. van Anders, Jeffrey Steiger and Katherine L. Goldey, 'Effects of Gendered Behavior on Testosterone in Women and Men', PNAS, 112: 45 (10 November 2015).

11. 'The Double-Bind Dilemma for Women in Leadership', Catalyst (2007).

12. Anonymous interview, London (2016).

13. Interview with Andrew Davidson: Virgin Money CEO Jayne-Anne Gadhia on glass ceilings and financial disruptors, *Management Today* (23 February 2016).

14. Vicki Owen, 'It's OUTRAGEOUS! Why Are You Giving Women Our Jobs?', *The Mail on Sunday* (9 April 2016).

15. Q&A, ABC TV (19 March 2009).

16. Michelle K. Ryan and S. Alexander Haslam, 'The Glass Cliff: Evidence that Women Are Over-Represented in Precarious Leadership Positions', *British Journal of Management*, 16: 2 (June 2005).

17. Ken Favaro, Per-Ola Karlsson, Gary L. Neilson, 'The 2013 Chief Executive Study: Women CEOs of the Last 10 Years', PriceWaterhouse Coopers (29 April 2014).

18. Alison Cook and Christy Glass, 'Above the Glass Ceiling: When are Women and Racial/Ethnic Minorities Promoted to CEO?', *Strategic Management Journal*, 35: 7 (July 2014).

19. Kunur Patel and Nat Ives, 'Who is Laura Lang, Time Inc.'s New CEO?', *Advertising Age* (30 November 2011).

CHAPTER NINE

1. 'Kamila Klingorová and Tomas Havlicek, 'Religion and Gender Inequality: The Status of Women in the Societies of World Religions'; Moravian Geographical Reports, 23: 2 (February 2015).

2. Mordechai I. Twersky, 'Girl, 8, Becomes Poster Child for Anti-Haredi Backlash', Haaretz (26 December 2011).

3. Interview with Steinunn Arnþrúður Björnsdóttir, Reykjavík (26 April 2016).

4. Kamila Klingorová and Tomas Havlicek, 'Religion and Gender Inequality: The Status of Women in the Societies of World Religions', *Moravian Geographical Reports*, 23: 2 (February 2015).

5. Interview with Ayisha Osori, conducted for this book by Jeremy Gaines via Skype (14 August 2016).

6. John Ward, Bernice Lee, Simon Baptist and Helen Jackson, 'Evidence for Action: Gender Equality and Economic Growth', Chatham House (September 2010).

7. 'Religion in China on the Eve of the 2008 Beijing Olympics', Pew Research Center (2 May 2008).

8. 'China Says its Gender Imbalance "Most Serious" in the World', Reuters (21 January 2015).

9. Valerie M. Hudson and Andrea Den Boer, 'A Surplus of Men, A Deficit of Peace: Security and Sex Ratios in Asia's Largest States', *International Security*, 26: 4 (Spring 2002).

10. Shaan Khan, 'What's Really Behind India's Rape Crisis', The Daily Beast (25 March 2016).

11. 'Not as Easy as It Looks', *Economist* (21 November 2015).

12. Kathy Matsui, '"Womenomics" Continues as a Work in Progress', *Japan Times* (25 May 2016).

13. Steve Mollman, 'Japan Cuts its Target for Women in Leadership Positions from 30% to 7%', Quartz (6 December 2015).

14. Matthew Garahan, 'China to Become World's Largest Movie Market within 2 Years', *Financial Times* (7 December 2015).

15. Kim Wall, 'Sex and the Law in China: The People Will Pull, and the Government Will Follow', *The Atlantic* (6 June 2013).

16. Jonathan Kaiman, 'In China, Feminism is Growing – and so is the Backlash', *Los Angeles Times* (15 June 2016).

17. World Economic Forum, Global Gender Index 2015.

18. *Ibid.*

19. Golnaz Esfandiari, 'Protesters Demand Afghan Government Action Against Acid Attacks on Women', Radio Free Europe (13 July 2016).

20. Atika Shubert and Bharati Naik, 'ISIS Soldiers Told to Rape Women "to Make Them Muslim"', CNN Online (8 October 2015).

21. Interview with Elizabeth Mitchell, London (27 July 2016).

22. 'Challenges for the Saudi Royal Family', Stratfor (11 September 2012).

23. Eli Lake, 'Boko Haram's Bin Laden Connection', *The Daily Beast* (11 May 2015).

24. Rahila Gupta, 'Rojava Revolution: How Deep is the Change?', 50:50 (20 June 2016).

25. Interview with Nimco Ali, London (4 August 2016).

26. 'Challenges for the Saudi Royal Family', Stratfor (11 September 2012).

CHAPTER TEN

1. Mary Anne Franks speaking at 100 years of Women's Civil Rights: International Conference Celebrating the Centenary of Women's Suffrage in Iceland (23 October 2015).

2. Helena Horton, 'Microsoft Deletes "Teen Girl" AI after It Became a Hitler-loving Sex Robot within 24 Hours', *Telegraph* (24 March 2016).

3. 'Will a Robot Take your Job?', BBC Online (11 September 2015).

4. Scheherazade, an artificial intelligence developed at the Georgia Institute of Technology.

5. Germaine Greer, *The Female Eunuch* (1970, new edn, Harper Perennial 2006)

6. Interview with Lea Coligado, Palo Alto (19 May 2016).

7. Sidney Fussell, 'This Woman Created the Tinder for Jobs to Shatter Hiring Barriers in the Tech World', *Tech Insider* (12 May 2016).

8. *Ibid*.

9. Meghan Casserly, 'Sheryl Sandberg Named to Facebook Board. Finally.', *Forbes* (25 June 2012).

10. Doug Bolton, 'Men are Angrier and More Argumentative on Facebook than Women, Study Finds', *Independent* (26 May 2016).

11. Anonymous, 'I Worked on Facebook's Trending Team – the Most Toxic Work Experience of my Life', *Guardian* (17 May 2016).

12. VCDiversity.org (2016).

13. Interview with Sarah Hunter, San Francisco (18 May 2016).

14. Interview with Stephanie Lampkin, San Francisco (17 May 2016).

15. Charlie Warzel, '"A Honeypot For Assholes": Inside Twitter's 10-Year Failure To Stop Harassment', BuzzFeed (11 August 2016).

16. Sam Shead, 'Google Hired at Least 65 European Government Officials in 10 Years', *Business Insider* (6 June 2016).

17. Interview with Margaret Gould Stewart, Menlo Park (19 May 2016).

18. Abigail Tracy, 'Google Moved Billions of Dollars to Bermuda to Avoid Taxes ... Again', *Forbes* (19 February 2016).

19. Rhiannon Williams, 'Facebook's 71 Gender Options Come to UK Users', *Telegraph* (27 June 2014).

20. Alex Hern, 'Facebook Relaxes "Real name" Policy in Face of Protest', *Guardian* (2 November 2015).

21. Craig Silverman, 'This Analysis Shows How Fake Election News Stories Outperformed Real News On Facebook', BuzzFeed (16 November 2016).

22. Michael Nunez, 'Former Facebook Workers: We Routinely Suppressed Conservative News', Gizmondo (9 May 2016).

23. Interview with Claire Rowland, London (29 March 2016).

24. Charles Duhigg, 'How Companies Learn Your Secrets', *New York Times Magazine* (16 February 2012).

25. 'Tech Giants to Freeze Eggs for their Female Employees', BBC Online (15 October 2014).

26. Society of Human Resources Management (2015).

27. Jodi Kantor and David Streitfeld, 'Inside Amazon: Wrestling Big Ideas in a Bruising Workplace', *New York Times* (15 August 2015).

28. David Streitfeld and Jodi Kantor, 'Jeff Bezos and Amazon Employees Join Debate Over Its Culture', *New York Times* (17 August 2015).

29. Dina Vaccari, 'I was quoted in the NY Times article about working at Amazon. Here is my story', LinkedIn (31 August 2015).

30. Jathan Sadowski, 'Why Silicon Valley is Embracing Universal Basic Income', *Guardian* (26 June 2016).

CHAPTER ELEVEN

1. Ursula Le Guin, 'Is Gender Necessary?', 1976 essay reprinted with author's own annotations in *The Language of the Night* (The Women's Press, 1989).

2. Interview with Alvin Níelsson, Reykjavík (25 April 2016).

3. Edward Robinson and Omar Valdimarsson, 'This Is Where Bad Bankers Go to Prison', Bloomberg (31 March 2016).

4. Interview with Auður Styrkársdóttir, Reykjavík (25 April 2016).

5. Þóra Kristín Þórsdóttir, 'Iceland: From Feminist Governance to Gender-Blind Austerity', *Gender, Sexuality and Feminism*, 1: 2 (December 2014).

6. Louise Armistead, 'Women Hedge Fund Managers Outperform the Men', *Telegraph* (16 January 2014).

7. 'Woman' by Ingibjörg Haraldsdóttir, trans. Salka Guðmundsdóttir; quoted in Jóhanna Sigurðardóttir, 'Iceland's First Female PM: Europe Needs its Women Leaders after Brexit', *Newsweek* (30 June 2016).

8. Interview with Drífa Snædal, Reykjavík (25 April 2016).

9. Interview with Sara Riel, Reykjavík (26 April 2016).

10. UK Government consultation on Modern Workplaces: Government Response on Flexible Parental Leave – Impact Assessment (November 2012).

11. John Ward, Bernice Lee, Simon Baptist and Helen Jackson, 'Evidence for Action: Gender Equality and Economic Growth', Chatham House (September 2010).

12. 'The Power of Parity: How Advancing Women's Equality Can Add \$12 Trillion to Global Growth', McKinsey Global Institute (September 2015).

13. Interview with Védís Guðjónsdóttir and Þuríður *Pétursdóttir*, Reykjavík (26 April 2016).

14. Interview with Steinunn Arnþrúður Björnsdóttir, Reykjavík (26 April 2016).

15. Merlind Theile, 'No Gender, No Problem?', *Spiegel* (13 October 2011).

16. Interview with Védís Guðjónsdóttir and Þuríður *Pétursdóttir*, Reykjavík (26 April 2016).

17. Interview with Margrét Pála Ólafsdóttir, Reykjavík (26 January 2016).

18. Valdis Jonsdottir, Leena M. Rantala, Gudmundur Kr Oskarsson and Eeva Sala, 'Effects of Pedagogical Ideology on the Perceived Loudness and Noise Levels in Preschools', *Noise and Health*, 17: 78 (2015), 282–93.

CHAPTER TWELVE

1. bell hooks, *Talking Back: Thinking Feminist, Thinking Black*, (1989 new edn, Routledge 2015).

2. Catherine Mayer, 'My Sister's Cancer Exposed a Gross Gender Bias in Medicine – and How It Treats Women', *Telegraph* (15 September 2016).

Select Bibliography

Acemoglu, Daron and James A. Robinson, *Why Nations Fail: The Origins of Power, Prosperity and Poverty* (Profile Books, 2012).

Adichie, Chimamanda Ngozi, *We Should All Be Feminists* (Fourth Estate, 2014).

Ball, Ros and James Miller, *The Gender Police: A Diary* (Epub, 2015).

Banyard, Kat, *Pimp State: Sex, Money and the Future of Equality* (Faber & Faber, 2016).

———, *The Equality Illusion: The Truth about Women and Men Today* (Faber & Faber, 2010).

de Beauvoir, Simone, *The Second Sex* (Vintage, 1997).

Blome, Nikolaus, *Angela Merkel: Die Zauder-Künstlerin* (Pantheon, 2013).

Bohnet, Iris, *What Works: Gender Equality by Design* (Belknap Press, 2016).

Clinton, Hillary Rodham, *Living History* (Simon & Schuster, 2013).

Coates, John, *The Hour Between Dog and Wolf* (Fourth Estate, 2012).

Cochrane, Kita, *All the Rebel Women: The Rise of the Fourth Wave of Feminism* (GuardianShorts, 2013).

Crawford, Alan and Tony Czuczka, *Angela Merkel: A Chancellorship Forged in Crisis* (Wiley/Bloomberg, 2013).

El Feki, Shereen, *Sex and the Citadel: Intimate Life in a Changing Arab World* (Chatto & Windus, 2013).

Eltahawy, Mona, *Headscarves and Hymens: Why the Middle East Needs a Sexual Revolution* (Weidenfeld & Nicolson, 2015).

Faludi, Susan, *Backlash: The Undeclared War Against Women* (Vintage, 1993).

Fine, Cordelia, *Delusions of Gender: The Real Science Behind Sex Differences* (Icon Books, 2010).

Frank, Thomas, *Listen, Liberal: What Ever Happened to the Party of the People* (Scribe Publications, 2016).

Friedan, Betty, *The Feminine Mystique* (Penguin Books, 1963).

Glezerman, Marek, *Gender Medicine: The Groundbreaking New Science of Gender – and Sex-Related Diagnosis and Treatment* (Duckworth Overlook, 2016).

Greer, Germaine, *The Female Eunuch* (Harper Perennial, 2006).

Hawklsey, Lucinda, *March, Women, March: Voices of the Women's Movement from the First Feminist to Votes for Women* (André Deutsch, 2013).

Hoff Sommers, Christina, *Who Stole Feminism: How Women Have Betrayed Women* (Simon & Schuster, 1994).

hooks, bell, *Ain't I a Woman: Black Women and Feminism* (Pluto Press, 1987).

———— *Outlaw Culture: Resisting Representations* (Routledge, 2006).

Hudson, Valerie M. and Andrea M. den Boer, *Bare Branches: The Security Implications of Asia's Surplus Male Population* (MIT Press, 2004).

Isaacson, Walter, *Steve Jobs,* (Hachette Digital, 2011).

Kornelius, Stefan, *Angela Merkel: The Chancellor and her World* (Alma Books, 2013).

Laqueur, Thomas, *Making Sex: Body and Gender from the Greeks to Freud* (Harvard University Press, 1990).

Le Guin, Ursula K., *The Left Hand of Darkness* (Hachette Digital, 1969).

Lorde, Audre, *Sister Outsider: Essays and Speeches* (Crossing Press, 1984, 2007).

Mansfield, Harvey C., *Manliness* (Yale University Press, 2006).

McMillen, Sally G., *Seneca Falls and the Origins of the Women's Rights Movement* (Oxford University Press, 2008).

Millett, Kate, *Sexual Politics* (Virago, 1977).

Morojele, Naleli, *Women Political Leaders in Rwanda and South Africa: Narratives of Triumph and Loss* (Barbara Budrich, 2016).

Morrison, Toni (Ed.), *Race-ing Justice, En-gendering Power: Essays on Anita Hill, Clarence Thomas, and the Construction of Social Reality* (Pantheon Books, 1992).

Newton-Small, Jay, *Broad Influence: How Women Are Changing the Way America Works* (Time Books, 2016).

O'Toole, Emer, *Girls Will Be Girls: Dressing Up, Playing Parts and Daring to Act Differently* (Orion, 2015).

Pankhurst, Emmeline, *My Own Story* (Eveleigh Nash, 1914).

Rowlatt, Bee, *In Search of Mary: The Mother of All Journeys* (Alma Books, 2015).

Rosen, Robert, *Beaver Street: A History of Modern Pornography* (Headpress, 2013).

Sandberg, Sheryl, *Lean In: Women, Work, and the Will to Lead* (WH Allen, 2013).

Simons, Margaret A., *Beauvoir and the Second Sex: Feminism, Race and the Origins of Existentialism* (Rowman & Littlefield, 1999).

Slaughter, Anne-Marie, *Unfinished Business* (Oneworld, 2015).

Steinem, Gloria, *My Life on the Road* (Oneworld, 2015).

———— *Outrageous Acts and Everyday Rebellions* (Holt McDougal, 1995).

Susskind, Richard and Daniel Susskind, *The Future of the Professions: How Technology Will Transform the Work of Human Experts* (Oxford University Press, 2013).

Thatcher, Margaret, *The Downing Street Years* (HarperCollins, 1993).

Vincent, Norah, *Self-Made Man* (Viking Penguin, 2006).

Wittenberg-Cox, Avivah and Alison Maitland, *Why Women Mean Business* (Wiley, 2009).

Wollstonecraft, Mary, *Vindication of the Rights of Woman, With Strictures on Political and Moral Subjects* (Vintage Classics, 2015).

Index

The Women's Equality Party is listed as WE throughout this index, apart from its own entry where the name is spelled out in full.